THE SUICIDE SYNDROME

THE SUICIDE SYNDROME
*Origins, Manifestations, and Alleviation
of Human Self-Destructiveness*

Larry Morton Gernsbacher, Ph.D.
*Founder-Director
The Institute of Professional Suicidology
Albuquerque, NM
Tyler, TX*

HUMAN SCIENCES PRESS, INC.
*72 FIFTH AVENUE
NEW YORK, N.Y. 10011*

Copyright © 1985 by Human Sciences Press, Inc.
72 Fifth Avenue, New York, New York 10011

Printed in the United States of America
987654321

Library of Congress Cataloging in Publication Data

Gernsbacher, Larry Morton.
  The suicide syndrome.

  Bibliography: p.
  Includes index.
  1. Suicide. 2. Self-perception. I. Title
RC569.G47 1985   616.85′8445   84-19759
ISBN 0-89885-232-3

To my wife and colleague, Mary Willson Williams,
and to Ronald, David, and Morton Ann Gernsbacher.

CONTENTS

PREFACE

In this book I set forth an original and radically different approach to the meaning and motives of suicide. But this book is not about suicide as an isolated phenomenon unrelated to everyday life. It is about everyday human beings and a comprehensive process shaping the character of our lives, influencing the societies we comprise, and questioning the ultimate meaning of our existence.

Since these issues touch the lives of virtually everyone, I address them to the general reader. Scholars and professionals will find concepts and methodologies germane to clinical practice, study, and research. But they will find them phrased in the popular vernacular.

The process I describe is an evolutionary one. Each phase of its development evolves from those preceding it and founds those to follow. I therefore recommend this book first be read through from its beginning. Mediation and alleviation processes I describe are designed to be employed only with proper training, educated judgment, and professional responsibility.

Due to sociocultural influences, two of the three suicidal personality types presented in this book are preponderantly male. For this reason and for lack of a wieldy alternative, I arbitrarily use the masculine gender except when specifically referring to the feminine. I sincerely hope this will not be misconstrued by members of either sex as indicative of a prejudicial position. Names are fictitious and case histories are fictional accounts. Any resemblance to any real person, now living or ever having lived, is purely coincidental.

A. Gerald Spalding first confirmed the value I found in the rudimentary ideas upon which this book is based. Richard Pesqueira, Douglas Ferraro, Norman Katz, Sheila Sweet, David Scheinbaum, Richard Lichman, and Ben Davis read parts or all of a longer version in progress. Each offered valuable challenges, insights, and suggestions. Fain Williams aided in cutting the manuscript down to publishable size. And from earliest concept through final draft, my wife and colleague, Mary Willson Williams, provided me with her invaluable encouragement, perspicacity, love, and companionship.

Larry Morton Gernsbacher
Albuquerque, New Mexico

INTRODUCTION

Most people feel like committing suicide at least one time in their lives. Many do more than just feel like it. They are out to kill themselves any way they can. Some attempt suicide again and again until they finally succeed. Others succeed quite succinctly on their very first try.

Many people secretly savor the idea of committing suicide as a final resort, should all other efforts for fulfillment seem to fail. Many other people experience sudden and inexplicable suicidal impulses. Still others live out their lifetimes scarred by a haunting and pervasive suicidal urge.

But however they experience suicidal feelings, very few people escape them. If asked if they ever felt like committing suicide, most people would probably answer, "Hasn't everyone?"

On the surface, there appears to be a vast difference between feeling like committing suicide and going so far as attempting it. But appearances can be very deceiving. Regardless of how impulsive a suicide attempt may appear, one must feel like committing suicide before actually attempting it.

On the other hand, some obviously suicidal people can honestly say they never consciously consider committing suicide. Yet the way they live their lives tells a radically different story. Even the most casual observer of their blatant self-destructiveness must conclude they are out prematurely to end their lives, one way or another.

The same unconscious goal underlies all these conditions. One person actually commits suicide. Another attempts it again and again. Still another just feels suicidal. And still another never consciously feels suicidal but is unconsciously determined to die before his or her time. Despite their apparent differences, their underlying suicidal goals are the same.

Suicide affects every age group, every community, every economic level, every social status, every vocation. It is indiscriminate: rich or poor; young or old; famous or obscure—anyone can fall victim to it.

The suicide rate is rapidly accelerating among our youth. Our children, adolescents, and young adults are committing suicide by the thousands every year. Suicide ranks second only to accidents as the cause of death between the ages of fourteen and twenty-four. And we have no way of determining how many so-called accidents are, in fact, suicides.[2]

The suicide rate is equally alarming among our older people. Many of our elders apparently prefer suicide to the kind of extended lifestyle our society allows them. They often do themselves in quite handily. They simply quit living.

But suicide is not the exclusive property of our very young and our very old. Businessmen, housewives, and engineers; attorneys, physicians, and teachers; secretaries, street people, and scientists; professors, laborers, and unemployed industrial workers; people of every race, religion, and station in life are killing themselves by the hundreds every day.

Records show over 35,000 people commit suicide in the United States each year. But many more suicides go unrecognized or unreported. Pioneer suicidologists Edwin Shneidman and Norman Farberow estimate the real number to be over 85,000. They also believe over three times that many attempt suicide every year.[3]

We read about the suicides of well-known people in newspapers and magazines. We learn about them on television. A relative, a neighbor, a friend overdoses. A business acquaintance fires a bullet through his head. An entire religious group—over 900 people—commit the sensational mass suicide of the century.[4] The World

Health Organization estimates that over 1,000 people commit suicide every day.[5]

Confronted by such numbers, we can visualize a whole world determined to do itself in, individually or collectively. We can easily understand why Freud endowed us with a death instinct;[6] why Ernest Becker believed a universal fear of death paradoxically drives us to it.[7]

Are we helplessly driven to self-destruction by deep and mysterious forces beyond our control? Is our uniquely human ability to foresee our own inevitable death so frightening that we are forced to hasten its day? Do we possess some terrible flaw in our makeup plunging us towards an early end? Is the drive to suicide a psychological paradox we can neither solve nor avoid?

Or is it a social paradox that cannot be alleviated? Are there some awesome but inescapable factors in our societies driving us to mindless self-destruction? Are we culturally conditioned indiscriminately to kill ourselves? Do the differing suicide rates between various countries indicate that geography, politics, economics, or social conditions dictate to us how many of us will kill ourselves and even how and when?

But suicide is not a recent phenomenon. It has been with us throughout our history. Nine hundred members of the Peoples Temple committed suicide at Jonestown in 1978. But just as many Hebrew zealots suicided at Masada almost 2,000 years before. Much like our daily news reports, our history books teem with the suicides of celebrated persons. But neither our history books nor our news reports call attention to the thousands of more obscure people who commit suicide in proportion to each of the more celebrated ones.

Suicide is so rampant and has been with us so long, one would think we would have learned all there is to know about it. But ignorance has prevailed. Even among those we would think would have all the answers—or those who would have us think they do—suicide has been an enigma.

As incredible as it may seem, the modern sciences of psychiatry, psychology, and sociology have all failed to discover the real reasons people commit suicide. Psychiatry may seem to know, but appearances are considerably weakened by some little-known and disturbing facts.

For example, hospitalized psychiatric patients commit suicide six to ten times—according to whose data you use—more often than other people. The medical profession, of which psychiatry is a part, has the highest suicide rate of all professions. And, finally, among the medical specialties, psychiatry itself has the highest suicide rate.[8]

Psychiatric explanations for suicide are usually founded on psychoanalytic theory. This entails—depending on which faction you listen to—either endorsement or rejection of the Freudian Death Instinct. But Freud's most knowledgeable biographers, Ernest Jones[9] and Marthe Robert,[10] claim Freud developed this theory very late in his formulations and under such circumstances—the recent death of his daughter Sophie—that even Freud feared for its acceptance.

The endorsement of the death instinct theory would automatically interpret suicide as resulting from an instinctual drive which must be mediated, displaced, or sublimated for survival. But the absence of suicide in all other living creatures would imply that only human beings—the least instinctually motivated of creatures—would possess the death instinct. Or it would imply the equally untenable view that other animals have intellectually learned better to resist it.

On the other hand, rejection of the death instinct leads psychiatry into a forest of its own medical obscurities. The "bible" of psychiatry for decades, the *Diagnostic and Statistical Manual of Mental Disorders*—DSM II, contained no category for suicidal disorders. In fact, it did not even mention the word "suicide." It did, however, cite "suicidal behaviors" as an adult reaction to situational stress, along with fear in battle.[11]

The more recent DSM III, several years in the making, does little better. It still ignores suicide as an issue worthy of special mention or, more accurately, as one for which there is a medical solution. It mentions "suicidal behavior" no more than a half-dozen times, and then only as a possible side effect to such obscure-sounding conditions as Tourette's Disorder.[12]

Furthermore, only one of about 250 articles in the *Standard Textbook of Psychiatry* deals with suicide. It is written by a psychologist, Edwin Shneidman, not a psychiatrist.[13]

While psychiatric literature abounds with case studies of suicide, none provide a satisfactory assessment of it. Only in the widely dissimilar views of Karl Menninger and Karen Horney can one find concepts even approaching a comprehensive overview of suicide. Menninger emphasizes the often subtle but all-pervasive aspects of human self-destructiveness. But by failing to discern any cause other than the death instinct, he undermines his case.[14] Horney saw the neurotic search for glory as inherently self-destructive. But by failing to see suicide as the ultimate expression of the glorified self-image, she missed the comprehensive whole.[15]

Now, over 70 years later, psychiatry can only repeat Freud's own observation made after the Vienna symposium on suicide in 1908. Freud observed that he and his colleagues had examined much evidence and heard many theories, but they could still not reach any definite conclusion as to why people commit suicide.[16]

Academic psychology is equally baffled. No historical or theoretical system approaches the suicide phenomenon from a comprehensive view or even incorporates suicide into its multifactorial, scientific system. In fact, most theories and textbooks fail to even address it.

Psychology usually categorizes abnormal behavior along the same lines as the psychiatrists' DSM. And just as in the model, suicide is ignored. The word "suicide" is not found in the indexes of many abnormal psychology textbooks. Nor are the complexities of its dynamics usually studied in graduate psychology courses.

Only sociology has attempted a comprehensive explanation for the suicide phenomenon. But most contemporary studies are modeled on the nineteenth century work of the French sociologist, Emile Durkheim. Paradoxically, contemporary sociologists themselves have repeatedly proven Durkheim's data shot with error and his conclusions highly suspect.[17]

Although the kinds of statistical data used by Durkheim have been proven so inaccurate as to be virtually useless—the two reporting branches of even such a closed system as the United States Army can't even agree on how many of its active members die each year, let alone how many commit suicide[18]—sociologists still try to use these kinds of data as bases for their theories rather than adjuncts to them.

Indeed, variations on the theme by Durkheim are still with us. Gibbs and Martin play the numbers to interpret suicide as resulting from a "lack of status integration," a more modern term for Durkheim's "anomie."[19] Ronald Maris tries to mix Durkheim with Freud, arriving at the solution that suicide can only be avoided by transcending inherent self-destructiveness through social assimilation.[20]

A more modern French sociologist, Jean Baechler, properly dismisses his predecessor as the establishment moralist he was. Some of Baechler's categorizing is insightful, but he sees suicide mainly as an individual solution to socially propagated problems. Suicide is unfortunate, but unavoidable.[21]

Another contemporary sociologist, Jack Douglas, has recognized the impossibility of abstracting explanations for individual acts such as suicide from social theory.[22] But his concepts regarding the individual meanings of suicide have been generally ignored by social science as too psychological. And they have been ignored by psychology as too sociologically esoteric.

Lacking a sound and comprehensive theoretical foundation upon which to base its research and prevention techniques, the new science of suicidology has floundered in the wake of the past. Since its ranks are filled with psychiatrists, psychologists, and sociologists, the confusion is understandable. Research projects often end inconclusively and prevention methods operate solely on empirical observation.

While suicide prevention centers can rightfully claim effectiveness, they are hard pressed to prove their case. And while pioneers in the study of suicide have collected important data and succeeded in dispelling many commonly held superstitions, fallacies, and myths, the fundamental dilemmas remain.

Until now, there has been no etiology, no typology, and, most importantly, no prescription for a preventative methodology. Indeed, the contemporary dean emeritus of suicidology, Edwin Shneidman, begins his article on suicide for the 14th Edition of the Encyclopaedia Britannica by echoing Freud's Vienna observation: "No one really knows why people commit suicide."[23]

But past failures to discover a comprehensive concept explaining the whys and wherefores of suicide obviously entail consequences extending far beyond the purview of scientific curiosity. For the value of any knowledge must be measured in purely human terms. It is in this real human cause that I have tackled these dilemmas and originated the comprehensive construct of the origins, manifestations, and alleviation of suicide that I present here.

Paramount, of course, is the tragic loss of human life as the price of continuing neglect. But the complex phenomena leading to suicide entail far more pervasive and widespread consequences than these senseless deaths. To be sure, suicide extracts a terrible toll in tragic human deaths. But the process from which it stems extracts an infinitely more sweeping toll in tragic human lives. For suicide does not arrive unheralded from out of the blue as an immediate consequence of social conditions or the casualties of life. It arrives as the supreme guest of honor of a comprehensive life process unconsciously designed to entertain it.

This process ultimately dictates the lives of those who live in accordance with its strictures. And it helps shape the societies they comprise. It is so well entrenched, pervasive, and enculturated that the real enigma is not why so many people commit suicide. The real enigma is why so many people do not.

This enigma emerges as a tribute to the intrinsic vitality of the human organism. And it constitutes our saving grace. For only by calling on our most vital intrinsic qualities can we prevent suicide and can we eradicate the comprehensive self-destructive process from which it stems.

I call this comprehensive process The Suicide Syndrome.

Part I

GENESIS OF THE
SUICIDE SYNDROME

Chapter 1

THE SUICIDE SYNDROME

Human beings, like all other living creatures, naturally strive to survive, to propagate, to realize their intrinsic natures. But human beings, unlike all other living creatures, can abandon these natural strivings in favor of an artificial process originally holding forth great promise but inevitably leading to pernicious self-destructiveness. This self-destructive process is so subtle and widespread, we hardly recognize it except in its most extreme forms. Yet it is so pervasive, very few of us are fortunate enough to escape it.

Suicide—the termination of one's own existence—obviously stands out as the most extreme form of human self-destructiveness. But suicide is not an isolated phenomenon unrelated to the vicissitudes of everyday life. Suicide is the ultimate expression of this artificial self-destructive process herein called the Suicide Syndrome. And any person who lives by its strictures—*whether he ever consciously considers committing suicide or not*—is herein called a Suicide.

25

MANIFESTATIONS OF THE SYNDROME

The Suicide Syndrome is manifested in the intrapsychic, interpersonal, and existential processes of the Suicide. It colors his feelings and beliefs about himself. It determines his goals in life and his values. It shapes his personality and the ways he relates to other people. It influences his attitudes regarding work, creativity, and accomplishment. It molds the character of the societies he comprises. It even defines the meaning and purpose he attributes to his life. Finally, and most tragically, it dictates his motivations to die.

Yet despite its comprehensive and pervasive influence, the Suicide Syndrome develops and operates unconsciously.[1] Many of its consequences occur in the all too glaring light of awareness. But its main theme and basic process remain unconscious. A person can live according to the Suicide Syndrome and never be aware of it.

Because the syndrome develops and operates unconsciously, the Suicide often feels helplessly driven by it. And since it makes little sense for him to feel helplessly driven by motivations of which he is unaware, he usually devises numerous rationalizations to explain his feelings and behavior. Paradoxically, the rationalizations the Suicide usually identifies as the reasons for his feelings and behavior are consequences of the Suicide Syndrome. They are not the causes of it.

The Suicide especially identifies the consequences of the syndrome as the reason for his suicidal impulses. For these consequences are overwhelming indeed. The syndrome generates endless desperation, frustration, and guilt. It produces anxiety, fears, and phobias. It stimulates emotional suffering and underlies a pervasive lethargy and lack of genuine motivation. It manifests acute and chronic depression.

The syndrome plays havoc with the mannerisms, habits, and behavior of the Suicide. It stimulates alcoholism and other drug abuse. Many accidents and illnesses result from its dynamics. It underlies chronic failure and misfortune. It breeds habitual overwork, stress, and strain. On its account, the Suicide can run afoul of the law or other authority.

The syndrome invades the Suicide's relations with other people. It influences his choice of lover, spouse, and friend. It writes the script for relationships to them. It delineates their meaning and importance. And it prescribes their tragic bent.

The Suicide's sexuality is especially vulnerable to the syndrome, which shapes its pattern and character. For the basic tenets of the syndrome comprise the very antithesis of natural sexuality.

The syndrome dominates the Suicide's thinking processes. It colors his perceptions. It dictates his concepts. It distorts the ways he sees himself and others. It twists his sense of reality. Most ominously, it determines his beliefs regarding the nature of life and the immutable finality of death.

The syndrome shapes the Suicide's social systems. It prescribes their character and their goals. It determines their moral values. It sets his role within them. At times, it turns his societies against him. And it nourishes the roots of his discontent with them.

The consequences of the Suicide Syndrome are so all-pervasive, it is easy to see why the Suicide usually points to them as the grounds for his unhappiness; why he believes he feels suicidal on their account. But the reasons the Suicide believes to be the roots of his self-destructiveness are its effects, not its cause.

For the Suicide Syndrome is inherently self-destructive. It turns the Suicide against himself. It destroys his self-esteem. It disrupts his relations with others. It crushes his hopes for the future. But its real unconscious goal is the absolute destruction of the Suicide's sentient self.

ORIGINS OF THE SYNDROME

Although the Suicide Syndrome unconsciously aims at human self-destruction, it ironically originates in those very characteristics we associate with the best of human nature. It derives from that unique combination of assets that distinguish human beings from other animals: those that go into making human beings human.

First of all, it derives from the human capacity to learn.[2] For our capacity to learn obviously extends well beyond learning simple responses to simple stimuli. Humans learn extremely complex responses to equally complex stimuli. We even learn to learn. Furthermore, we incorporate our learning into an extremely complicated, highly interdependent repertoire of concepts, affects, and behaviors. And we tend automatically to repeat this repertoire without necessarily being aware that we do so.

Secondly, the syndrome derives from human conceptual creativity. We humans use our imagination to form new and complex concepts. We reorganize our previous perceptions into these concepts. And, most importantly, we respond to these concepts as we would respond to the real thing.

The syndrome also derives from our human emotions. For we humans develop manifold emotional responses to our own perceptions and conceptions. In other words, we learn extremely complex responses not only to external stimuli, but also to the conceptual products of our own imagination. And we experience these responses as feelings or emotions.

The syndrome further derives from the human capacity to symbolize. We create symbols and communicate them to others in the form of language and other signs. And we tend to ignore the distinction between these symbols and what they symbolize.

In addition, the syndrome derives from our expanded human awareness. Through the use of concepts, symbols, and communication, we can expand our awareness beyond the confines of our immediacy. We are aware of our past. We can conceive of our future. We can even be aware of our own impending death.

The syndrome also derives from what we call the human intellect or mind.[3] We can abstract concepts and ideas from beyond the limits of our immediate experience. We interpret these abstractions according to our human rules of logic and reason, thus reinforcing them. And we can repress both our real experiences and abstract concepts alike from our immediate awareness.

The syndrome also derives from the human tendency to form close personal ties. We humans tend to form lasting sexual bonds and build family groups around them. We greatly extend parental license over our young, lending extensive influence over their development.

Moreover, the syndrome derives from human socialization. Humans normally exist as social animals. We organize inclusive social systems. We identify with membership in the group. And we develop social institutions, endowing them with a symbolic existence all their very own.

Finally, and most ironically, the syndrome derives from human aspirations. For humans aspire to live beyond the redundancies of a barren animal existence. We impart purpose to our lives, and we strive towards its fulfillment.

Like an insidious parasite, the Suicide Syndrome feeds on the very best its host has to offer. And therein lies its tragic paradox. For the Suicide Syndrome turns the greatest human gifts against the human being.

CHARACTERISTICS OF THE SYNDROME

The Suicide Syndrome comprises a logical, artificial, and self-sustaining system of beliefs, feelings, and behaviors paradoxically aimed at this self-destructive goal. But as paradoxical as the syndrome outwardly appears, it contains an internal logic all its very own.

In fact, once a person accepts the basic premise which lies at the heart of the Suicide Syndrome, actual suicide becomes his only logical objective. Fortunately, human beings rarely behave so logically. Most Suicides spend their entire lives compromising with the logic of the syndrome, never carrying it out to its obvious conclusion.

Although the syndrome contains an internal logic, its basic premise does not. But the Suicide accepts this basic premise at a time, age, and circumstance when logic does not prevail. Once the premise fails to meet the test of rationality, the Suicide's belief in it is repressed. It then becomes the unconscious foundation for the syndrome's further development.

The basic premise of the Suicide Syndrome is disarmingly simple. But the process founded on it grows to infinite complexity. It burgeons into an elaborate interdependent system of beliefs, behaviors, and relations, each sustaining and counter-reinforcing the others. It grows so pervasive and complex that it seems to have an existence all its very own.

Thus, the Suicide Syndrome operates as an orthogenetic system. Each development derives from those preceding it and germinates those to follow. A diversion might form here, a delay or new twist there, but the general development of the syndrome progresses in the life of every Suicide with amazing uniformity. But because the syndrome operates unconsciously, the Suicide is rarely aware of its development.

The Suicide also remains unaware of the syndrome because of its virtual universality. He encounters the signs of the syndrome in other people at his every turn. Even entire social systems fall prey to it. But despite its universality, the Suicide Syndrome is an essentially artificial process. It is antithetical to intrinsic human nature. And, because it is an artificial process, the syndrome can be reversed.

People, individually and collectively, can rid themselves of the syndrome. Suicide can be prevented. And its inherent tragedy can be eradicated through the understanding and alleviation of the Suicide Syndrome.

Chapter 2

THE FANTASTIC SELF

The Suicide's unconscious conviction in his Fantastic Self lies at the heart of the Suicide Syndrome. His Fantastic Self is born in fantasy, endowed with fantastic characteristics, and unconsciously experienced by the Suicide as his own true self. His unconscious conviction in it causes him virtually unlimited shame, humiliation, and despair. It underlies all his self-destructiveness. And it alone foments his impending suicide.

In contrast to his conscious concept of himself but essential to his experience of it, his Fantastic Self comprises all the Suicide unconsciously conceives himself to be. To the extent he cannot manifest its attributes in his behavior, he experiences them as his potential. To the degree that other people fail to ratify its existence, this he blames on their stubbornness, callousness, or stupidity. To the measure the course of his life fails to affirm it, he looks to an inexplicable promise of his future.

His Fantastic Self is perfect, flawless, and infinitely powerful. It is all-knowing and all-understanding. It is immune to the foibles, weaknesses, and vulnerabilities of the ordinary human condition. It is invincible to the casualties of everyday life.

His Fantastic Self is pure, selfless, and ultimately altruistic. It is infinitely lovable, virtuous, and deserving. It is absolutely benign, innocuous, and good. It cannot even know evil, let alone manifest it.

His Fantastic Self is incomprehensible. It exists beyond the confines of mundane experience, above the contingencies of worldly life. Its wisdom is infinite, its existence ethereal and supreme.

In short, his Fantastic Self is Omnipotent, Innocent, and Transcendent. And consequently, it is immortal. His Fantastic Self is also impossible. Yet the Suicide remains unaware of its impossibility. He may realize he harbors impractical expectations of himself, but he refuses to acknowledge their ultimate impossibility. He may feel superior, misunderstood, or estranged from other people, but he blinds himself to the impossibility of his expectations in regard to them. He may experience discontent, ennui, or desperation with the course of his life, but he never allows the utter impossibility of his actually existing as his Fantastic Self to surface into his awareness.

Most importantly, the Suicide remains unaware that he even believes he is his Fantastic Self, let alone facing its impossibility. He cannot grasp its essential nature as a fantasy, nor can he realize he endows it with fantastic characteristics. It never fully registers in his consciousness that what he unconsciously believes himself to be is, in fact, a fantastic self.

The Suicide was not born believing in his Fantastic Self, but it is not a capricious invention of later years. His unconscious belief in it stems from imperatives invoked by his earliest life experiences. He creates his Fantastic Self and he becomes unconsciously convinced he is it because of conditions beyond his volition.

CONTAMINATION OF INTRINSIC GROWTH

If provided ideal conditions, an acorn grows into an oak. While the principle is the same, intrinsic human growth is infinitely more complex. However, conditions conducive to intrinsic human growth are rarely ideal for anyone. They may, in fact, be sufficiently deleterious to corrupt his intrinsic growth in favor of an artificial development compelling him towards creating his Fantastic Self.

These deleterious conditions can exist within his family milieu, the social ambience, and cultural mores. They profoundly distort his experience of himself, other people, and the essence of life. In the process, they corrupt the growth of his intrinsic autonomy, empathy, and spontaneity.

Intrinsic autonomy naturally grows out of the realization of one's own efficacy as a functioning human being. Its growth is corrupted by the imposition of overt and covert extrinsic authority. Rather than learning to actualize his intrinsic sense of inner sovereignty, our budding Suicide learns to perform according to these extrinsic standards, and he learns to judge his own performance in the light of these standards.

The degree of corruption of his intrinsic autonomy is generally contingent with first, the artificiality of imposed standards; secondly, the quality of either overt stringency or covert insidiousness under which they are imposed; and thirdly, their relative inconsistency with his natural development. Capricious criteria, either harshly or insidiously imposed at a time and circumstance guaranteeing his inability satisfactorily to fulfill them, are the most deleterious. They virtually assure that the growth of his autonomy will be completely corrupted.

However, an infant or child experiences his own efficacy through the autonomous development of those skills associated with natural human growth. Thus, at the same time that these conditions corrupt the growth of his intrinsic autonomy, they also cause him to experience himself as intrinsically inefficacious.

Likewise, intrinsic empathy with other people evolves directly out of experiencing genuine empathy emitted from them. Its growth can be contaminated or aborted by significant others in his environment setting idiosyncratic conditions he must meet in order to gain satisfaction of his bona fide needs.

Rather than learning to relate empathetically with other people, our developing Suicide learns strategies of relating to them. Furthermore, he learns to employ these strategies as unconscious pretenses in order to gain satisfaction of his needs.

The degree of corruption of his intrinsic empathy is generally contingent with first, the range of idiosyncratic conditions employed by significant others; secondly, the quality or quantity of unconscious duplicity he must employ in return; and thirdly, the artificiality of these pretenses. Spurious criteria, hypocritically or inconsistently employed, have the most corrupting effect.

However, an infant or child experiences his being loved as the empathetic recognition and unconditional satisfaction of his genuine needs. Thus, these conditions not only corrupt the natural growth of his intrinsic empathy, they cause him to experience himself as intrinsically unlovable.

Finally, intrinsic spontaneity normally grows out of the unhampered expression of natural responses to stimuli, including self-expression, self-interest, and sexuality. Its growth can be blocked by the environmental imposition of artificial constraints designed overtly or covertly to control them.

Rather than respond spontaneously to natural stimuli, our future Suicide learns to artificially control his responses. Furthermore, he learns to divert the energy he would otherwise spontaneously expend to inhibit psychophysiologically his own intrinsic responses.

The degree of corruption to his intrinsic spontaneity is generally contingent with first, the artificiality of these constraints; secondly, the amount of overt or covert pressure used in applying them; and thirdly, the quality or quantity of energy he learns to deploy to inhibit his own responses. Essentially artificial constraints, pervasively applied, accompanied by subtle rewards for inhibition have the most deleterious effect.

However, the developing child experiences his organismic integration into life through his spontaneous expression of natural responses to stimuli. Thus, these constraints do not just corrupt the development of his spontaneity. They also teach him to inhibit his own vitality, thereby blocking his integration into the mainstream of organic life.

This comprehensive contamination process pervades the neophyte Suicide's early life experiences. No single aspect or event could produce an effect so overwhelming. He sometimes valiantly struggles against it—no one forfeits his autonomy, empathy, and spontaneity without a struggle—but because of social reinforcement of the process, it eventually conquers.

Should he survive without succumbing either to death from mysterious causes or lack of resistance to disease, or to personality disintegration, we now find him in an untenable situation. We find him devoid of his autonomy, empathy, and spontaneity, experiencing himself as inefficacious, unlovable, and inhibited in meeting life. As he grows older, these conditions combine to generate profound and unbearable feelings of insignificance, anxiety, and tension.

But he does have an apparent solution. Although he cannot regain his autonomy, empathy, and spontaneity, he can relieve the unbearable feelings resulting from their loss. This he can do by creating his Fantastic Self.

CREATION OF THE FANTASTIC SELF

He uses his emerging powers of imagination to create an imaginary self-concept. And he can reorganize this self-concept any way he sees fit. He can endow it with strength and power to ameliorate his inefficacy. He can give it goodness and virtue to allay his unlovableness. He can grant it self-sufficiency to offset his alienation from the mainstream of life.

Furthermore, in order to overcome his feelings of insignificance, anxiety, and tension, he can so reify his self-endowed characteristics that they can become all that really matter. The more insignificant he feels, the more anxiety and tension he experiences, the more he must glorify the characteristics of his new self-concept.

He eventually so glorifies his new self-concept as to make it into a Fantastic Self on two accounts. In the first place, it is born of fantasy. It is but the product of his imagination. In the second place, he endows it with fantastic characteristics. He so glorifies them that he eventually renders them ultimate and absolute.

He creates his Fantastic Self to compensate for his loss of autonomy, empathy, and spontaneity, and to relieve his feelings of insignificance, anxiety, and tension. To these ends, his Fantastic Self attains a resounding success. But his elation is not long-lasting. Inevitably, reality enters the picture. And it is the harbinger of new sources of pain, anxiety, and tension.

He begins to compare his new Fantastic Self with his real experiences of himself as inefficacious, unlovable, and inhibited. Again, he is brought up short as he faces the painful comparison. And once again, he suffers a new source of anxiety—the dread that he really is inefficacious, unlovable, and inhibited rather than radiating all the glories of his Fantastic Self.

Having come this far, he now has no choice. He must alleviate these new sources of pain and anxiety. He must retreat into himself and achieve the irrevocable conviction that he really is his Fantastic Self.

DEVELOPMENT OF THE FANTASTIC SELF

This is truly a momentous decision. Once he becomes convinced he is truly his Fantastic Self, he faces profound and disastrous consequences. First of all, he diverts all his energies into the development of his Fantastic Self rather than devoting them to his natural growth and development. This process is analogous to contrived manufacture as opposed to natural growth. Instead of the natural spontaneous growth of his intrinsic qualities, he employs a self-conscious forming, shaping, and forcing of himself in trying actually to be his Fantastic Self.

Thus, the developing Suicide abandons his innate growth in favor of his Fantastic Self's development. As a result, he actually becomes arrested in his genuine growth. And since this process occurs in the child, whenever genuine autonomy, empathy, or spontaneity do appear in his later behavior, they appear in childish ways.[4]

Moreover, with his innate growth arrested, his need further to nurture his Fantastic Self becomes insatiable. Inevitably, he finds himself under its complete control. For although he is the creator of his Fantastic Self, his Fantastic Self now requires everything of him. Having abandoned his true growth in favor of the development of his Fantastic Self, he puts himself at its mercy.[5]

Finally, and most ironically, he attempts to manifest the glorified characteristics of his Fantastic Self in his behavior. Once again, reality intervenes. And once again, he faces a painful discrepancy. Now utterly convinced he is his Fantastic Self and devoting everything he has to its development, he finds he cannot manifest its glorified characteristics in his everyday life.

REPRESSION OF THE FANTASTIC SELF

Faced with this new dilemma, the young Suicide must either abandon his sense of consensual reality, withdrawing into a world of his own, or repress his belief that he is his Fantastic Self.[6] But once he represses it, his Fantastic Self becomes even further removed from the mediating confines of reality. He is now free to escalate his Fantastic Self's characteristics to the absolute.

His glorification of strength and power turn into absolute Omnipotence. His goodness and virtue turn into absolute Innocence. His detached self-sufficiency turns into absolute Transcendence. Released from the mediating effects of reality, his Fantastic Self evolves into the absolute All.[7]

Furthermore, his repression of his Fantastic Self not only allows it to evolve into the impossible, it also renders his Fantastic Self inaccessible to his awareness. This carries a double-binding effect, for in the future, the more his Fantastic Self conflicts with reality, the deeper he must repress it. And the deeper he represses it, the more inaccessible to his awareness it becomes. Thus, the more unconsciously convinced he is in his Fantastic Self, the more readily he abdicates the course of his life to its control.

Our neophyte has now evolved into a full-fledged Suicide. Having suffered the corruption of his intrinsic autonomy, empathy, and spontaneity, he experiences himself as inefficacious, unlovable, and inhibited from organic life. As a concomitant result, he incurs feelings of insignificance, anxiety, and tension. To compensate for the loss of his intrinsic growth and to relieve his feelings of insignificance, anxiety, and tension, he creates a glorified self-concept, his Fantastic Self, and he convinces himself he is it. As his convictions conflict with reality, he represses them, allowing his Fantastic Self to assume the absolute attributes of Omnipotence, Innocence, and Transcendence.

Furthermore, by repressing his convictions in his Fantastic Self, he turns over to it the whole course of his life and the goal of his death. Arrested in his intrinsic growth, he makes the sole unconscious purpose of his life—and the underlying goal of his impending suicide—the impossible actualization of his Fantastic Self.

Chapter 3

THE EMPIRICAL SELF

The young Suicide unconsciously believes he is his impossible Omnipotent, Innocent, and Transcendent Fantastic Self. Yet he must function within the realm of the possible. He must become a real person, relate to other people in a real world, exist in the cold glaring light of reality.

But with the growth of his intrinsic autonomy, empathy, and spontaneity diverted in favor of an artificial development, he has no real substance to him. Believing himself to be the absolute in every way, he has no real selfhood with which he can relate to others. Convinced in the fantasy of himself, he possesses no functional reality. Superficially, he may appear to be progressing through the natural stages of personal growth, but this essential dilemma pervasively haunts him.

To the careful observer his dilemma can show itself in manifold ways. It can surface in an unsettling artificiality. One can never be quite sure of him. There appears a subtle duplicity, a bland denial, a comprehensive artificiality, an occasional blatant falsehood.

It can also appear in a deep sense of anxious insecurity. New experiences elicit acute anxieties. Sleep brings nightmares, tensions mount under situations relatively free of stress, fears arise in the absence of the apparent threat.

It can also appear in a preoccupation with a private world of the Suicide's own, coupled with a mistrust of virtually everything outside it. However he delineates his private world—whether he includes a handful of peers or siblings or limits it to just himself—his world is all that counts and all he can trust.

But the ways in which his dilemma may show itself on the surface are but superficial intimations of a far deeper and more profound existential one: the self he unconsciously believes he is, is but an illusion. In order to live in a real world of real possibilities, he must somehow become a real person, one who actually exists and who actually relates to other people. The person he becomes is his Empirical Self.[8]

THE ADOLESCENT PREDICAMENT

The Suicide must negotiate a difficult and harrowing experience in order to become his Empirical Self. Unconsciously believing he is his Fantastic Self, he attempts to manifest its absolute attributes in his behavior, feelings, and thought processes. But how can he even attempt to manifest omnipotence, innocence, and transcendence simultaneously? How can he be powerful and benign, masterful and compliant, competitive and detached, humble and aloof, all at the same time?

Because of this diverse opposition of his Fantastic Self's attributes, he suffers a severe lack of intrapsychic unity. At one moment, he feels master of all he surveys—at the next, a faithful and obedient slave. At one moment he believes he loves everyone—at the next, he wants nothing more than to withdraw into an isolated cave.

This lack of unity colors all his inner processes. His values and objectives vacillate from one radical extreme to another. Racked by his own diffusion, he has no existential continuity to him, no reality. His feelings, beliefs, and behaviors are unpredictable, even to him. This diffusion and confusion urge him towards some kind of unity, if only an artificial one.

Secondly, this confusion and diffusion also enter into his relations with other people. Neither he nor they really know who he is. As a consequence, he incurs a profound need for identity.[9]

His need for identity is a powerful one. For stripped of his intrinsic responses and struggling to manifest an impossible Fantastic Self, he has no real identity to count on. Other people experience him as an unpredictable and unidentifiable unknown. Is he a strong leader or a dependent follower? Is he a generous friend or an acquiescent recipient of other people's kindness? Is he a self-reliant victor over the obstacles of life or a dependent burden on others?

His lack of identity is far from illusionary. To the contrary, it is strictly on account of his illusions that he lacks an identity. There is no real self to identify. The self he believes real is a fantasy. Yet he still must deal with real people in a real world. He must, therefore, find some way to establish an interpersonal identity.

Finally, regardless of the universality of his Fantastic Self's attributes, they are useless to him in a world of reality. He must function in a real world. He must actually *be*, in a real existence. But he forfeits his real existence to the pursuit of a mirage. Worse, he makes this mirage all that he is. Consequently, he simply does not exist as a real person; he exists only in the realm of his imagination. Although he rarely, if ever, consciously perceives this immutable fact, the existential anxiety resulting from it constantly haunts him.

In order to function in the realm of reality, he is forced to create a functional existence. By the necessities invoked by his very being in this world, he must contrive a utilitarian selfhood that at least gives the appearance of functional utility.

The adolescent Suicide does not know what he is, who he is, or even *that* he is. Anxious, confused, and diffused because of the opposing attributes of his Fantastic Self, he cannot even vouch for his own existence. In order to live a real life, he must devise a real self. He achieves a real selfhood by means of an unconscious resolution of his confusion, diffusion, and conflicts. He thereby actually becomes his Empirical Self.

THE ADOLESCENT RESOLUTION

The Suicide's Empirical Self is that person whom he, other people, and the existential environment empirically experience in everyday life. His Empirical Self functions, relates to other people, actually exists. Regardless of the Suicide's unconscious convictions otherwise, he really *is* his Empirical Self.

He becomes his Empirical Self through an unconscious resolution of his conflicts. He unconsciously achieves unity, identity, and functional utility by means of repression, fixation, and idealization.

First, the Suicide unconsciously represses two of his Fantastic Self's diverse attributes. Simultaneously motivated in three contradictory and opposing directions, he achieves intrapsychic unity by unconsciously cancelling two of them. His repression of these attributes does not diminish their absolute nature. He merely submerges them deeper in his unconsciousness.

Secondly, the Suicide forms an unconscious fixation on the remaining attribute of his Fantastic Self, thereby gaining an interpersonal identity. His fixation influences his concepts, feelings, behavior, and relations with regard to himself, other people, and the core of his existence. It determines his personality, his goals, his objectives in life.

Thirdly, the Suicide begins to idealize his fixed attribute and despise his repressed attributes. This idealization of his fixed attribute goes beyond providing him unity and identity. It provides him functional utility. It validates his existence. It gives him something to stand for, principles to believe in, concepts to build on, purpose to exist.

Through this process of repression, fixation, and idealization, the adolescent Suicide attains unity, identity, and functional utility. Now he exists. Now he can function. He knows who and what he is. He can relate to himself, to other people, and to his existence as a whole person. That this entire process comes about unconsciously and artificially is of little or no importance, at least for now. For although the Suicide actually becomes his Empirical Self, he still does not abandon his conviction that he is his Fantastic Self.

CHOICE OF TYPE

The Suicide's Empirical Self results from his selective repression, fixation, and idealization of his Fantastic Self's three diverse attributes. Those two attributes he represses and the one he fixates combine to establish his type in the Suicide Syndrome. There are three general types:

The *Antipathic Type* represses the Fantastic Self's Innocence and Transcendence. He fixates and idealizes its Omnipotence.

The *Synpathic Type* represses the Fantastic Self's Omnipotence and Transcendence. He fixates and idealizes its Innocence.

The *Apathic Type* represses the Fantastic Self's Omnipotence and Innocence. He fixates and idealizes its Transcendence.

While most of this unconscious resolution takes place during the

Suicide's adolescence, the process actually begins much earlier and continues into his adulthood. The Suicide begins selecting his particular role at the earliest stirrings of life. His attitudes towards his own efficacy in the light of external authority, the strategies he learns to employ in relation to other people in order to gain satisfaction of his needs, the character of inhibited control he learns to use, all effect his later choice of type.

But a myriad of other factors can also influence the process. These may be physiological, genetic endowment, physiological and psychological trauma, birth order, socioeconomic conditions, and cultural influences. Yet the most important factor is the degree of respective contamination of his intrinsic autonomy, empathy, and spontaneity.

The Antipathic Type, by fixating and idealizing the Fantastic Self's Omnipotence, and by repressing and despising its Transcendence and Innocence, seeks his autonomy lost in childhood. During the Antipathic Type's development, his autonomy suffers significantly more corruption than his other intrinsic responses. But as we will soon see, the kind of autonomy he attempts to gain appears as but a parody of its intrinsic expression. He unconsciously attempts to reestablish his sense of autonomy, exaggerating it to the extent of making himself absolutely Omnipotent.

On the other hand, the Synpathic Type, whose intrinsic empathy was corrupted in childhood, represses and despises the Fantastic Self's Omnipotence and Transcendence, and fixates and idealizes its Innocence. But again, there is such a gross exaggeration of expressions of empathy as to render them but a travesty of the genuine article. Thus, the primary unconscious goal underlying the Synpathic role is exaggerating this sense of empathy, even to the extent of becoming absolutely Innocent.

Finally, the exaggeration of the Apathic Type's expression of spontaneity to impossible proportions, coupled with the evasion of expressions of autonomy and empathy, indicates its particularly severe corruption in early childhood. Robbed of spontaneous participation in the essence of organic life, the Apathic Type tries to transcend it. Thus, the main unconscious goal in the Apathic role is regaining his lost spontaneity, but in the gross form of absolute Transcendence.

None of the three intrinsic responses—autonomy, empathy, and spontaneity—could suffer complete contamination while the others remain intact. All three incur such corruption as to cause the Suicide to abandon them in favor of seeking an imaginary selfhood. Yet a more comprehensive contamination of one particular area always underlies his unconscious choice of role.

However, once he selects his particular role, the Suicide pursues its ends with all the vigor his illusions provide him. His choice eventually determines his personality. It sets the tone of his life, how he relates to others, how he feels about himself. Finally, it determines his primary motivation towards suicide.

Part II

SUICIDAL TYPES

Chapter 4

COMMON CHARACTERISTICS

The Suicide's Empirical Self is who and what he really is. It is, never-theless, founded on the impossible attributes of his Fantastic Self. His Adolescent Resolution does lend him a superficial unity, identity, and functional utility. It defines what kind of person he is, how he relates to other people, and the meanings he imparts to life. But behind the results of his resolution he is unequivocally, albeit unconsciously, de-termined to actualize his Fantastic Self.

His choice of type merely establishes the ways he goes about man-ifesting this secret goal. For instance, everything the Antipathic Type does is unconsciously calculated to manifest his omnipotence. His be-liefs about himself, his attitudes regarding work and accomplishment, how he treats other people, the values he strives towards in life, all grow out of his unconscious goal. And the parallel holds true for the other two types. Underneath their every act lies Synpathic innocence or Apathic transcendence. Thus, each Suicidal Type differs dramati-cally from the others in countless superficial ways. However, the com-mon conviction in his Fantastic Self automatically results in certain Common Characteristics for them all.

45

The personality of each type might tend to camouflage some particular common characteristics and accentuate others. But strictly because of his conviction in his Fantastic Self every Suicide becomes characterized by unconscious pride, egocentricity, narcissism, perfectionism, compulsiveness, obsessiveness, arrogant superiority, and apparent irrationality.

UNCONSCIOUS PRIDE

Unconscious Pride is by far the most significant and potentially destructive common characteristic, for it renders the Suicide infinitely vulnerable to the realities of his existence. But because he believes he is his Fantastic Self, the Suicide must constantly reinforce his impossible belief with pride.[1]

Pride growing out of the Suicide's conviction in his Fantastic Self must be distinguished from fulfillment gained through realizing intrinsic autonomy, empathy, and spontaneity. Certainly, realization of one's own efficacy, mutuality with others, and integration into the natural processes of existence contains inherent rewards. But these rewards are genuine, durable, and substantiated by experiences in everyday life.

In contrast, the Suicide's pride seeks rewards only in the apparent confirmation of his Fantastic Self. And, as a consequence, his rewards are spurious, fleeting, and inevitably contradicted by the vicissitudes of everyday life.

The Suicide invariably ignores this fundamental distinction. Consequently he keeps escalating his pride, rendering himself further vulnerable to the pain resulting from its contradiction. He may seem to give up bits of it from time to time but, in reality, the Suicide merely represses his pride; he cannot sacrifice it.

The superficial aspects of the Suicide's pride can often be confusing, but not when we remember what it is of which he is proud. To be sure, the Antipathic Type's pride often shows through clearly in all its shining glory. He knows he is Omnipotent, and is proud of it. But the pride of the Synpathic Type rarely shows in ways we customarily recognize as pride. Pride in Innocence contains an inherent contradiction. And the Apathic Type's pride can also be paradoxical. Pride in Transcendence is not of this world.

But whichever attribute of his Fantastic Self the Suicide fixates, he must reinforce it with pride. The Omnipotent Antipathic Type must be proud of power, strength, and mastery. The Innocent Synpathic Type must be proud of altruism, lovableness, and benignity. The Transcendent Apathic Type must be proud of unworldliness, self-sufficiency, and cosmic universality.

As confusing as the Suicide's pride in his fixed attribute can sometimes appear, he further complicates the picture by growing unconsciously proud of his repressed attributes. Since these attributes are simply repressed, not diminished, they still are essential to the comprehensive concept of his Fantastic Self and they must be reinforced with pride. While pride in his repressed attributes is rarely as apparent as pride in his fixed attribute, it nevertheless renders him increasingly vulnerable to mysterious pain resulting from its contradiction.

Ultimately, the Suicide grows proud of the illusion of his Fantastic Self, simply as an illusion. Pride in his illusion of his Fantastic Self overflows into pride in all his illusions and in his other mental processes as well. Consequently, every Suicide also grows proud of his powers of intellect, reason, and will.

Because of pride in his illusions, he clings to them tenaciously. Although he may occasionally recognize their illusionary nature, he feels that he would dissolve into nothingness should he forego them.

Because of pride in his intellectual powers, he believes he is knowledgeable in everything. He may appear uninformed or even ignorant, but he judges himself all-knowing.

Because of pride in his reasoning powers, he never doubts his impossible dream. Unquestionably believing he is his Fantastic Self, it is only reasonable that life should prove him out. While others may judge him stubborn or fatuous, he knows he is the paragon of reason. Given his basic premise—the belief in his Fantastic Self—it is only logical for him to pursue its ends.

Finally, because of pride in his will power, he never waivers from his singular course. He knows he can do it, simply because he has the will. And while his convictions cost him dearly in the face of real situations, he never loses faith in the power of his will.

The Suicide's pride costs him even more dearly in many other ways, as we shall see, but it is essential to him. Without the reinforcing effects of his pride, his Fantastic Self would collapse in the face of reality. This could mean chaos in a void, because his real Empirical Self is founded on it. Regardless of its price, as long as the Suicide clings to the conviction that he is his Fantastic Self, he must reinforce it with pride.

EGOCENTRICITY

The second characteristic growing out of the Suicide's unconscious conviction in his Fantastic Self is an underlying egocentricity.[2] This is not ordinary selfishness nor blatant self-concern. While these may superficially indicate an underlying egocentricity, the Suicide's outward behavior often belies his egocentricity.

He may appear to be completely absorbed in his work, or wholly dedicated to some social cause. He may seem to be devoted to the happiness and welfare of other people. He may profess to having no rights, no power to influence others, nor the ultimate course of his own life.

Nevertheless, the Suicide's egocentricity is a subjective and profound one. The Suicide Syndrome has an utterly private scope. It absorbs every aspect of the Suicide's life into the centricity of itself, like an astronomical black hole. The Suicide has his private religion: the belief in his Fantastic Self. He has his private dogma: the pride he invests in his being his Fantastic Self. He has his private rituals: his behavior aimed at actualizing his Fantastic Self. He even has his private heaven: the immortality of his Fantastic Self.

He is the measure of all things. He perceives himself, other people, and the panorama of life only through the periscope of his submerged egocentricity. Whether he behaves as uncompromisingly selfish or utterly self-sacrificing, gregariously personable or friendless and withdrawn, the Suicide is profoundly egocentric. His belief in his Fantastic Self lies at the very core of his egocentricity.

NARCISSISM

Because of his conviction in his Fantastic Self, the Suicide also grows narcissistic. Ordinarily, we consider a narcissistic person as being in love with himself. But the Suicide's narcissism more closely resembles the original myth. He does not love himself. Quite on the contrary, as we shall soon see, the Suicide grows to hate himself. But like Narcissus, who falls in love with his image reflected in a pool of water, the Suicide falls madly in love with his image of himself. The Suicide loves his Fantastic Self.[3]

He idealizes his Fantastic Self. He is awestruck by its potential and magnitude. He humbles himself before it. He closes his mind to its imaginary nature and to its irrational grounds.

He preoccupies himself with his Fantastic Self. He devotes all his energies and resources to its actualization. All that he is, he puts into its service. His Fantastic Self dominates his every thought, dictates his every action, prescribes his every feeling. It is the object of his dreams, the subject of his fantasies, the sole purpose of his daily life.

Like Narcissus, the Suicide's love for his image of himself is exclusive. It leaves no possibility for genuine love for anyone else. And, like Narcissus, he can be eventually destroyed by it.

PERFECTIONISM

Because of the absolute attributes of his Fantastic Self, the Suicide becomes perfectionistic. We usually picture a perfectionist as one who strives for outward perfection in any of the manifold functions of human endeavor. Such behaviors may certainly characterize it, but they are not necessarily the perfectionism of the Suicide.

Just as often, the picture we observe might be one of a person who neglects the details of his work, his appearance, his health, and the condition of his personal environment, or who is sloppy in his habits and whose affairs are in constant disarray. However, the Suicide whose virtually every mannerism reflects his striving for outward perfection and the one whose mannerisms reflect just the opposite, both have a Fanastic Self which is already perfect.

If his fixed attribute is Innocence, manifested through perfect love and sacrifice for others, then certainly he could not be occupied with selfish concern about his own welfare, health, appearance, or the organization of his own affairs. Or if his fixed attribute is Transcendence, manifested through perfect freedom and independence, then surely he could not be bothered with such mundane responsibilities. If he is Omnipotent and capable of perfect mastery over all the larger aspects of life, he should not have to bother with such petty details.

So, despite the appearance or lack of what we ordinarily picture as perfectionism in his behavior, underneath the picture poses his perfect Fantastic Self.

COMPULSIVENESS

Because of the absolute attributes of his Fantastic Self, the Suicide becomes compulsive. He simply must feel, behave, and respond in accordance with the fixed attribute of his Fantastic Self. Since he unconsciously believes this image is all he really is, he becomes literally driven towards the futile effort to actualize it.

All that is compulsive in the Suicide Syndrome has this headlong plunging towards the fulfillment of his Fantastic Self as its motivating force. Accordingly, the Suicide displays a callous disregard for his genuine best interests. A most blatant example is the obvious one of his very contemplation of suicide. Yet this disregard for his genuine best interests shows up in many other subtle and obvious ways.

The compulsive nature of his behaviors also appears in their indiscriminateness. Regardless of his present situation, condition in life, intrinsic capabilities, inherent limitations, or early environmental conditions, he simply must be what he believes himself to be. He takes into consideration none of the realities pertaining to himself, other people, prevailing socioeconomic conditions, nor the character of the course of human life.

Finally, his compulsiveness grows out of the Fantastic Self's insatiability. The criteria of his Fantastic Self are never met. No amount of power, goodness, independence is ever quite enough. Only the absolute would suffice. The Suicide must constantly accelerate his efforts to fulfill these criteria. There is no end, no completion, no lasting satisfaction.

The Suicide's compulsiveness shows through in manifold ways. Despite his belief that his feelings, behavior, and motivations are all his own doing, his belief in his Fantastic Self compels him accordingly. At often incalculable cost to his genuine best interests, he remains compulsively driven towards the impossible fulfillment of his Fantastic Self.

OBSESSIVENESS

The Suicide's unconscious conviction in his Fantastic Self also causes him to become obsessive. Here again, we ordinarily depict an obsessive person as obviously engulfed by an ideal, concept, or mission in life, to which he subjects his behavioral repertoire. Although this may represent the outward behavior of some Suicides, others unconsciously disguise their true obsessiveness.

Many Suicides act as though they have no apparent sense of purpose, no active strivings towards any goal, no real deliberateness in anything they think, feel, or do. Yet, underneath, the Suicide is truly obsessed with his Fantastic Self.

When he is not trying outwardly to behave as his Fantastic Self, he is inwardly thinking about it. This usually means he is worrying about it. To the objective observer, even to those people in his immediate surroundings, he may seem completely unconcerned with the purpose and meaning of his own life. He may display a remarkable detachment in regard to the real conditions of his daily life, to the purposeful structuring of his time, to the long-term directions in which he moves. Nevertheless, his cognitive process is at work, worrying about being his Fantastic Self.

On the other hand, he may be fantasizing about it. He is obsessed with the essential fantasy of himself. As a result, his fantasy life may be rich with daydreams of great heroics, monumental achievements, ethereal goodness. He may submerge himself in visions of infinite wisdom or reveries of universal or passionate love.

Yet some Suicides can honestly say that they have little or no conscious fantasy life, and that they really do not worry about much of anything. Their entire behavior might reflect a phlegmatic indifference toward themselves, other people, and the course of their life in general.

But in no way does their apparent indifference signify an absence of obsessiveness: it merely indicates the transcendence of the Fantastic Self. Convinced of a Fantastic Self that transcends mundane life, the Suicide becomes obsessed with manifesting it through obvious indifference toward his everyday mundane affairs.

Arrogant Superiority

Because of the absolute attributes of his Fantastic Self, the Suicide always becomes characterized by arrogant superiority. Although many Suicides display the boasting pompous air we usually associate with an arrogantly superior person, many do not. But whether the Suicide's outward behavior or conscious self-concept reflects it or not, arrogant superiority automatically results from his secret conviction that he is his Fantastic Self.

First, he arrogates qualities to himself which he cannot possibly manifest in actual behavior. Secondly, he so idealizes both these arrogated qualities and those he might actually possess as to render himself unmistakably superior to others.

His arrogant superiority may appear in many subtle ways. He may evince self-abnegating humility while harboring beneath it a holier-than-thou attitude. He may parade self-deprivation while inwardly feeling above the selfish hedonists around him. He may even elicit abuse from others while maintaining a moral advantage. He may hold himself aloof from the pursuits of the common herd, all the while feeling superior to their triviality.

The behavior of those Suicides who do openly and indiscriminately display an air of arrogant superiority is familiar to us all. But whether or not the Suicide openly displays his arrogant superiority, or is even consciously aware of it, it is always present. His Fantastic Self is superior in every way, thereby automatically rendering him arrogant by virtue of his belief he is it.

Apparent Irrationality

Despite the intellectual origins of the Fantastic Self, the Suicide invariably appears irrational. He makes no rational assessment of his egocentricity in a world composed of interdependent autonomous human beings. He ignores the rational evaluation of the universal human condition. He rationalizes away his own particular limitations in favor of a private myth. He forfeits the sure knowledge of himself and the quiet self-confidence which would accrue, to the anxious pursuits of an impossible dream. Finally, he irrationally idealizes the dream itself, thereby glorifying his own irrationality.

The Suicide's conviction in his Fantastic Self automatically renders him proud, egocentric, narcissistic, perfectionistic, compulsive, obsessive, arrogantly superior, and irrational. These characteristics are shared by all Suicides alike, regardless of how evident in overt behaviors.

Some Suicides may outwardly act more compulsive or more perfectionistic, for example, but appearances can be very deceiving. Just because the Suicide fails outwardly to display these characteristics in the ways we are accustomed to seeing, in no way means he is free of them.

Yet the overt behavior of the Suicide does carry paramount significance in many other ways. The aggregate of his behavior not only characterizes his type, but it reflects how and what he feels in relation to himself, what he thinks and feels about other people, and how he relates to the essence of his very own existence.

Chapter 5

HAROLD — THE ANTIPATHIC TYPE

The Antipathic Type Suicide fixates omnipotence and represses innocence and transcendence. Harold Roberts, our typical Antipathic Type, unconsciously believes he is his Omnipotent Fantastic Self. This unconscious belief constitutes the foundation upon which his real Empirical Self is based. It shapes his personality and determines the way he relates to himself, to others, and to life. It also establishes his Primary Motivation to suicide.

The characteristics, goals, and values of the Antipathic Type are heavily reinforced by our society, especially in our men.[4] Women living in the Antipathic role usually do so secretly, surreptitiously, or vicariously through their men.

But an Antipathic man can drive himself to suicide, and most people will not have even noticed anything was wrong until after the deed is done. Even then, they may be mystified or disbelieving.[5] Our society so idealizes the characteristics of the Antipathic role for its men, it refuses to recognize the destructiveness of those characteristics.

Intrapsychic Factors

But destructive they are: and in Harold Roberts' case, ultimately self-destructive. Harold believes in power, mastery, and control. He so glorifies this belief as to render it but a travesty of his previously crushed autonomy, which he unconsciously seeks. Harold unconsciously makes the impossible manifestation of his imagined omnipotence his primary goal in life.

Like most Antipathic Types in our culture, Harold utilizes his work as the main route towards manifesting this goal. In his work, there is no problem too great for Harold to solve, no task too difficult for him to master. Whatever his actual situation may be, he sees himself as the Chairman of the Board, the real Power behind the Throne, or at least, the unrecognized Brains of the Outfit. He overestimates his own contributions and he minimizes the contributions of others.

Harold makes comprehensive and often secretly grandiose plans. He drives himself mercilessly to complete them. He briskly plunges into his work first thing in the morning. He spends his lunchtime working or talking shop. He uses the afternoon berating his co-workers. He brings a briefcase full of work, or stories of his real or imagined achievements, home with him at night. On Harold's desk or locker door may be his motto: "The difficult I do right away, the impossible takes a little longer."

The irony of his slogan is that Harold really believes it of himself. He believes he is capable of everything. He is masterful, he is strong. He is always right, he is never wrong. His values are the standards of humanity: his ethics, its universal laws. He believes all of this about himself, and he makes sure to let other people know about it, too.

Harold usually strives for a leadership position. If conditions prevent him from leading, he eventually loses interest in the venture —unless he can maneuver into some prominent role. He especially likes playing Expert-from-out-of-Town, Authority-in-his-Field, or simply Diamond-in-the-Rough.

Of course, all this requires a tremendous expenditure of Harold's energies. He must always strive for control. But to Harold, his relentlessly driving himself is simply normal ambition or self-discipline. Although he may occasionally complain of the contingencies of his condition, he harbors no real sympathy for his helplessly driven self.

This is understandable. For Antipathic Harold represses the other two attributes of the Fantastic Self, Innocence and Transcendence. And he despises and depreciates the feelings and behaviors characterizing them.

To Harold, altruistic love is cheap sentimentality. Compassion is for fools. After all, it's every man for himself. And as far as benign compliance with others is concerned, that would make him appear weak or helpless: so how could he show compassion, even for himself? The same holds true for transcendent freedom, objectivity, and detachment. Who could Harold defeat and control if he were isolated and alone?

Above all, Harold must be the master. He must always be in control. The impossibility of effecting these standards in his everyday life always escapes his awareness. It may be the only thing Antipathic Harold does *not* know.

INTERPERSONAL FACTORS

In his interpersonal relations, Harold is always on the offensive. Here too, he must always be in control. He can be outright sadistic in his treatment of other people. But he may employ some skill at human relations. If so, Harold can be pleasant and outgoing. He can be generous, gregarious, and entertaining. But his motives are not to bring others genuine joy or pleasure. He is out to gain admiration, to exert control, to manipulate others into liking him—for his own motives, or just to enhance his public image.

His relations with other people in work situations are normally strained. His behavior may vary from open contempt for subordinates, through intimidation of peers, to subversive derision of superiors. He may disguise his motives behind a warm handshake, a fixed smile, a shallow camaraderie, or a bumbling ineptitude. But even so, wherever he circulates, he leaves those in his wake with a feeling of having been *had*.

He carries these same techniques into his close relationships. He still must be in control. The less control he attains at work or other endeavors, the more he must assert at home. He assesses his mate or lover on the basis of her usefulness to him. He uses her in terms of service, to care for his possessions, his personal needs, to bear his children, to service him sexually, to entertain his pals, customers, or superiors, to help further his goals.

But her purpose is more than just to serve his actual needs. He also uses her to provide social status, to enhance his public image, to lend him the appearance of success or security. Even though he may keep her in the background, she still forms an essential link in his life's master plan, and her inevitable failure to fulfill all these functions to his total satisfaction provokes his unmitigated rage. Yet the harder she tries to satisfy him, the more he escalates his demands.

He has an uncanny ability unconsciously to choose a Synpathic Type mate who is always anxious to please. Regardless of how strong a front she may present, he sees right through it. He can spot her inherent weakness at a glance. And for reasons of her own, she is drawn to him like a magnet. Their relationship is nearly always turbulent. She suffers from his open hostility and he chafes from unfilled demands.

For Harold will not hesitate to assert his demands upon his mate or upon anyone else. He believes he deserves their total satisfaction. On this account, he rarely feels any obligation to those who satisfy them. Yet nothing will provoke Harold's rage more quickly than the frustration of his demands. He automatically feels cheated and insulted. He will take up the challenge as a personal vendetta. He will go to almost any lengths to get his way.

If satisfaction is still not forthcoming, he feels utterly defeated. But only temporarily. He then reacts with vehement retaliation. He is out to get an enemy any way he can. In the end, he must be the victor, one way or another. Thus he brings his competitiveness into all his relationships.

It would be far too limiting to consider Harold's competitiveness only in respect to those who are his actual rivals. Harold does not confine it to competing for a particular advantageous goal, status, or position. Instead, he competes with everyone with whom he comes into contact.

He sets his own private criteria in measuring up the competition. His scale of values may be based on almost anything; it need not be appropriate to the situation at hand. He just has to find some way to compete in which he is assured of winning.

He even chooses his associates on a competitive basis. He must appear superior to them in some obvious way. But they cannot be so obviously inferior as to reflect on his prestige. This is important, because he also chooses friends on the basis of reflected glory. He tries to befriend those people who can provide him prestige by virtue of the association.

Harold does not necessarily restrict any of these strategies to gaining any useful advantages. Real gains are rarely his goal. Yet that picture serves as an excellent analogy of how Harold views his entire life. His is an all-encompassing struggle to be on top.

EXISTENTIAL FACTORS

Harold sees life as the eternal struggle of all-against-all. He wins friends. He conquers women. He overcomes obstacles. He defeats enemies. He subdues competitors. He surmounts challenges. He masters situations. He gains advantages. He acquires power. In his consuming drive to triumph over life, he relinquishes any hope of genuinely loving or being loved. He willingly sacrifices his freedom and independence on the altar of symbolic victory.

Harold attempts to offset his existential alienation by turning against himself, other people, and mundane existence. He tries to conquer life rather than simply live it. Obviously, Harold must fail.

In the first place, Harold must fail because his fixation on omnipotence automatically ends as hollow. Failing to see the impossibility of his Omnipotent Fantastic Self, he believes himself capable of everything. Yet the realities of life inevitably prove him wrong.

Because of his exaggerated expectations of himself, he takes on challenges he cannot possibly overcome. Because of his competitiveness and need to defeat others, he rarely receives their sincere cooperation in his endeavors. Because of his overestimation of his real capabilities, he underestimates the time and efforts required to complete any task. Because of his conviction in his supreme knowledge, he concentrates his efforts only on what he thinks important rather than on what is more universally valued. And, because of his belief in his unlimited powers, no actual achievement ever measures up to his inflated expectations.

As a result, Harold is invariably denied the real power, mastery, and control he so ardently desires. In the absence of significant proof of his omnipotence, Harold falls back on arrogance to convince himself and others of his powers. Thus, Harold plays the high and mighty. Regardless of real evidence otherwise, Harold must act all-knowing, all-powerful, all-sacrosanct. His unconscious idealization of omnipotence automatically turns into commonplace petty arrogance.

In the second place, Harold's repression of innocent compliance with other people also fails him. For even though he turns against other people, he has urgent need for them. He needs them for manifold reasons. He needs them to manipulate, to experience his power over them, to compete against. He needs them for their actual assistance, resources, and prestige. He needs them so he can have someone to defeat, and for their admiration and recognition. Without other people, he feels powerless and ineffectual. And since he measures his own worth in terms of his ability to defeat others and prove his superiority over them, he feels weak and impotent in their absence. But despite his needs for other people, Harold's relations to them are invariably characterized by hostility.

In the third place, Harold's repression of transcendent freedom and independence also fails him. Obviously, he is neither free nor independent. He is but a slave to his work, his ambitions, his competitiveness. He is so bound by his needs that the very idea of independence is absurd to the objective observer of his ways. He is bound by his needs for other people, by his needs for work, by his needs to prove his powers and mastery. Actually, he is bound in every conceivable way by his insatiable need to master life.

But how can the omnipotent Harold admit to an inherent lack of freedom? Rather than admit to his slavery, Harold embraces it. By turning against himself, he suppresses his own inner feelings. As a result, Harold becomes mechanically rigid and inflexible. He cannot bend. He cannot give in. He carries this inherent rigidity into every aspect of his demeanor. It appears in a multitude of important and incidental ways. It shows up in his dress, in his demeanor, in his intolerance, in his resistance to changes of any kind. He wears his rigidity like a suit of armor.

Harold's attempt to master life in order to actualize his Omnipotent Fantastic Self inevitably fails on all these accounts. He can be resourceful, strong, knowledgeable, seemingly invincible. He can drive himself, force himself, tirelessly compel himself. He can control other people or defeat everyone with whom he comes into contact. But his unconscious goal is still out of reach. The more he strains for power, mastery, and control, the more he must fall back on their surrogates. Through all his efforts to prove his omnipotence, Harold merely becomes arrogant, hostile, and rigid.

Chapter 6

RUTH — THE SYNPATHIC TYPE

Ruth Parsons, our typical Synpathic Type Suicide, fixates innocence and represses omnipotence and transcendence. She unconsciously believes she is her Innocent Fantastic Self and she shapes her real Empirical Self accordingly. How she relates to her own inner processes, how she relates to other people, and how she relates to her very own existence is determined by her conviction in her Innocent Fantastic Self. It also determines her Primary Motivation to suicide.

The personality characteristics of the Synpathic Type are more readily recognized in women in our society than in men. This is not to say that they are exclusively feminine characteristics. They are not. But our society, even considering recent social changes, heavily reinforces these characteristics in women. Conversely it depreciates them in men. Synpathic Type men usually disguise their roles behind a secondary facade or alternative life style. On the other hand, a Synpathic Type woman can drift into pervasive self-destructive behavior, and many people will say that she is merely acting "just like a woman."

Intrapsychic Factors

Synpathic Ruth does not merely repress the fixed attributes of the Antipathic and Apathic Types. She fears and despises their expression, especially in herself. Yet Ruth cannot rid herself of them. They remain just as compulsive as ever, only now they are unconscious. As a result, Ruth secretly envies and admires their characteristics. This is one of her best-kept secrets, especially from herself.

Ruth outwardly fears and despises all those personality aspects characterizing Antipathic power and aggressiveness. Anger, open hostility, outward expressions of power, strength, or assertiveness are just not Ruth's way. She rarely admits to hatred or resentment of other people. She may really believe herself to be completely free of prejudices. She thinks she cannot possibly carry a grudge for long. She believes she can never be openly arrogant or competitive, even should she try.

Ruth also fears and despises the expressions of Apathic independence and self-reliance. The idea she is essentially a free agent is beyond her conscious comprehension. She may intellectually acknowledge her capacity for independence, but she never really feels it in her gut. Although she may be faced with undeniable evidence of her available freedom, she will not accept the responsibility for it. She may be confronted by irrefutable indications of her competence and capacities, but she just does not believe in them.

For Ruth actually represses her independent assertive capacities. As a result, she cannot actually exercise her full range of inherent capabilities. She rarely, if ever, takes positive action on her own toward any constructive and comprehensive goal on her own behalf. Whenever Ruth does accomplish anything of merit, she does so only with a great deal of help, support, encouragement, or grateful appreciation from other people.

In her work, she may be able passively to comply with a series of small assigned tasks, but she is usually overwhelmed by any long-range project to be completed over a considerable period of time. Nor can Ruth tap her own creative resources to devise original and imaginative work. She is definitely not a self-starter. Unless Ruth is told, she simply does not know how to start or where to end.

Yet she can thrive with a great deal of praise and encouragement or if she occupies a position of appreciated service to others. But her goals are not the value of the work accomplished for her own satisfaction. Her goals are to gain praise or appreciation, which she experiences as affection; or actual expressions of grateful affection from other people. For Ruth usually suppresses any open and obvious expression of independent assertiveness.

On the other hand, Synpathic Ruth does not merely fixate her Fantastic Self's Innocence. She idealizes all its expressions. She secretly believes she is infinitely good. Her main goals in life are to manifest her lovableness, altruism, and benignity—so that as with most Synpathic Types in our culture, Ruth turns to love to validate her innocence. To her, loving and being loved are all that really matter in life. But Ruth's concepts of loving and being loved are essentially affectual. She does not experience them as expressive activities of human endeavor. Love, to Ruth, is simply a symbiotic feeling.

This brings us to the very crux of Ruth's internal processes. Ruth is essentially enmeshed in her feelings. In fact, she virtually drowns in them. And she actually fears she might.

Ruth feels love. She feels understanding, tolerance, and sympathy—she even feels her ideals. She does not arrive at her idealized values of innocent love, goodness, and altruism through philosophic, religious, or ethical concepts. She simply feels them. Engulfed by her feelings, Ruth is consequently blinded by them. She is completely unaware that feeling something is not the same thing as being or doing it.

INTERPERSONAL FACTORS

Because she represses her aggressive independence, Ruth relates to other people with compliant dependency. And because she idealizes her feelings of love for other people, compliant dependency is her way of loving.

Her dependency needs appear in a multitude of large and small ways. They are so profuse, she often seems a parasite. She depends on other people for virtually anything. Her dependencies range from constant emotional support to considerable material help. She feels inadequate to provide much of anything for herself. But Ruth does not just feel inadequate. She has vested interests in actually being so. Her inadequacies justify her dependencies, free her of obligation to others for help received from them, and reinforce her illusions of innocence.

Her need to comply with others is equally profuse. Regardless of how much she may inwardly rebel against it, she cannot help but outwardly comply with the needs, wishes, and demands of other people. Her dependence and compliance are also her ways of proving her innocence.

But beyond that, Ruth is simply not a fighter. Because of her innocence and repressed aggressiveness, Ruth cannot take an active stand and stick to it under formidable opposition. She can only fight through passive defiance.

Because of her secret admiration of aggressiveness and independence, she invariably feels attracted to those very characteristics in other people. This is especially true with respect to her love objects. Ruth simply must fall in love with an aggressive Antipathic Type or an independent Apathic Type. And usually with disastrous results.

She has no defenses to protect her from the Antipathic Type's aggressiveness. She may do everything she can to appease him, but she usually ends up suffering from the onslaught. On the other hand, the Apathic Type virtually starves her needs for affection. She yearns for his attention and will try anything to draw him out of his detachment. But she usually winds up despairing that he will ever love her. At least, not the way she needs to be loved.

For the way Ruth needs to be loved is comprehensive. It entails total satisfaction of her compliant dependency. Just as importantly, it requires total acquiescence to her fear of independent aggressiveness. Ruth is blind to this obvious contradiction. She cannot get satisfaction of her compliant dependencies from someone lacking independent aggressiveness. And she carries this double-binding expectation into all her relationships.

But Ruth does not limit her needs to just a few romantic relationships. It is absolutely essential for Ruth to feel loved—or, at least, liked—by virtually everyone with whom she comes into contact. Her need for other people's approval, or at least their passive acceptance, is insatiable.

Ruth also tends to subordinate herself to other people. She not only appeases their aggressiveness, but she must not appear to be openly aggressive to them. Although something in her makes her yearn for the spotlight, she also shrinks from it. She rarely leads. She automatically follows.

When circumstances put her in an unavoidable leadership position, she demurs from taking firm charge. She procrastinates. She makes exceptions to her decisions on personal appeal. Even her decisions, when she does make them, are primarily aimed at pleasing those she is supposed to lead.

In addition, Ruth must appear to be the paragon of goodness and humility. She measures her own worth in terms of being a "nice" person. And she believes other people value her in the same way. Whenever friction does enter her relations, she retreats from it, rather than resolving it. Whenever inevitable difficulties with others arise, she always feels innocent of blame.

But despite Ruth's pervasive need to be liked by other people, romantic relationships are normally central to her life. She is always in love, either in her own reality or in her fantasies of the past or future. But she does not just idealize love. She hopelessly idealizes love relationships. She expects them to be completely free of any and all conflict. Even though Ruth consciously, even cynically, denies it, she really believes love will conquer all.

Because of her idealization of love relationships, Ruth may subject herself to all kinds of real and imagined abuse just to maintain them. She will feel belittled and deprived. She will feel used and despoiled. She may actually provoke abuse just to sustain her innocence and subjugation. She may feel that almost anything is worth the price in her quest for the perfect love.

Paradoxically, Ruth does not know what to do with love once she actually gets it. First of all, because Ruth experiences love strictly as a feeling, she cannot recognize the genuine article. Also, for reasons we will later explore, Ruth eventually loses interest in her pursued love object, once she is convinced she has finally won him over. In addition, since Ruth represses her aggressiveness and independence, she projects the resulting feelings of deprivation and lack of freedom onto her love object. After all, he is the core of her existence and the source of all good and evil. He must be the one to blame for her chafing under her own repressions.

Finally, and most importantly, Ruth's own capacity to love actively is blocked, if not completely aborted, by her previously crushed intrinsic empathy. In short, although love becomes the central meaning and purpose to her life, Ruth can neither love nor let herself be loved.

EXISTENTIAL FACTORS

As with Harold, Ruth is existentially alienated from the mainstream of life. But in contrast to Harold, Ruth attempts to resolve her alienation by moving towards her own inner feelings, other people, and life itself. But Ruth's effort to ally herself with life no more resolves her alienation than Harold's struggle to conquer it.

First of all, by repressing her aggressiveness and independence, Ruth deprives herself. She denies her own capacities as a fully functioning human being. Yet, since her repression does not diminish their compulsiveness, her aggressiveness and independence surface in passive and ineffectual ways.

Ruth supplants overt active aggressiveness with covert passive defiance. She is no less free from the need to defeat other people than Antipathic Harold. She merely does it passively. People close to her may call her headstrong, stubborn, or willful. Those more distant see her simply as relatively pleasant but as ineffectual, naive, or forgetful.

Despite her repressed aggressiveness, Ruth secretly harbors an enormous and competitive ambition. It is unlike Harold's, whose conscious and open ambition is tempered by the test of reality. Instead, Ruth's competitive ambition, just because it remains so deeply repressed and untested, can grow to infinite proportions. Yet it still remains undercover. The only evidence of its existence shows in her passive defiance of others by constantly disappointing their expectations of her.

Furthermore, at the same time that Ruth manifests her repressed aggressiveness through passive defiance, she manifests her repressed independence through passive withdrawal. Rather than actively assert her capacity for independence, Ruth simply withdraws from other people. Despite her intense need for other people's affection, her detachment is no less than the Apathic Type's. Again, people close to her feel the void of this estrangement. Meanwhile, those more distant become confused by her dichotomous need for their company alternating with her passive withdrawal from it.

Because of her passive withdrawal from others, it seems that she makes no demands on them. In contrast to Antipathic Harold, Ruth rarely even expresses expectations, let alone feels justified in making demands. Likewise, in contrast to the Apathic Type who really believes he is self-sufficient, Ruth knows she needs other people. And she needs a great deal from them. Yet her repressed independence keeps her from openly expressing her needs. She can only withdraw into herself, thereby creating a vacuum for other people to fill for her.

Together, Ruth's repressions always add up to her feeling—and indeed being—abused, inadequate, and deprived. She must accentuate her inadequacies to express her passive aggressiveness. And she must deprive herself of the affections of others in order to express her passive independence. Regardless of her repressions, her existential alienation prevails. She still finds herself a stranger in a foreign land.

But Ruth's fixed idealizations also end in disaster. By idealizing only the affectual aspects of innocent love, Ruth never really experiences it. Since she expects so much from love, it invariably disappoints her. Because of her own incapacity to love, she never really attains it.

Confirmation of her Innocence through love is everything, yet Ruth is invariably denied it. This denial causes her to feel all the more inadequate and deprived. In fact, all this combines to make her feel massively abused.

Ruth's idealization of innocent love, goodness, and compliant understanding of others invariably ends with her feeling abused. Her repressions of aggressiveness and independence cause her to feel inadequate and deprived. These three feelings summarize everything there is to know about Ruth. Feeling abused, feeling deprived, and feeling inadequate are the hallmarks of the Synpathic Type Suicide.

Chapter 7

CARL — THE APATHIC TYPE

Carl Goldman, our typical Apathic Type Suicide, fixates transcendence and represses omnipotence and innocence. Unconsciously believing he is his Transcendent Fantastic Self, he shapes his real Empirical Self accordingly. This unconscious belief forms the basis for the way he relates to his own existence, and to others around him. This conviction of his Transcendent Fantastic Self establishes his Primary Motivation to suicide.

The Apathic Type Suicide so glorifies and idealizes freedom and independence as to render them but preposterous imitations of the real thing. In his lifelong quest for transcendent freedom and independence he overlooks one essential fact. His quest, in itself, becomes compulsive. He becomes a prisoner of his own unconscious motivations toward ultimate self-destruction. Apathic Type Suicides are usually treated by our culture as its rebels.

Intrapsychic Factors

As with the Antipathic and Synpathic Types, Carl represses and despises the characteristics of the other two types of Suicides. Initially, he represses Antipathic drives for omnipotent power and aggressiveness. Actively striving for achievement and recognition is utterly repulsive to Carl. He sees such activity as an unacceptable infringement on his liberty. To strive for mastery over other people, things, or institutions is equally offensive to him. It would require far too much of his time and energy either to strive for such power or to execute it.

Secondly, Carl represses Synpathic drives for innocent mutuality with other people. Love, to Carl, is something other people pretend to feel. It is almost impossible for him to make any kind of commitment to anyone else. The very idea of a permanent attachment can send him into panic or deep depression.

On the other hand, Carl so idealizes transcendental freedom and independence that he makes absolute self-sufficiency his singular purpose in life. His sole purpose for existence is to eliminate his needs. He simply must feel that he never needs anyone or anything.

Although alienation is characteristic of all three types of Suicides, to Carl, it takes on a special meaning. In order to manifest his goal of transcendence, he must necessarily escalate his alienation. As a result, Carl strives for ultimate detachment. In fact, this may be his only active striving. He instills this sense of detachment into all aspects of his life. It characterizes his relations with the outside world. It even enters his internal relations with himself.

As with Harold and with Ruth, Carl's repressed attributes are not extinguished, but remain powerfully lurking in the depths of his unconsciousness. His internal detachment alienates Carl from his own real feelings. He is, therefore, far more susceptible to the sudden surfacing of his repressions than either Harold or Ruth. His repressed attributes can sneak up on him, robbing him of his equilibrium and tranquil detachment.

When his Synpathic innocence surfaces, love enthralls him. He feels that he will die unless he finds it. When his Antipathic omnipotence surfaces, ambition overwhelms him. He feels compelled to aggressive activity by mysterious and irresistible forces. When both repressions surface, he feels as though he is coming apart at the seams. These disturbances reinforce his determination for ultimate detachment—from himself, from other people, from the world. He must be on constant guard to protect it.

To fortify his detachment, Carl tends to impersonalize. If he must work to survive, he seeks work as empty of personal involvement as possible. Although he may be quite creative and original, he looks upon the products of his creativity as if he had nothing to do with them. He feels that he is but an instrument through which they are expressed by their own miraculous volition.

His attitudes in this respect differ markedly from Harold's or Ruth's. Harold quickly claims exaggerated personal credit for anything with which he is even remotely connected. Ruth only reluctantly admits responsibility for what little she does create, minimizing its importance. In contrast, Carl stands back and admires his creation, but impersonally, as though his creation actually created itself.

Because of his detachment, Carl works best alone. Able to tolerate some impersonal contact with other people, he finds it almost impossible to collaborate with them. In large organizations, Carl is the loner working on a special project down the hall. He abhors regulation and regimentation, therefore ignores regular working hours. He usually arrives at work early, or, if tolerated, late. He lunches at an unusual hour, by himself and lingers past quitting time to avoid leaving with the herd. In smaller organizations, such isolation is usually impossible. Carl then strives for an isolated niche. He detaches himself as much as possible from the people and activity in his surroundings. When engaged in a preferred vocation allowing him to work alone, he avoids the friction of competition. He may market the fruits of his labor far below their actual value, just for sustenance, like the painter Gauguin. He may passively allow a friend or relative to handle his affairs for him, as another artist, van Gogh did.

But if possible, Carl will avoid committing himself to work altogether. He may do odd jobs just to earn minimal sustenance. He may survive on welfare. In the extreme, he may become a vagrant or a derelict. He will suffer almost any deprivation to avoid commitment or obligation.

Above all, Carl must be free. He must be independent. He must be detached. He must be objective. It may never occur to him that absolute transcendence is absolutely impossible.

INTERPERSONAL FACTORS

Carl brings all of this into his interpersonal relationships. In fact, they can hardly be called relationships. Antipathic Harold moves against other people, attempting to crush all positive feelings for them. Synpathic Ruth moves towards other people, enmeshing herself in her feelings for them. In contrast, Apathic Carl moves away from other people. He simply transcends feeling anything for anyone.

To Carl, love is a trap. It is nothing but a pretense. In fact, he is quite adept at piercing through the pretenses of love such as Ruth's or Harold's. He accurately sees their "love" as compliant dependency or compulsive manipulation of other people. On the other hand, he is blind to love's authenticity.

He may say he loves, but, at most, he feels a warm but distant affection. Yet he can sustain a lasting relationship with a mate or companion provided she meets at least three conditions. She must never make any demands on him. She may never expect any open commitment from him. And she can never initiate any active moves towards a closer relationship.

Carl may omit sex from his relationships, or occasionally participate with relative strangers. He may be an old hand at one-night stands, or he may utilize sex strictly for physical release. But above all, sex, like everything else, must be impersonal. It must not implicate contingencies—especially contingencies of personal involvement.

Just as he abhors regulation and regimentation, Carl is repelled by personal obligation. Harold feels omnipotently deserving, and therefore never feels obligated. Ruth feels innocently inadequate, and therefore cannot be obligated. But because it challenges his transcendence Carl actually fears and despises obligation itself.

His mate or lover must not allow a situation to evolve that could cause him to feel obligated. If she should expect favors, attention, affection, or sex from him, she will languish lonely and unsatisfied. She may even provoke his anger because she is setting up a situation causing him to feel obligated. Although he can be very generous with unexpected gifts or favors, he is a master at forgetting promises, birthdays, anniversaries, or other occasions to which he ascribes an obligatory nature. Carl experiences obligation as the ultimate infringement on his liberty. He simply will not tolerate it.

Yet, in his peculiar way, Carl is extremely tolerant of other people. He will endure all kinds of obnoxiousness in others without the slightest hint of revulsion—as long as they keep their emotional distance. Just as he represses his feelings of love, Carl also represses his feelings of hostility. Unlike Ruth, it is not that he cannot fight. He simply refuses to get involved.

Lastly, Carl cannot allow himself to need other people. And on this account he will suffer almost any degree of loneliness and isolation. Harold needs other people for their usefulness, and to provide him with their recognition and admiration. Ruth needs them for their love and affection, and to provide satisfaction of her dependencies. But Carl needs them only to leave him alone.

We can now understand the difficulty in calling Carl's interpersonal relationships by that term. For, in essence, relationships for him do not exist. In his transcendent drive for self-sufficiency, he will not allow himself a need for other people. In his endless quest for absolute freedom, he can form no lasting ties with anyone. In his mindless compulsion for ultimate independence, he cannot allow commitment nor obligations to another.

EXISTENTIAL FACTORS

As with Harold and Ruth, Carl Goldman is existentially alienated from the mainstream of life. But rather than moving against or toward mundane life, other people, and his own inner processes, Carl moves away. Rather than alleviate his alienation, Carl actually escalates it. For in order to manifest his transcendence, Carl tries to detach himself from his own inner processes, relations with others, and involvement with mundane life.

Obviously, Carl's resolution of his existential alienation is no resolution at all. His external and internal detachment may impart an apparent aura of inherent serenity, but it is a facade. His detachment inevitably fails him.

In the first place, his external detachment actually cripples his ability to live a full and satisfying life. He has more than ample freedom *from* everything, but he has absolutely no freedom *towards* anything. And Carl inherently fails to see this vitally important distinction. Carl is not free to love, fight, or actively strive for anything. He is not free to set goals, to plan for his own future, to relate closely with others. He is hamstrung by his own detachment.

Carl is completely unaware that his external detachment keeps him isolated and alone, never realizing that it prevents his accomplishing much of anything. He cannot understand that it prevents him from manifesting his full range of capabilities. He blinds himself to the fact that he cannot strive for gratifying achievements, satisfying personal relations, and existential fulfillment. He simply mysteriously finds himself without friends, without love, without family, without goals, without accomplishments, and without material possessions.

In the second place, Carl's internal detachment causes great disturbance to his otherwise serene equilibrium. Since he is so detached from his own inner processes, his repressed attributes are free to introject themselves indiscriminately into his feelings and behavior at any time. Suddenly, he simply must find love or companionship. Unexpectedly, he gets caught in the clutches of unlimited ambition. Without warning, he finds himself torn apart by totally opposing drives. But they not only oppose each other, they oppose his transcendence.

When his repressed innocence surfaces, he simultaneously feels compelled toward love and compelled to resist it. When his repressed omnipotence surfaces, he simultaneously feels compelled toward aggressiveness and compelled to resist it. When both surface at the same time, he feels compelled toward insanity.

More than either of the other two types, Apathic Carl is subject to this terrifying ambivalence. He tries to avoid its anxieties by escalating his detachment, but often to no avail. His escalation of internal detachment precludes his ever really knowing what he wants out of life. His escalation of external detachment keeps him from ever putting anything into it. Consequently, he ends up wanting nothing, and receiving nothing.

In the third place, Carl's ambivalent detachment leads him straight into apathic inertia. He never knows what he wants from life. He never willingly puts himself into it. His history may be punctuated by periods of significant achievement. It may include sporadic love affairs, even marriage. Yet the overall picture is of drifting with the tide.

Power, mastery, and control are everything to Harold. But he ends up being denied it. Loving and being loved are everything to Ruth. But she, too, ends up denied her goals. So it is with Carl. Transcendent freedom and independence are the promised land. But, like Moses, Carl is barred from it. His detachment enslaves him. His ambivalence commands him. His inertia confines him. Carl becomes but a prisoner to his insatiable quest for absolute transcendence.

Chapter 8

COMMON CONSEQUENCES

Although the Suicide is his Empirical Self, he does not abandon his unconscious conviction that he is his Fantastic Self. To the contrary, his Empirical Self is cast in a mold shaped by the primary attribute of his Fantastic Self. While the impossibility of his Fantastic Self remains beyond the scope of his awareness, he shapes his personality, his behavior, his feelings, his relationships, his goals, and his values all in conformance with its criteria.

Antipathic Harold unconsciously believes he is omnipotent. He tries to manifest his omnipotence through power, mastery, and control. But rather than realize his omnipotence, Harold actually becomes hostile, arrogant, and rigid. Synpathic Ruth unconsciously believes that she is innocent. She tries to manifest her innocence through goodness, love, and compliance with others. But rather than realize her innocence, Ruth actually becomes abused, inadequate, and deprived. Apathic Carl unconsciously believes he is transcendent. He tries to manifest his transcendence through freedom, objective independence, and self-sufficiency. But rather than realize his transcendence, Carl actually incurs ambivalence, detachment, and inertia.

72

As each of their lives unfold, the harrowing discrepancy between what the Suicide unconsciously believes himself to be and the reality of what he actually is comes to the fore. This conflict between his Fantastic Self and the reality of himself, his relations to other people, and of his mundane existence operates as a fundamental conflict from which all the other processes of the Suicide Syndrome derive.

However, the unique characteristics of each suicidal type rarely appear as neatly and distinctly as they do with Harold Roberts, Ruth Parsons, or Carl Goldman. Yet despite their disparate personalities, Harold, Ruth, and Carl share far more with each other than they differ.

COMMON DEVELOPMENT

In the first place, all three got where they are through the same developmental process. All were victims of the corruption of their intrinsic growth. All underwent the same process leading to the creation of their imaginary selves. Each of them created a Fantastic Self. Each of them endowed it with absolute attributes. And each of them became convinced of being that Self.

Secondly, all three underwent an adolescent predicament. And they all arrived at an Adolescent Resolution. Each of them repressed two of their Fantastic Self's attributes and fixated the other.

Thirdly, they all developed the same Common Characteristics on account of their unconscious convictions. They each became proud, egocentric, perfectionistic, narcissistic, compulsive, arrogantly superior, and irrational. Although one or more of these characteristics may appear more pronounced in the outward behavior of one type compared with another, all of them are present in the personality of every Suicide, regardless of how well disguised.

Fourth, they all become existentially alienated on account of their secret convictions. And while each of them attempts to resolve his existential alienation a different way, each solution inevitably miscarries. Regardless of whether they move against, toward, or away from their own inner being, other people, and mundane life, the move inherently fails.

Fifth, they all end with ironic characteristics of their Empirical Selves. Harold seeks power, mastery, and control. But he ends with hostility, arrogance, and rigidity. Ruth seeks altruistic goodness, love, and symbiotic compliance with others. But she ends up feeling abused, inadequate, and deprived. Carl seeks freedom, independence, and self-sufficiency. But he ends with ambivalence, detachment, and inertia. Every Suicide's empirical characteristics ironically reflect his secret convictions.

Finally, they all share the common processes resulting from their common development. For every Suicide's belief in his Fantastic Self inherently conflicts with reality. And this inherent conflict eventually influences the entire course of his life.

COMMON PROCESSES

This inherent conflict automatically enters every aspect of the Suicide's existence. It enters his intrapsychic processes. He believes he is omnipotent, innocent, and transcendent. And he inevitably incurs shame on account of his inability to actually manifest these attributes in his everyday life. As a result, his Fantastic Self, inexplicably tied to his Empirical Self, but inherently shamed by it, inevitably grows to hate it.

This impossibility also taints his relations with other people. He knows he is his Fantastic Self, but other people somehow fail to get the message. They treat him only as his actual Empirical Self. And he will not forgive them this humiliation. Inevitably, he grows vindictive toward them.

Finally, this impossibility contaminates his existential processes. His omnipotent, innocent, and transcendent Fantastic Self is automatically at odds with the reality of mundane existence. He inevitably despairs of ever existing as his Fantastic Self.

His shame, humiliation, and despair automatically generate Self-Hatred, Vindictiveness, and Hopelessness. These constitute the three exclusive Suicidal Motivations of the Suicide Syndrome. They are always present in the life of every Suicide, and their expressions and his defenses against them dominate his very existence.

COMMON DISGUISES

However, the expressions of his Suicidal Motivations in combination with his defenses can often disguise the true condition of the Suicide. In fact, he may not consciously feel or outwardly appear suicidal, but even should he feel or appear suicidal, his true motivations are nearly always disguised. The Suicide may single out almost anything other than his true motivations as grounds for his suicidal impulses.

Moreover, the expressions of his Suicidal Motivations in combination with his defenses against them can somewhat disguise his type. For instance, the Antipathic Type normally strives for power, control, and mastery over life. But, as we will see, because of his defenses, he may outwardly appear appeasing and withdrawn. On the other hand, the Synpathic Type normally strives for compliant symbiotic relations with others. But because of her defenses, she may outwardly appear hysterically vituperative, and aloof. Likewise, the Apathic Type normally strives for detachment. But because of his defenses, he may appear deeply involved, even willing to comply with the wishes of others.

But beyond the confusion lent by his expressions in combination with his defenses, the Suicide can employ other disguises as well. His choice of type may poignantly conflict with that assigned to him by our social system. The Antipathic female or Synpathic male fails to conform to our society's conventions. And, as a result, they often learn unconsciously to disguise their true fixation.

The Antipathic female often expresses her drives for power vicariously through her mate. He knows her to be hostile, arrogant, and rigid. But the public only sees her characteristics through her insatiable ambitions for him. The Synpathic male also often hides behind his mate. In public, he makes half-hearted gestures towards fitting the social ideal. But at home, he invariably sinks back into a passive dependence.

Suicides belonging to socially conflicting roles often join the Apathic of either gender and generally shun social conventions or merely pay them lip service. And while homosexuality entails infinitely more complex dynamics than conflict with conventional social roles, this conflict usually plays a part. Dedicated lesbians are often Antipathic Types, and male homosexuals often manifest Synpathic ideals of universal love or innocent dependence.[6]

Because of his disguises, the Suicide may seem to possess a proverbial multiple personality. For instance, he may appear antipathic at work, synpathic at home, and apathic in more general social situations. But he runs the risk of encountering situations entailing all three conditions. The office party or company picnic would constitute such a situation. And his usual extreme discomfort at such affairs attests to the difficulty of maintaining such disguises.

Finally, the Suicide may disguise his true type through a secondary resolution. For example, he may emerge from his Adolescent Resolution a predominately Antipathic Type, incur a severe crisis, and then apparently shift to the Synpathic mode. After a similar disturbance, he may then move on to outwardly appearing Apathic.

Such profound shifts must always entail a crisis of massive dimensions. They often involve a harrowing brush with fate, a serious suicide attempt, a bout with the law or the psychiatric ward, a near-fatal illness, accident, or alcoholic episode—the virtual end of his being as he and others know it.

This secondary resolution always results from a mixture of his conscious and unconscious efforts on behalf of his real survival and the survival of his Fantastic Self. What conscious efforts he does make are invariably intertwined with his unconscious need to maintain his Fantastic Self in the form of any of its attributes. And while his Adolescent Resolution was an artificial one in the sense that he only repressed two of his Fantastic Self's attributes rather than achieving riddance of them, this secondary resolution becomes even more artificial, tenuous, and pretensive.

But however the Suicide's true type may be disguised on the surface, his underlying conflict prevails. The discrepancies between his Fantastic Self and the reality of himself, other people, and his mundane existence cannot be so readily resolved. As we will see in the following chapters, he cannot escape the Self-Hatred, Vindictiveness, and Hopelessness this conflict inevitably brings him.

Part III

THE MURDEROUS TYRANT WITHIN

Chapter 9

ORIGINS OF SELF-HATRED

Self-Hatred results from the shame the Suicide experiences from his inability to actualize his Fantastic Self. For although his Fantastic Self soars to absolute omnipotence, innocence, and transcendence, it is still attached to his Empirical Self, with feet on the ground. The Suicide invests his pride in his ability actually to be his Fantastic Self. By virtue of his making this investment, he subjects himself to severe and pervasive shame.

Despite undeniable evidence otherwise, the Suicide remains unconsciously convinced he really is his Fantastic Self. His convictions result in three tragic consequences. One, he must compare his actual Empirical Self with his imaginary Fantastic Self. Naturally, his Empirical Self falls painfully short. Two, he cannot help but fear that he really is his Empirical Self, rather than his Fantastic Self. This fear, usually unconscious, results in acute and chronic anxiety. And, three, further to alleviate this resulting pain of comparison and anxiety, he resorts to a system of autoreinforcement. He becomes proud of being his Fantastic Self.

Harold is proud of his omnipotent aggressiveness, of relentlessly driving himself, of striving for total mastery. He is proud of his strength, perseverance, and high standards. Because he represses human warmth and affection, he is proud of being above cheap sentimentality. Because he represses spontaneity, he is proud of his hard self-discipline. He is proud of his bold candor, courageous invincibility, singular strength of purpose. Harold actually becomes proud of his pride.

Ruth differs greatly in this respect. She refuses even to acknowledge her pride. Yet Ruth's pride in her imagined attributes is just as great and pervasive as Harold's. Ruth is paradoxically proud of her innocent modesty, humility, and selflessness, of her quiet civilized mannerisms, of her refusal to lower herself to primitive anger. And, since she represses aggressiveness and self-sufficiency, she grows proud of her passivity and willingness to comply with and depend on others.

Ruth takes great pride in not voicing demands on anyone; pride in not openly expecting anything from them. She is proud of her flexibility and of her sympathetic understanding of other people. Her pride in never asserting her own rights, wishes, or self-interest, is as powerful as Harold's pride in his aggressiveness, assertiveness, or exaggerated self-esteem. She is even proud of her inadequacies. She often boasts of her own limitations. But more than anything else, she is proud of her inherent innocence, lovableness, and tolerance of other people.

Carl also grows proud of his idealized and imagined attributes. He is proud of his serene isolation, of never needing anything or anyone. Since he represses both aggressiveness and mutuality with others, he grows proud of being above the competitive rat-race. Because he so stringently limits his needs, wishes, and desires, he grows proud of his stoicism, intellectualism, or asceticism.

But transcendental freedom and independence is where Carl invests the greatest amount of pride. He believes he simply cannot be bought: not for love; not for money. And he deeply reinforces this imagined purity of spirit with pride. Carl is proud of being his own man. No person, no passion, no ambition can shake his imperturbable detachment. His pride will not be tempted.

But the Suicide cannot actually be his Fantastic Self despite the reinforcement of his pride. The undeniable reality of life and of his real situation in it, shakes his pride to its very roots. When reality interferes with his ability actually to be his Fantastic Self, he suffers unbearable shame.

CRITERIA OF THE FANTASTIC SELF

Blind to the impossibility of actualizing his Fantastic Self, he cannot understand why he fails to live up to its potential. Yet his ability to incorporate the criteria of his Fantastic Self into his daily life is, of course, impossible.

It is impossible because only the absolute will satisfy. His Fantastic Self has absolute potential. It is absolutely omnipotent, innocent, and transcendent. Therefore, he must absolutely be whatever he believes himself to be. No real amount of mastery, goodness, or self-sufficiency is enough. It must be total and absolute.

Harold, who believes he is omnipotent, will cite missed opportunities—times when he could have worked harder or when he did not absolutely assert his mastery. Regardless of how powerful, how ingenious, how diligent he may have been, he will recall examples of when he just could not overcome an obstacle. And, since absolute omnipotence is all that will satisfy, Harold will inevitably feel shamed by his weaknesses.

Ruth, who believes she is absolutely innocent, will dwell on the times she could have been more lovable, more attractive, more desirable, more willing to please. She will remember times when she failed to win another's affections, times when she actually appeared callous, uncaring, or intolerant. And, since absolute innocence is all that will satisfy, Ruth cannot help but feel shamed by her failures.

Carl, who believes he is transcendent, recounts the few times he really did rely on someone else to help him out. He will enumerate the examples of his benefiting from fortunate circumstances. He will recall feeling that he really did need something or someone. And, since absolute transcendence is all that will satisfy, Carl cannot help but feel shamed by his own needs.

Worse, Harold, Ruth, and Carl experience these instances, themselves, as absolutes. These instances are absolute proofs of their absolute failure absolutely to be what they absolutely believe themselves to be. Regardless of how closely their behavior may resemble the fixed attribute of their Fantastic Self, it is never close enough.

If you should ask them if they really did expect all this of themselves, of course, they would immediately deny it. But the proof to the contrary is evidenced by their reaction of shame to each instance of what they see as their failures.

Furthermore, even though the Suicide's behavior may closely resemble his fixed attribute, his repressed attributes still operate. Ironically, he cannot help but feel ashamed that he fails in respect to them, also.

Harold feels shamed by his obvious lack of freedom and spontaneity. Ruth feels shamed by her inability to stand up for her own rights, to assert herself, to set significant goals, and to strive toward achieving them. Carl, who because of his inner detachment is more susceptible to the surfacing of his repressed attributes, is constantly shamed by his inability to fulfill them. For example, he simultaneously feels shamed by his inability to love, and shamed by his inability to fight. But regardless of whether the Suicide is Antipathic, Synpathic, or Apathic, his inherent inability to fulfill the demands of his repressed attributes greatly increases his shame.

LIMITATIONS OF THE EMPIRICAL SELF

The Suicide's fixed and repressed attributes of his Fantastic Self cause him unlimited shame. But they also profoundly affect his personality. They actually place great limitations on his range as a functioning human being. As a result, he also feels shamed by the limitations they place on his Empirical Self.

For example, Harold believes he is Omnipotent. Yet he is far from being infinitely powerful and masterful. Instead, Harold is actually hostile, arrogant, and rigid. Furthermore, Harold's hostility, arrogance, and rigidity actually stand in the way of his more effectively actualizing his powers.

Harold strives for power over other people. But his hostility inevitably makes any reasonable recognition a joke. He strives for achievement. But his rigidity blocks his progress at every turn. The limitations placed on Harold's Empirical Self actually prevent him from realizing progress towards his one-sided goals.

Ruth believes she is Innocent. She believes in her infinite lovableness, goodness, and compliant understanding of other people. Yet Ruth actually feels abused, inadequate, and deprived by them. In addition, her feeling abused, inadequate, and deprived actually blocks her progress towards her ideals.

Ruth strives for symbiotic love. But her feeling inadequate invariably blocks love's fulfillment. Ruth strives for infinite goodness. But her feeling abused counteracts her strivings. Ruth strives for symbiotic compliance. But her feelings of deprivation continually stand in the way.

Carl believes he is Transcendent. But Carl is far from free from mundane life. Instead, he is imprisoned by his own detachment, ambivalence, and inertia. And these very characteristics block his progress towards his ideals.

His detachment prevents free access to anything. His ambivalence blocks any concentrated effort he might initiate towards real independence. His drifting inertia ensures that he can never gain real self-sufficiency in a real world.

In other words, the potential of the Suicide's fixed attribute is absolutely impossible. The demands of his repressed attributes are equally impossible. But more than that: the limitations placed on his Empirical Self—strictly on account of his fixed and repressed attributes—actually impede the progress he might otherwise make towards achieving a modicum of his ideals.

Finally, and most importantly, his Fantastic Self is simply not of this life. Regardless of how masterful, loving, or self-sufficient the Suicide grows, he still must function in the world of reality. He can shape himself, force himself, stringently compel himself. But he can never actually *be* his Fantastic Self.

Consequently, his Fantastic Self must inevitably hate his Empirical Self, not just because of his special limitations, not just because of his inability to satisfy occasionally surfacing repressions, not just because of his inability to fulfill his fixation. His Fantastic Self must inevitably hate his Empirical Self simply because he is real.

The Suicide unconsciously identifies with his Fantastic Self. He unconsciously but uncompromisingly believes he is his Fantastic Self, not his actual Empirical Self. Yet, the more he tries to actualize his Fantastic Self, the more his Empirical Self gets in the way. As a result, his Fantastic Self is constantly and pervasively shamed by his only real self. But regardless of how much his only real self shames him, he cannot exist without it. His shame grows into an inexplicable and paradoxical Self-Hatred.

REPRESSION OF SELF-HATRED

The Suicide inherently ignores the existential dichotomy implicit in his Self-Hatred. That one can only hate an object outside himself always escapes his awareness.

But it did not escape the penetrating insight of Freud. He stated that the Ego must "objectify" itself in order for suicide to occur. For this is exactly what happens. The Suicide unconsciously experiences himself as two distinct entities.[1] He identifies with his Fantastic Self. And he objectifies his Empirical Self. And because his Empirical Self causes his Fantastic Self so much shame, he must grow to hate it.

This inherent duplicity is so automatic and unconscious, we often take it for granted. Such common statements as "I get so angry at myself," can only reflect such an implied but inherent dichotomy.

However, the Suicide must automatically repress his true Self-Hatred on three essential accounts. First, for him to admit to the true nature of his Self-Hatred would not only reveal the impossible dichotomy it implies but would further reveal that he is not really his Fantastic Self. For if he really were his Fantastic Self, he would have no reason to hate himself. Secondly, to admit to the true nature of his Self-Hatred would constitute admission of why he hates himself. This could only cause him further shame, further escalating his Self-Hatred. Third, and most important, should he openly express his Self-Hatred, he would have no defenses against it. He must repress it simply to keep himself alive.

Even though he may occasionally feel that he hates himself—this is especially true of the Synpathic and Apathic types—his true Self-Hatred remains repressed. As we will see, he simply makes the mistake of identifying some of its expressions as the real thing. For his Self-Hatred grows to such overwhelming proportions, he simply must express it.

Because of his unconscious Self-Hatred, his condition becomes analogous to that of a captive slave living under the rule of a hateful, cruel, and ruthless tyrant. In this analogy, the hateful tyrant would invoke a multitude of dictatorial rules to which the slave must adhere under the threat of severe punishment. He would hold his captive in contempt, for certainly humane respect would not be his due. To keep his victim subservient, the tyrant would constantly accuse, punish, and defeat him. And, lastly, the tyrant might—in a fit of hateful rage—actually destroy his despicable slave.

Chapter 10

EXPRESSIONS OF SELF-HATRED

The Suicide's Fantastic Self becomes his cruel and hateful tyrant. His Empirical Self—his one true self—becomes the despised and hated slave. He sometimes wonders why he treats himself so cruelly, but the full ramifications of his comprehensive Self-Hatred remain deeply embedded in his unconscious.

Yet the failure of his Empirical Self to measure up to the impossible criteria of his Fantastic Self fuels the fires of his Self-Hatred. His inevitable failures regarding his repressed attributes fan the flames. The special disabilities of his Empirical personality add tinder to the fire. And the reality of life and of his condition in it whips the flame into a fury. Even though he manages to keep the true nature and overwhelming power of his Self-Hatred under wraps, it burns with such intensity he must find ways to express it.

INNER DICTATES

The first way the Suicide expresses Self-Hatred is through Inner Dictates. These are a multitude of dictatorial rules and decrees to which he must adhere under threat of severe punishment.[2] They consist of a combination of injunctions and taboos aimed at complete control of all his feelings, behavior, and relations. They are absolute and irrational in nature, and ultimately self-destructive in content. They are easily recognized on account of the additional shame and Self-Hatred resulting from his violating them.

Although the Suicide shapes his inner dictates generally in accordance with his particular fixed attribute, their extent and potency are never so limited. What they really boil down to is that nothing should be impossible for him.

Because of their absolute coercive power over him, his inner dictates can appear as moral codes, personal ethics, or inner conscience. But when we examine them closely, we note that they lack the serious convictions of genuine human ideals. And because he borrows some of their content from outside sources, his inner dictates can resemble cultural and parental injunctions and taboos.[3] But to interpret them strictly as introjections or conditioning would be much too circumscribing as to their origins and scope.

The Suicide, alone, incorporates material borrowed from parental and social edict, value systems, and moral codes, into his own inner dictates. He alone embellishes, expands, selects, and culls them to suit his own fixation and repressions. And he alone instills them with absolute coercive power over his own life.

His inner dictates result only from his unconscious Self-Hatred which in turn results from pride in his Fantastic Self, and so on, back to our beginning. Their coercive power over him is based solely on his irrational conviction in his Fantastic Self. Absolutely nothing should be impossible for him.

Yet the Suicide is mostly interested in his apparent adherence to his inner dictates. He only must appear never to violate any of his injunctions and taboos. This behavioristic adherence is our key to understanding the grounds from which his inner dictates originate. His enslaved Empirical Self must appear to adhere to the dictates of his tyrannical Fantastic Self. Regardless of what behavior might naturally arise in any given situation, he can only behave as he should or suffer the consequences.

Because of the severity of these consequences, he becomes painfully aware of those inner dictates he occasionally violates. He has little doubt about them. On the other hand, he is almost never aware of those inner dictates to which he normally adheres. He simply feels that he acts the way he does because he wants to.

The Suicide normally experiences his inner dictates in accordance with his type. Antipathic Harold identifies with his inner dictates. His injunctions and taboos are who and what he is. What Harold believes he should be, Harold believes he is. He should be strong, therefore he is strong. He should be wise, therefore he is wise. He should be persistent, therefore he is persistent. He should always control himself and others, therefore he always controls. Because Harold identifies with his inner dictates, he lends them even more coercive power over him.

Synpathic Ruth passively accepts her inner dictates. Her injunctions and taboos are just the way she is. Instead of feeling she should be compliant and inadequate, Ruth simply is compliant and inadequate. Instead of feeling she should be helpless and dependent, she simply is helpless and dependent. Instead of feeling she should be humble and pacific, she simply is humble and pacific. Ruth's bland acceptance of her inner dictates also adds to their potency. Since she never questions them, they are always just the way she is.

Apathic Carl feels obligated by his inner dictates. Of course, he resents them. How paradoxical for Carl! How can he free himself from his own injunctions that say he must be free? How can he rebel against his own taboos lodged against compliance? Characteristically, Carl attempts to transcend his own inner dictates. He pretends they are not there. Other people see ample evidence of Carl's adherence to his inner dictates, but he blocks his own awareness of them. By ignoring his inner dictates, Carl further surrenders to their coerciveness.

Regardless of type, the Suicide becomes completely controlled by his own inner dictates. His injunctions and taboos destroy what little autonomy he might have left. Although he may grow acutely aware of those inner dictates which he occasionally violates, he blinds himself to those he usually adheres to. Still, even a minor violation of any of them plunges him into abject shame and increased Self-Hatred.

Nothing should be impossible for him. Yet his own illusions prevent him from executing the readily possible. Although he may believe that he hates himself because he violates his inner dictates, the sequence is just the opposite. The Suicide's inner dictates are the primary expression of his unconscious Self-Hatred.

SELF-ACCUSATIONS AND SELF-CONTEMPT

The second way in which the Suicide expresses his unconscious Self-Hatred is through Self-Accusations and Self-Contempt. It sometimes seems as though the Suicide hates himself as a result of accusing himself. But, again, the sequence is just the opposite. The Suicide accuses himself and holds himself in contempt because he unconsciously hates himself. Self-accusations and self-contempt are conscious expressions of his unconscious Self-Hatred.

Only when seen in this light can his otherwise senseless self-accusations and self-contempt make any sense. For his self-accusations are limitless. If and when he recites them to someone else, he goes on and on. No amount of reassurance can mollify him. But his self-accusations and self-contempt make sense when we see how both come about.

The Suicide's Fantastic Self is both the Judge and the Prosecutor. His Empirical Self is the Defendant. The Bill of Indictment is endless; the verdict of Guilty-as-Charged is a foregone conclusion. And, because he chafes under the process, he is constantly held in Contempt of Court.[4]

Although the Suicide usually accuses himself of failing to adhere to his equally endless inner dictates, his self-accusations go beyond that. They amount to nothing less than his guilt of not being the absolute in every respect.

His self-contempt is contingent with his self-accusations. They go hand in hand. Because he is so guilty, he is utterly contemptible, so that at bottom he judges himself completely worthless.

These worthless feelings are distinct from the similar feelings he experienced earlier as a result of the contamination of his intrinsic autonomy. These particular feelings grow directly out of his current Self-Hatred. From his Fantastic Self's point of view, his Empirical Self deserves only contempt.

How the Suicide experiences his self-accusations and self-contempt again depends on type. Again, Antipathic Harold's hostility, arrogance, and rigidity enter the picture. Again, Synpathic Ruth's feeling abused, inadequate, and deprived come into play. And, once again, Apathic Carl's detachment, ambivalence, and inertia are involved.

Harold's self-accusations are the voice of his conscience. But he fails to see they are directed against him rather than for him as would be the admonitions of a constructive conscience. His self-contempt often appears as blatant or subtle discountings of his achievements or accomplishments.

Despite his arrogance, Harold often sells himself short. His achievements may be remarkable, but because of his self-contempt, they are never gratifying. He fails to see the poignant irony in mercilessly driving himself to attain some goal, then immediately deprecating its importance once he attains it.

Ruth's self-accusations and self-contempt mesh perfectly with her feeling abused, inadequate, and deprived. Typically, she abuses herself, accuses herself, and thereby deprives herself. She, too, discounts everything about herself on account of her self-contempt. She simply cannot accept a compliment, regardless of how sincere. "Such a pretty dress," a friend may comment. "This old rag?" is Ruth's classic reply.

Ruth's inherent feelings of deprivation automatically reinforce her self-contempt. She must depreciate other people's affection and regard for her, or their efforts on her behalf. It may mystify other people that she yearns for their help and affection but discounts it when she gets it. Worse, her self-contempt causes her to discount the people, themselves, who come to her aid or offer their affection. To use a well-worn example from Groucho Marx, Ruth certainly would not want to associate with someone whose standards are so low that they would accept her.

The way Carl discounts his whole life illustrates his self-accusations and self-contempt. Although he desperately tries to rise above his self-accusations, they still pull him down. He cannot wholeheartedly strive for any kind of gratification. And he constantly accuses himself on this account.

Carl's self-contempt also lurks behind subtle devaluations of his life. He belittles his motives, what meager objectives he may strive for, what small gains he may make. His self-contempt often hides behind witticisms or sarcastic put-downs of himself. He jokes about his lack of motivation, his lack of roots, his spiritual and material impoverishment. As with all such humor, it contains a hard kernel of truth.

These ways of experiencing self-accusations and self-contempt are never so distinct in any one Suicide. All may incur any kind of self-accusation and self-contempt. But regardless of how they experience them, their self-accusations and self-contempt have one common aspect. The Suicide's real Empirical Self is held to be infinitely guilty and contemptible by his unconscious Fantastic Self.

SELF-DEFEAT AND SELF-PUNISHMENT

Self-Defeat and Self-Punishment constitute the third way the Suicide expresses Self-Hatred. Accused and judged infinitely guilty and contemptible, he must be punished accordingly. And since he cannot live up to the demands of his inner dictates, he must suffer the consequences. The punishment and consequences are severe, indeed. They range from the simplest petty frustrations to actual psychic and physical abuse.[5]

The ways he finds to punish himself are virtually unlimited. For example, he denies himself satisfaction of simple needs and pleasures such as rest, relaxation, and recreation. He deprives himself of genuine enjoyment of holidays and vacations. He will be habitually generous with extravagant gifts and favors to others, yet deny himself inexpensive necessities. He procrastinates in his work, financial affairs, or social relations, denying himself their full benefits. He preoccupies himself with problems, doubts, and fears, filling himself with anxious forebodings for the future.

He overworks, overeats, or overdrinks to the point of severe discomfort and threat to his health. He neglects routine health care. He grows habitually careless in respect to his own welfare, incurring loss of property, jobs, social status, or friendship. He becomes unkempt in his appearance or disorganized in his personal strivings, leading to social isolation, waste of time and energies, and loss of material possessions.

He frequently displays social awkwardness, blushing ineptitude, or gross clumsiness in public. He acts stupid, aloof, or offensive among friends and acquaintances. He elicits rejection or provokes hostility from others, or makes himself look foolish. He blinds himself to obvious opportunities for advancement in his career, forming new friendships, or attracting a potential lover.

He flirts with dangerous sports or other high-risk activities. He takes chances with his health, safety, and security. He recklessly gambles with his best prospects in a job or marriage. He experiments with drugs or plunges into addiction. He neglects laws, rules, and regulations, laying himself open to trouble with the law or other authority.

He subjects himself to useless and repeated surgeries. He suffers from mysterious and undiagnosable pain. He subjects himself to unwarranted psychological, physical, and emotional stress. He contracts a debilitating or fatal illness.

The list is virtually endless. It goes far beyond his not looking out for his own best interests, or even not taking care of himself. What it really amounts to is that he is out to defeat and punish himself any way he can.

Despite his complaints, frustration, and deprivation, those

around him can often discern his intent. They may even perceive his secret glee. Part of him fails, and the other part of him gloats over it. Friends, relatives, co-workers, and especially therapy groups, often note his "gallows humor" when he relates his misfortunes. He shows off self-defeats like hard-won trophies. Even though they become a source of further shame and Self-Hatred, he cannot help but let other people know about them.

He even enlists the aid of other people in the war against himself. He slyly or blatantly provokes, encourages, or seduces other people into helping him defeat or punish himself. He seeks their admiration for the skill and resourcefulness he uses in defeating himself. But other people cannot become too helpful in the campaign. He will instinctively fight back should they threaten to rob him of the pleasures of pure self-defeat.

Here lies the key to the nature of self-defeat and self-punishment. He must do it to himself. Antipathic Harold will fight to the death with anyone who even hints at standing in his way. But he blocks his own progress at every turn. Synpathic Ruth will suffer any indignity to win the affections of others. But she provokes their rejection at the drop of a hat. Apathic Carl stubbornly struggles against any real or imagined infringement on his liberty. But he imprisons himself in his own tight little world. They will not let anyone else interfere with their lofty goals. They must do it to themselves.

On the surface you might think Harold could strive beyond self-defeat. But more than either Carl or Ruth, he is deeply affected by it. Just as he hones his skills for accomplishment, he polishes his abilities to defeat himself. Despite all Harold's efforts, real success always lies beyond his grasp.

Whether he works as a maintenance man or as a corporation president, the products of his labor are inevitably flawed. But because of his perfectionism, Harold sees any flaw, however insignificant, as spoiling the whole. No accomplishment satisfies him for long. None lives up to his inflated expectations. And because of his exaggerated belief in himself, he underestimates the difficulties involved in his work or the time and efforts required to complete it. His efforts often go to waste, and he invariably fails to obtain the success he so ardently desires.

Ruth's middle name is Self-Defeat. It is part and parcel of who and what she is. Yet Ruth seems far less disturbed by self-defeat than Harold. Because of her inadequacies, Ruth expects it of herself. Her self-defeat makes her feel terribly abused and deprived. But she feels powerless to do anything about it. That her inadequacy is what inevitably defeats her is a paradox beyond her comprehension.

Ruth's history may be punctuated by little peaks of near fulfillment, but she cannot bear real accomplishment, in love or in work. She may not even be able compliantly to accept it. She eventually has to do something—or, usually, not do something—which messes everything up. She usually brings defeat about by sins of omission. Ruth defeats herself best by not doing anything at all.

Like Ruth, Carl may be almost oblivious to self-defeat. Since close relations with others or worldly success are usually anathema to Carl, failure to achieve them are his signs of success. But his detachment, inertia, and ambivalence eventually catch up with him.

Carl lets himself drift into unbearable situations. He gets caught up by the norms of society, the whims of others, or the vacillations of his own ambivalence. His very lack of specific worldly goals defeats him in his pursuit of his unconscious transcendent goal. He suddenly looks around to find himself imprisoned. Where did these obligations come from? Who made these commitments? In a panic, Carl reacts, but always to his own detriment. He invariably deprives himself of the ultimate rational freedom: the freedom to choose what he wants for himself and to get it.

On the surface, it appears as though the Suicide hates himself because he defeats himself. But on close examination, the origins and character of his self-defeat and self-punishment become obvious. Just as with his injunctions and taboos, just as with his self-accusations and self-contempt, his self-defeat and self-punishment result from Self-Hatred rather than cause it.

Chapter 11

DEFENSES TO SELF-HATRED

Completely controlled by his inner dictates, judged infinitely guilty and contemptible, and punished and defeated accordingly, the Suicide remains blind to the forces behind it all. His Self-Hatred remains inaccessibly unconscious, but its consequences profoundly affect him.

His Self-Hatred grows out of his shame at his failure actually to be his Fantastic Self. Yet its consequences ironically add to his shame. He struggles to adhere to the inner dictates controlling him. But he hates himself for not being able to break free of them. He tries to stop accusing himself. But he ends by accusing himself for making self-accusations. He punishes himself accordingly. But he inevitably feels shamed by the effects of the punishment. He defeats himself, then condemns himself for his failures.

This entire ever-worsening process intensifies his shame, which in turn adds to the Self-Hatred that initiated the process. His Self-Hatred grows so intense as to threaten the very illusion in his Fantastic Self from whence it came.

While this turn of events takes a terrible toll on Ruth and on Carl, to Harold it becomes a matter of life or death. How can the proud omnipotent Harold admit that he is powerless in the face of his own inner dictates, that he crumbles before his self-accusations, that he holds himself in contempt, that he defeats himself at every opportunity, and that he punishes himself without mercy? And worse, that he is helpless in the face of it all?

For Harold to survive, he must find some ways to defend his illusions of omnipotence from the consequences of his own Self-Hatred. To this end, he develops a system of unconscious defenses aimed at protecting his illusions. Although these defenses protect his illusions from further injury, they exact a heavy toll on his real life. But to him they are worth the price, to salvage his imagined omnipotence.

CHECKS AND AVOIDANCES

The first way in which Antipathic Harold defends his illusions of omnipotence from the consequences of his expressions of Self-Hatred is through evasion. He dodges the consequences by employing Checks and Avoidances. This defense has serious debilitating effects.

First of all, he avoids contact with other people, any of whom can inadvertently stimulate his Self-Hatred. For other people inevitably fail to show him sufficient deference and regard. And when they do ignore him, defy him, or omit to shower him with accolades, they evoke his self-condemnation. He should be so important as to never be disregarded. He should be so powerful as to never be defied. He should be so admired as never to be denied tributes.

Furthermore, Harold can always find people who have accomplished more than he has. Yet because of his competitiveness, he must compare himself with them. For example, at a baseball game he condemns himself for not being the All-Star Home-Run King; at a concert he condemns himself for not being the greatest conductor of all time; at a business seminar he condemns himself for not being Chairman of the Board of the world's largest corporation. Any kind of contact with people—if only to read of them in the newspaper—can arouse his self-condemnation. As a consequence, Harold must do his best to avoid contact with other people simply to protect his illusion of omnipotence.

In the second place, Harold also tries to avoid facing himself. He acts as though he is attached to some stranger. "This is not the real me," he tells himself. And he will go to any lengths to prove it.

Consequently, he avoids taking himself seriously. He will not—he cannot—face himself and his true condition in life with clear recognition.

He finds a variety of ways to avoid facing himself. He plunges into a frenzy of work, sex, athletics. He daydreams. He sleeps excessively. He travels incessantly. He hangs out in bars and clubs. He stays drunk or drugged. He gambles compulsively. He goes to countless movies or spends endless hours lost in television. He does anything he can to avoid being idle and alone with just himself.

In the third place, Harold avoids active strivings on his own account in order to protect his illusions. Since his goals for himself are impossible, he is bound to fail. And since any new failure triggers immediate self-condemnation, it's best to leave well enough alone and quit trying. However, as long as he harbors unfulfilled goals, he condemns himself for not fulfilling them. His choice is clear. He must put an unconscious check on even the devising of new goals, let alone striving to fulfill them.

This very important point changes our outward picture of the Antipathic Type Suicide. Up to now, we see him as literally compelled towards the fulfillment of his particular goals. Although this is always true of his inner processes, it is not necessarily the image he presents. Instead, because of this unconscious check on goal-making and striving, he may very likely present a picture of drifting lethargy.

Since Harold's Fantastic Self is omnipotent, he cannot admit to having any goals he must struggle to obtain. He therefore automatically converts all such goals into inner dictates. This process is so automatic and unconscious, he may never be aware of it. Before he even has a chance to experience a genuine desire to do anything, it automatically becomes a *must*. Harold rarely feels that he *wants* to do anything. He only feels that he *should*.

But every unfulfilled inner dictate ends with additional self-condemnation. He must cease wanting to do anything just for himself. Others may profit from his efforts. His family, his business, his employer, even society, may benefit. But he may not. What goals and strivings he does offer are only to appease his Fantastic Self, solely to enhance his image.

Harold's inner dictates drive him. But his checks on goals and strivings hold him back. Inwardly, he feels driven. But, outwardly, he cannot act. Coupled with his other avoidances, this check on goals and strivings entails a terrible debilitating effect. By avoiding other people, he condemns himself to isolation. By avoiding himself, he denies himself the genuine satisfaction in the richness of life. By putting this check on goals and strivings, he prohibits himself from attaining even a sample of his idealized goals.

Constantly working against himself, he hovers at the point of explosion. Like a vehicle running at full speed with its brakes locked, Harold tends to burn himself out. Coronaries, ulcers, hypertension, and similar impairments always pose a threat. But the most dangerous potential crisis of all is Harold's discovering the truth about himself.

Antipathic Harold's evasion defenses actually add to his Self-Hatred. But regardless of their consequences, he must necessarily invoke his checks and avoidances. To do anything else would expose his omnipotence to the full impact of the consequences of his unconscious Self-Hatred.

DISPLACEMENT: EXTERNALIZING

The second way in which the Antipathic Type defends against Self-Hatred is to displace it. He unconsciously Externalizes his own Self-Hatred onto other people. Thus, he does not consciously hate himself. He hates other people instead.

Obviously, externalized Self-Hatred increases Harold's hostility, arrogance, and rigidity. But beyond that, it entails further debilitating effects on his relations with other people. In the first place, externalized Self-Hatred entails an unconscious reaction which automatically triggers Harold's hostile rage towards others. Something happens which causes Harold shame, thus eliciting his Self-Hatred, and he immediately externalizes his rage onto someone else as a consequence.

This unconscious reaction is so automatic, Harold may never be aware of the shame and Self-Hatred which triggers it. All he usually experiences is the event and the rage against others that follows. And, since virtually anything can trigger his Self-Hatred, he constantly rages against them.

In the second place, externalized Self-Hatred lies at the roots of Harold's paranoid behavior. Since virtually anything can trigger his unconscious reaction and since he automatically rages against other people when it does, he has every reason to suspect them. Since they are to blame for everything, he would be a fool not to distrust their intentions.

In the third place, while Harold usually remains unaware of this automatic process, other people suffer its full exposure. His increased hostility, sudden rages, suspiciousness, and diatribes cannot but provoke other people's hostility in return. Ironically, their aversion operates as another salvation of his illusions. See, he doesn't hate himself after all! Other people hate him.

All these debilitating consequences are counter-reinforcing. Other people's hostility reinforces his paranoid suspiciousness. His paranoia reinforces his own hostility towards them. His automatic reaction of rage against others when anything goes wrong reinforces his arrogance. And, of course, in the face of all this hostility, he must remain rigidly in control.

But regardless of its price to him in his relations with other people, Harold must externalize his Self-Hatred. Otherwise, he would expose his illusions of omnipotence to the full impact of its expressions.

TOKEN CONCESSIONS

The third and most destructive way in which Antipathic Harold tries to defend against his Self-Hatred is for him to compromise with it by making Token Concessions to it. He actually allies himself with his hateful Inner Tyrant. He salvages his illusions of omnipotence, but in the process he virtually destroys himself.

Token concessions often look like additional forms of self-defeat or self-punishment. But by this stratagem, Harold seems to attain a certain tranquil satisfaction. Through making token concessions he buys a temporary peace.

He offers up a concession to his hateful inner tyrant with the secret hope that he may win peace, if only for a little while. In a sense, he perpetrates a partial self-murder. He almost destroys himself, or completely destroys something of value to him. It usually works. Afterwards, friends or relatives may remark, "He seems to be a different person after his near-fatal car accident. He's taking life easier now. He seems to be at peace with himself. It's like it's the best thing that ever happened to him."

Token concessions range in severity from dangerous accidents or illnesses to seemingly trivial sacrifices such as the loss of something of value—a sum of money or a piece of jewelry. They all have the same unconscious placatory intent, but they vary in effectiveness in proportion to their severity.

Personal disasters, serious illnesses, near-fatal accidents, radical surgery, the actual loss of an eye or limb, all bring a profound and lasting relief. It might dismay friends or relatives that he can incur a terrible disaster, then suddenly seem happy, content, and at peace with himself while they remain shocked and concerned for his welfare.

The same effect can be gained by provoking misfortunes. He may get fired from his job, trigger rejection by a mate or lover, be arrested for driving while intoxicated, sleep through a crucial professional exam, incur a big loss at the race track. It is as if Harold offers blood sacrifices on the altar of his insatiable inner god—paying mounting blackmail to an internal collector, forever on the take.

Naturally, he feels upset: but not nearly so much as one would expect. The relief he gains by buying off his Self-Hatred more than compensates him for the disturbances to his life.

Possibly the most dismaying aspect of token concessions is the timing. They often occur just when everything seems to be going so well. But outside appearances can be deceiving. When things look to be going well for Harold may be the very time when his Self-Hatred reaches its peak—for several reasons.

In the first place, periods of good fortune deny Harold's Self-Hatred its usual outlets of self-defeat and self-punishment. Secondly, good luck can serve as another reminder of the limitations of reality compared with his Fantastic Self's infinite potential. And thirdly, good fortune often aborts his other defenses such as checks and avoidances and the hostility he expects from externalizations. Thus, the aggregate effect of favorable aspects can elicit more Self-Hatred than a streak of bad luck for the Antipathic Type.

Of course, token concessions have their sobering effect. The greater their severity, the more they subdue. But to other people's dismay, and often to Harold's own, he keeps executing them. He may gain some insight into their dark purpose, but this does not deter him for long precisely because his Self-Hatred grows beyond his control. A passing glimpse of the power of his own Self-Hatred can throw him into a suicidal panic.

Of course, it is exactly this at which his Self-Hatred aims. It is designed specifically to destroy him. How can his Fantastic Self ever be actualized until his hated Empirical Self is out of the way?

Part IV

THE ULTIMATE WEAPON

Chapter 12

ORIGINS OF VINDICTIVENESS

Vindictiveness results from the humiliation the Suicide experiences because other people do not relate to him as his Fantastic Self. For though he creates his Fantastic Self partly to compensate for his original loss of empathy with other people, through its creation, he learns to relate to other people, not *with* them. As he develops his Fantastic Self, he concomitantly develops his strategies. He learns to move against, towards, or away from other people as a means of gaining illusionary satisfaction of his own needs. He may attack at one moment, temporarily surrender at another, beat a hasty retreat at still another. But always there is a calculated strategy.

As he becomes convinced he really is his Fantastic Self, reality intervenes. Consequently, he must summon pride to reinforce his conviction. Now, mutuality with others is no longer the question. Instead, his pride renders him infinitely vulnerable. When other people hurt his pride, he suffers unbearable humiliation.

Other people must inevitably hurt the Suicide's pride because he expects through his relations with them the absolute confirmation of his Fantastic Self. This is beyond their power. They must fail him. His mounting humiliation grows into rage. And his rage automatically results in Vindictiveness.

EXPECTATIONS OF THE FANTASTIC SELF

Other people are bound to fail him because of the absolute attributes of his Fantastic Self. No real amount of power, love, or independence can satisfy him. Just as he mercilessly drives himself in its service, he conscripts others into its service, too. His family, friends, or co-workers find themselves drafted into the ranks. He makes them all, as he makes himself, subordinate to his Fantastic Self.

But even this will not suffice. In the first place, the people closest to him obviously do not have the power to make him into his Fantastic Self, even though he chooses them because of their apparent willingness to try.

Antipathic Harold surrounds himself with people he can defeat. His wife is submissive. His children are usually terrified of him. His co-workers learn better than to challenge him. And, of course, they all depend on him one way or another.

Synpathic Ruth associates only with those people upon whom she can depend. Her husband must be strong and capable. She trains her children to be the kind of people upon whom she can rely. Her friends have qualities, strengths, and resources she can tap. And her co-workers know there is much they must do to help her or encourage her with her tasks.

Apathic Carl picks people who will not bother him. His wife, lover, or sometime-companion knows not to make any demands or expect anything from him. His children, should he have any, quickly learn self-reliance or suffer the deprivation. His acquaintances accept that Carl may be here today and gone tomorrow. Those who might work with him know that it is his task, and his alone, that concerns him. They all learn never to obligate him.

But to Harold, Ruth, and Carl, none of this is enough. Each of their unconscious choices ironically work against the confirmation of the Fantastic Self simply by virtue of the fact they are tailored to fit. For example, just because Harold's wife submits to him does not prove anything to Harold. He knows she will submit to virtually anyone.

Furthermore, even though the Suicide surrounds himself with people who tend not to challenge his convictions about himself, they cannot absolutely confirm them. Yet only absolute confirmation will satisfy.

No amount of submissiveness from his wife can prove Harold's omnipotence. Besides, she still must reserve some elements of her life for herself, regardless of how stringently she restricts her pursuits in favor of his. There are bound to be some ways in which people deny Ruth her merited innocence. They, too, have their own lives to look after. Even those people around Carl look to him for some response other than transcendence. They have their own needs, even in connection with him.

But only total confirmation of the Suicide's Fantastic Self will serve, regardless of type. To make matters worse, other people's confirmation cannot be limited to his fixed attribute. It is not enough that they acknowledge Harold's powers. They must recognize his goodness and self-reliance, too. It is not enough that they cater to Ruth's innocence. They must verify her capabilities and individuality as well. It is not enough that they respect Carl's aloofness. They must also attest to his inherent strengths and love for humankind. Even though his fixed attribute always comes first, no other attribute of his Fantastic Self can be ignored.

Finally, despite the efforts of those around him to nurture his illusions about himself, there is still a whole world of people out there who fail to do so. The people in his immediate environment are not enough. They are far too few, and they cannot succeed anyway. What the absoluteness of his Fantastic Self really requires is for the world to be in his service.

But even when other people do try to nurture his illusions about himself, the Suicide fails to take it into full account. Their most sympathetic strivings often go completely unnoticed. He cannot recognize and appreciate other people's sympathy and efforts for him because he is so estranged from them. Their feelings are completely foreign to him. They may want nothing less for him than total satisfaction of all his needs, hopes, and desires. But his estrangement from them keeps him from ever realizing it.

Furthermore, his alienation prevents other people from realizing what his real needs are. It is virtually impossible for them to see through his facade. Harold holds himself back on account of his defenses. How can other people identify his specific burning ambition? Ruth withdraws from the very people she needs the most. How can they overcome her withdrawal to see that she yearns for their affection? Carl denies himself access to the very freedom he desires. How can others understand Carl if he will not allow them the most innocuous contact with him?

Even when people do get a fairly good picture of each type's innermost goals, this perception usually backfires. Others recognize the insatiability of the Suicide's expectations. Overwhelmed by their exorbitancy, other people realize there is little they can do to meet them. The net result is that other people lengthen their own estrangement from the Suicide in the face of such overwhelming odds.

Finally, other people are intimidated by his Fantastic Self. And on this account, he will forever be alien to them. He is not of their world. He is like a visitor from another planet. As much as they might want to confirm his glory, as mere mortal earthlings they lack the qualifications. Ironically, since the Suicide is unconsciously convinced he is his Fantastic Self, the favorable judgment and homage of those beneath him become meaningless.

Blind to this paradox, his resulting humiliation turns to rage. He will not forgive other people their transgressions. Because they are helpless to say or do anything for him that really counts, they grow ever more despicable in his eyes. By the very nature of his expectations of other people, he grows vindictive toward them.

Limitations of the Empirical Self

Yet his Vindictiveness comes about even when this is not the central issue. For simple genuine recognition of his actual assets will never do. What he really has to have is confirmation without caveat of his impossible Fantastic Self.

Even though he believes himself to be his imaginary Fantastic Self, other people can only relate to him through his actual Empirical Self. To complicate matters, all the limitations of his Empirical Self resulting from his unconscious convictions in his Fantastic Self hinder other people's relating to him on any plane.

How else can people relate to Harold except through his hostility, arrogance, and rigidity? They may try to befriend him, but his hostility invariably stands in the way. They may want to credit him with his achievements, but his arrogance discounts even their highest praise. They may attempt to establish a mutual relationship with him, but his rigidity specifies that it be only on his terms.

How can people prevent Ruth from feeling abused, inadequate, and deprived on account of their relating to her? Regardless of their kindness, she is bound eventually to feel abused by them. They may try to hide even their most trivial assets from her, but she still ends up feeling deprived. Nothing they can do can prevent her from comparing herself with them and feeling short-changed.

How can people get around Carl's ambivalence, detachment, and inertia? As soon as it looks as if they know him, his ambivalences carry him off in a completely different direction. Just trying to break through his detachment is virtually impossible. And as far as their adding something new to his life, his drifting inertia automatically nullifies such appeal.

What it boils down to is that the limitations of the Suicide's Empirical Self interfere with others relating to him in any way, let alone as his Fantastic Self. Blind to this irony, also, he holds other people accountable for it. They are at fault for not relating to him as his Fantastic Self. He grows increasingly vindictive as a result.

REPRESSION OF VINDICTIVENESS

His Vindictiveness grows to such overwhelming proportions, he simply must express it. But he cannot do so in the ways he experiences it. This would entail three very negative consequences.

First, should he openly express his Vindictiveness in its pure state, he would be admitting to himself and the world why he is vindictive. This admission could only cause him further humiliation. Secondly, should he openly express his Vindictiveness in its pure state, it would imply that he really is not his Fantastic Self. For if he really were, he would have no reason to be vindictive. Thirdly, should he openly express his Vindictiveness, it would subject him to immediate and overt retaliation from other people. Given the scope of his Vindictiveness, such massive retaliation would instantly disprove his absolute invincibility, infinite lovableness, or ultimate self-sufficiency.

These consequences are obviously prohibitive. The Suicide therefore has no choice but to repress his Vindictiveness. But he still must find ways unconsciously to express it. He may learn to disguise it. But regardless of how he hides it, he is out to get other people. He is out to get those closest to him, those in his social environment, those he casually encounters. He is out to get the whole world.

Chapter 13

EXPRESSIONS OF VINDICTIVENESS

Because of unconscious Vindictiveness, the Suicide embarks on a life-long campaign of vengeance. Like a convicted criminal, he unconsciously vows revenge upon his jurors. But in the case of the Suicide, the whole world is his jury.

His Fantastic Self's absoluteness assures his unconscious Vindictiveness. His estrangement from others whips it into a fury. The continued failure of others to relate to him as his Fantastic Self adds thunderous rage to the storm. His repressed Vindictiveness swells into a raging tempest. Despite its repression, it gains power enough to destroy everyone around him. The Suicide must find ways to vent his Vindictiveness, if only unconsciously.

EXTERNAL CLAIMS

The first way the Suicide expresses his unconscious Vindictiveness is by staking out External Claims against other people. His external claims are very much like his inner dictates. Instead of invoking countless injunctions and taboos upon himself, he invokes countless demands and restrictions upon other people.[1] Like his inner dictates, his external claims are irrational, absolute, and ultimately destructive. They are not aimed at simply disrupting his relations with other people, but at absolutely destroying them.

His demands and restrictions lodged against other people are virtually infinite. Although they are generally tuned to the confirmation of his fixed attribute, they are never so limited. What his external claims really amount to is that no one should ever deny him anything. Their sole unconscious purpose is the absolute control and exploitation of others in the service of his Fantastic Self. Like his inner dictates, his external claims can wear many disguises, but regardless of how he veils them, the essential Vindictiveness of the Suicide's external claims appears in three obvious ways.

First, the essential Vindictiveness of his external claims appears in their irrational absoluteness. His claims are insatiable. No amount of deference or recognition satisfies him. No amount of acquiescence to his needs is ever enough. No amount of approval or submission suffices.

He may experience his claims as reasonable hopes and desires, as passive longings for others' affection, help, or regard, or as an intellectual evaluation of the ways of the world. But, in truth, he never feels that he just desires something from other people, but that he deserves it.

Secondly, the essential Vindictiveness of his claims shows in the way he relates to others. He may seem quite concerned about other people, professing an egalitarian reciprocity of needs, regard, and consideration, even appearing self-sacrificing. But at best he sees other people's needs, hopes, and desires as only relative to his own. Theirs are not absolute, like his.

Thirdly, the vindictive essence of his claims always comes to light through his reaction to their frustration, which elicits his humiliation. This in turn elicits deeper Vindictiveness, further stimulating his need for retaliation. His humiliation, vindictive rage, and need for retaliation is so automatic he might not ever be aware of its source. Yet the frustration of his impossible claims is so ineluctable that he can never free himself from the cycle. Someone fails to satisfy a claim and he automatically reacts with vindictive retaliation. Thus, his external claims put him and others in a double bind. They cannot avoid frustrating his claims; he cannot avoid feeling humiliated. And, because he must retaliate, other people must incur his rage, however disguised.

Because of his automatic reaction, people may fail to recognize the frustration of his claims on the first occasion or so, though they are bound to recognize them later. But other people rarely recognize the claims they satisfy, until they make the mistake of failing to do so. The Suicide himself rarely realizes the extent and nature of his claims. But as with his other expressions, he lodges his external claims in accordance with his type.

Antipathic Harold identifies with his external claims. He is who and what his claims make him out to be. Since he believes he is infinitely masterful, powerful, and deserving of recognition, Harold stakes his claims accordingly.

Harold claims ultimate power, control, and recognition. Since ultimate power is inherently his, no one should ever stand in his way, assert himself in Harold's presence, or act independently of him. Since unlimited recognition is his inalienable gift, no one should ever question him, doubt him, or fail to praise him.

Because Harold exaggerates his powers, he believes virtually everyone is in his debt. His wife, his family, his co-workers, indeed, the whole world is obligated to him. They owe him gratitude, services, and recognition because of the benefits they accrue through his existence. And since he stakes his claims on the basis of his imagined potential, he really does not have to accomplish anything to deserve all of this. He deserves it because he exists.

Harold reacts to the inevitable frustration of his claims with amplified demands. When his claim for gratitude is frustrated, Harold exaggerates the value of the benefits others receive because of him. When his claim for recognition is frustrated, he exaggerates the importance of his accomplishments. When his claim for homage is frustrated, he exaggerates the assessment of his powers.

The frustration of his claims escalates Harold's hostility. The exaggeration of his powers and accomplishments bolsters his arrogance. The persistence of his demands reinforces his rigidity. The characteristics of Harold's Empirical Self and his vindictive external claims always go hand in hand.

Synpathic Ruth passively accepts her external claims. She accepts them so passively as to be unaware that she asserts them. Nothing would surprise her more than for someone to point out that she stakes impossible and exploitative claims against other people. But in many respects, the way Ruth stakes her claims is even more effective than Harold's.

Since Ruth believes herself to be absolutely Innocent, her primary claim is to be loved accordingly. But since she defines being loved as the total satisfaction of her compliant dependency, her seemingly simple claim becomes infinitely complex.

Ruth claims unconditional love. She must be loved simply because she exists, not because she develops any lovable qualities. Ruth claims absolute, exclusive, eternal, and comprehensive love. It must provide her with everything. Other people's love frees her from responsibility, even from herself. Naturally, Ruth fails to see the impossibility of this kind of love. The frustration of Ruth's claim for impossible love evokes her unbearable humiliation. But Ruth believes in her infinite goodness, understanding, and tolerance of others. As a result, her illusions prevent her from even feeling the resulting rage, let alone openly expressing it.

Therefore, whenever Ruth's claim for impossible love is frustrated, she experiences her humiliation by feeling massively abused, effectively expressing her unconscious rage by showing her frustrators how they abuse her. If satisfaction is still not forthcoming, she may even provoke abuse in order to back up her claim.

Since Ruth feels so inadequate in relation to others, she sees their attempts to satisfy her needs as directly proportionate to their regard for her. The more inadequate she is, the more other people must help her, and the more they help her, the more she feels loved. Thus, Ruth has a vested interest in being inadequate. It is her way of asserting her claim for love.

Finally, Ruth escalates her deprivation to assert her claim for love. But she cannot just feel deprived. She must show other people how deprived she is. Even in the face of abundance, Ruth accentuates her deprivation. If not deprived of material goods, then she is deprived of the spiritual. If not deprived of support, then she is deprived of her independence. If not deprived of the affection of her family and friends, then she is deprived of a career. Whatever Ruth's real situation, she always feels deprived. Other people deprive Ruth simply because they seem to have everything she feels she deserves. And because she is so good, she deserves everything. Therefore, anything anyone else has that Ruth does not, automatically deprives her. So everyone automatically owes her accordingly.

Obviously, Ruth not only has extensive external claims, but she asserts them very effectively. She asserts them by escalating her feelings of being abused, inadequate, and deprived. Worse, by passively accepting her seemingly simple claim to be loved, Ruth actually becomes even more abused, inadequate, and deprived.

Apathic Carl believes he is ultimately self-sufficient. For that reason, it would seem that Carl has no grounds for staking claims against other people. Wrong! Ironically, it is this very attribute of self-sufficiency on which Carl stakes his claims. Since he believes he transcends other people, Carl claims absolute exemption in relation to them. Carl unconsciously claims to be exempt from everything which he sees as obligation, commitment, ties, responsibility, and accountability.

Because his external claims are obviously irrational and impossible—even to him—Carl must deal with them the same way he deals with his inner dictates, pretending that they are not there. He must transcend his own external claims. Carl should not have to do anything.

All this is well and good until Carl's ambivalences enter his claims. Carl feels free indiscriminately to meet his own ambivalent needs without incurring obligations. He should be free to enjoy sexual relations without incurring intimacy. He should be free to work when he chooses without encountering competition or obligation. He should be free to benefit from friendships without having to maintain his end of the relationships. He should be free to come and go as he pleases at his own whim without other people's resentment. He should be able to enjoy the benefits of society without having to make any contributions.

Other people and society as a whole will tolerate Carl's claims only so far and so long. Inevitably, someone holds Carl accountable for something. So enters Carl's vindictive detachment. He expresses the resulting humiliation and rage by further distancing himself. When someone frustrates Carl's claims, he simply drifts away.

As with Harold and Ruth, Carl's external claims are counter-reinforced by the characteristics of his Empirical Self. Harold's claims work hand in hand with his hostility, arrogance, and rigidity. Ruth's are supported by her becoming more abused, inadequate, and deprived. Carl's reinforce his detachment, ambivalence, and inertia.

Each Suicide's external claims destroy what little empathy he might have left. Whether he ever becomes conscious of his external claims or not, they are the principle expression of his unconscious Vindictiveness.

CONTEMPT FOR AND ACCUSATIONS AGAINST OTHERS

The second way the Suicide expresses his unconscious Vindictiveness is by growing contemptuous of others and blaming and accusing them. Like his self-contempt and self-accusations, the contempt and accusations he lodges against others are limitless. And like his external claims, they are also absolute, vindictive, and irrational.

Some Suicides are openly contemptuous of others while some seem to be warm and friendly, even humble, on the surface, but somehow convey an uneasy feeling of contempt. Either overtly or covertly, they express unconscious Vindictiveness.

They blame and accuse others on the same account. The range and content of the accusations a Suicide actually lodges are usually commensurate with his type, yet those he actually feels can never be so limited. He generally accuses other people of character defects and of their treatment of him. But all his accusations contain a scarlet thread: he senselessly blames everyone for not treating him as his Fantastic Self.

Obviously, he has vested interests in not recognizing the character of his accusations, and in not even being aware that he makes them. He may delude himself that he is making justifiable criticisms and asserting his rights. He may experience his accusations as passive longings for change in those he would otherwise accuse. He may detach himself from involvement, indicating his cynicism about human nature. But those around him know the impact of his blame, openly expressed or not.

As you might expect, Antipathic Harold makes blatant his contempt and blame of others. He is not the least hesitant to express his scorn. Other people are stupid, inept, helpless, bungling, lazy, weak, crude, immoral. He may learn to mask his disdain but those who encounter him come away with the unmistakable feeling of having been put down, even if they cannot say exactly how.

But usually Harold does not bother to hide his derision. It is only right for someone with his superior powers to be openly contemptuous of others. No amount of evidence challenging his superiority deters him. He is quick to blame others for almost everything that goes wrong. And since he sees virtually nothing as ever going right, his accusations are endless. No one can ever please him for long. Even his own failures, misfortunes, or shortcomings are the fault of someone else.

Harold's hostility, arrogance, and rigidity reinforce his contempt and accusations. His contempt echoes his hostility. His accusations grow from his arrogance. And their persistence reflects his rigidity.

Synpathic Ruth, on the other hand, does her best to disguise her contempt and accusation of others. But she rarely succeeds in disguising them from anyone save herself. Her obliviousness does not diminish their potency. They are powerfully at work behind her innocent naiveté. Characteristically, Ruth shows her contempt for others by denying them their humanity, then accusing them of being inhuman.

Ruth's denial of others' humanity is comprehensive. It may never occur to her that other people have feelings she can hurt, rights she can impose on, needs she can ignore. She would be shocked to know she had hurt someone's feelings, since she believes they have none. She may, while in close-range situations, seem to guard against imposing on another's rights, but only to keep peace or win approval. As to needs, other people are luckily endowed with some mysterious strengths and self-reliance which are unfortunately missing from her own composition. She gives no consideration as to whether other people value her brand of love or desire her kind of efforts on their behalf. Behind all her efforts and pleas for mutual love and understanding lurks a comprehensive absence of real consideration for anyone else.

She will not recognize other people's efforts on their own behalf, discounting their struggles to improve their lives, blinding herself to their achievements. Other people are somehow graced with the knack of winning love, getting things for themselves, gaining independence, all without effort. Even when Ruth does seem to credit other people for their efforts and achievements, she does it obliquely or backhandedly, endowing them with the good fortune of being born motivated, a condition which she, alas, has been denied.

Other people are selfish, uncaring, callous, and insensitive, never giving her enough of anything—attention, affection, help, or material favors. They will not share any of those gifts or qualities with which they have been mysteriously endowed, while she has none. They have no feelings at all! Why can't they see she can't help being helpless? No matter how much she gives of herself, they still cheat her, deny her, and take advantage of her.

Thus, although she tries to hide them behind a screen of innocent naiveté, Ruth's contempt and accusation of others are comprehensive. How does she square her contempt and accusations with her innocence? After all, isn't she infinitely loving, understanding, and tolerant of other people?

Ruth reconciles the discrepancy by feeling abused, inadequate, and deprived. She feels abused by other people's inhumanity, inadequate in comparison, deprived because she lacks equal powers. But her suffering justifies it all. It enables her further to express her Vindictiveness by showing others how much they make her suffer.

In contrast to Harold and Ruth, Apathic Carl appears to be extremely tolerant of other people in many ways. He is usually uncritical of even the most obnoxious behavior. He seldom displays envy, anger, or impatience. On the surface, Carl seems to be virtually free of contempt and accusations against other people. That is, just as long as they keep their distance. But just try to question Carl's imagined immunity and you will meet his contempt head on. Just expect something from him and you will let yourself in for accusations ad infinitum.

Carl shows his contempt for others best by ignoring them. Other people don't rate. Nothing they do, think, or feel really matters. Their highest achievements, their sincerest feelings, their loftiest thoughts are insignificant to Carl. And behind his bland tolerance lurk accusations galore. Other people are rabble. They are vicious, stupid, and parasitic, wanting nothing more than to trap him and suck his life's blood dry.

Torn between overtly tolerating other people while covertly demeaning them, Carl drifts in and out of contact with them. Away from them, his Vindictiveness seems to subside. But whenever close contact is made, his contempt and accusations come to the fore.

"Who are you," he demands, "to try and trap me and drag me down to your level?" Then Carl consummates his contempt in his inimitable style. He stalks off from the trash around him.

Whether the Suicide openly expresses his contempt and accusations or only experiences them internally, they are always there making Harold more hostile—Ruth more suffering—Carl more alienated.

But however the Suicide reacts, the message he delivers through his contempt and accusations is the same. Other people are unworthy of him. And unworthy they will remain, as long as he is convinced he is his Fantastic Self.

VINDICTIVE RETALIATION

Vindictive Retaliation is the third way in which the Suicide expresses his Vindictiveness. Other people inevitably fail to satisfy his claims. And since he knows them to be utterly contemptible, they must suffer his retaliation.

He experiences his relations with them as a struggle of all against all. When they frustrate his claims, he feels that his whole being is threatened. When they deny his accusations, he feels utterly defeated. When they survive his contempt, he feels demolished.

Other people go about their daily lives never realizing that just by doing so, they frustrate his claims, deny his accusations, and survive his contempt. As a consequence, they cause him excruciating humiliation for which he must retaliate.

In fact, the better they survive, the greater his need for retaliation. This often puzzles those closest to him. They make constructive moves, find new avenues for self-expression and happiness, and these are the very times he strikes.

This is the first clue to understanding vindictive retaliation: what other people see as senseless hostility, he sees as a well-deserved reprisal. With him, the law of talion prevails: an eye for an eye, a tooth for a tooth. But just squaring accounts is never enough. Because he is his Fantastic Self, he must emerge the unmistakable victor. And since others cause him infinite humiliation, they are infinitely deserving of his revenge.

The second clue to understanding vindictive retaliation is that no amount of vengeance is too much. Simply evening the score will never do. The seemingly most insignificant frustration can cause a murderous rage within Harold. A slight which might cause most people to feel just a bit miffed can swamp Ruth with devastating humiliation. Carl's rage can reach overwhelming proportions in reaction to an utterly trivial obligation.

The final clue to understanding vindictive retaliation is that it appears irrational. It is not just senselessly out of proportion to the incident that touches it off. Beyond that, it is usually triggered by apparently irrational causes. However, it does make sense when viewed from the perspective of the Fantastic Self. From that point of view, it all adds up. Harold, infinitely masterful and powerful, naturally feels humiliated by anyone who even inadvertently denies his powers. Ruth, infinitely loving and deserving, of course feels humiliated by anyone who even remotely threatens her innocence. And Carl, infinitely free and self-sufficient, automatically feels humiliated by anyone who even questions his immunity.

Of course, Harold is out to get his enemies any way he can, and he doesn't care who knows it. Actually, after the fact, Harold wants everyone to know about it in detail. If they do not learn about it for themselves, he will be sure to tell them about it later.

Harold may temporarily camouflage his vengeance: but only because secrecy may be part of the plan. For Harold plans his revenge as a general plans an invasion. In fact, Harold may be so preoccupied with planning his revenge, he never gets around to executing it.

But Harold never forgets. He can carry a grudge for years. He has his own Enemies List, and it dates back to Year One. Although his enemies may grow ever more inaccessible, he remains obsessed with wreaking revenge, if only in his imagination. Those more available feel his reprisals, large and small, every day. He is quick to deny his enemies the simplest of pleasures. He likes nothing more than to belittle their most earnest strivings, achievements, and hopes for the future.

Harold can spot another person's vulnerabilities at a glance. And once he discovers them he rarely lets up. He harbors in his arsenal a wide variety of weapons. He can attack with stinging sarcasm, humiliating jokes, direct frontal assault. He is a master at vindictive denial, false promises, prolonged frustration. One of his favorite strategies is a combination punch of disappointing or frustrating others, then brushing off their valid complaints afterwards.

Those around him dread his terrible temper. He can grow so vituperative, he scares everyone around including himself. He can become physically violent, to the brink of murder and mayhem. Yet there is not much others can do to escape his vengeance. Their existence is enough to trigger his wrath.

Harold's empirical characteristics seem specifically designed for vindictive retaliation. His hostility, arrogance, and rigidity harmonize perfectly with it. Harold proudly and consciously develops his abilities to make people pay and pay and pay.

In contrast, Ruth's empirical characteristics appear to interfere with her directly and effectively exacting revenge. While Ruth feels so abused and deprived by others, she has all the more reason to strike back. But since she feels so inadequate compared with them, she must be extremely careful in how she does so. Above all, Ruth must appear innocent.

How does Ruth go about inflicting vindictive retaliation on others while still maintaining her innocence? She does it passively, by being helpless. She abuses other people by showing them how much they abuse her. She deprives them with her inadequacies. When others fail to satisfy her dependency claims, she retaliates by growing more dependent. When others deny her accusations that they are abusing her, she retaliates by provoking their abuse. When others ignore her contempt for their achievements, she retaliates by becoming more inadequate. Finally, when others threaten her innocence by questioning her motives, she retaliates by acting stupid, naive, and falsely accused. She cries. She fogs over. She withdraws. Throughout it all, she remains wide-eyed and innocent.

One of Ruth's favorite strategies is innocently to provoke another's hostility and then collapse in the face of it. Just as Harold is quick to spot other people's vulnerabilities, Ruth intuitively knows what will provoke their hostility. Other people, having grown accustomed to her tactics, may not react to her provocations at first. Ruth will then keep escalating until people finally react. For example, if her employer should try to ignore her coming to work late, she keeps arriving later and later until he cannot ignore it any longer.

Sometimes Ruth will make a half-hearted, ill-timed, inadequate gesture, just to recoup her innocence. She will get to work an hour early when there is nothing for her to do. Or she will start to reorganize the files but will not have time to complete the task, leaving everything in disarray. Then, when her employer reacts, she crumbles in a heap of injured innocence. "Nothing I ever do pleases you," she cries. How can one attack another who is so well-meaning, innocent, and defenseless? In the end, she leaves her object of vindictive retaliation just where she wants to: overcome with impotent rage. Ruth scores a vindictive triumph, yet remains innocent of it.

Carl retaliates through aloofness. He lets everyone know that at any moment they may never see him again. If they are able to form any kind of bond with him at all, it must be at their great risk. Despite his apparent tolerance, he will turn on them upon the slightest provocation. And his way of turning on them is for him to turn away.

But before he departs, he lets them know how little and insignificant they are. How far down do they want to drag him? Down to *their* level? How stupid do they think he is? As stupid as they are? How sickly ambitious do they want him to get? Be a rat in the rat race exactly like them? How emotional do they think he will be? As insipidly romantic as they?

He almost resembles Harold with his invectives. Yet, at the same time, he can employ much of Ruth's passive Vindictiveness. He may go on a drunk, lose his job, forget an important date or appointment, do anything he can to disappoint or frustrate the object of his rage. For in addition to his aloofness, Carl can score with both aggressive and passive Vindictiveness. This is one advantage—if we could call it that—to his ambivalences. He can retaliate against others in a broad spectrum of ways. But he scores best by manipulating them into being vulnerable to him, then simply walking away.

Others eventually learn to roll with his punches. Don't get too close. Stay detached. Don't count on him in any way. Always be ready for change. But don't try to effect a direction. Just drift along with the tide.

After a while you get an underlying message to the Suicide's Vindictiveness. He has the unconscious goal of making other people feel as he does. Harold's open Vindictiveness inevitably provokes other people's hostility. His singling them out for attack exaggerates their importance and brings out their arrogance. And they must become rigid to resist his dogged persistence. Other people soon feel hostile, arrogant, and rigid—just like Harold.

Ruth abuses other people with her passivity. She deprives them through her inadequacies. And she proves their inadequacy in the face of her helpless innocence. Inevitably, they begin to feel like Ruth—abused, inadequate, and deprived.

People must necessarily detach themselves from Carl. The only way they can protect themselves from him is to stay firmly on track under the power of their own inertia. But his comings and goings inevitably stir up their ambivalences. Just like Carl, they end with detachment, ambivalence, and inertia.

But other people feeling as the Suicide feels is still not enough. The law of vindictive retaliation says they must feel worse. This is one goal of his impending suicide. His goal is to make other people feel worse than he ever could.

Chapter 14

DEFENSES TO VINDICTIVENESS

Even though the Suicide represses his Vindictiveness, its modes of expression, like a raging holocaust, threaten to destroy him and everyone around him. They also threaten to destroy his illusions in his Fantastic Self. This is especially true for Synpathic Ruth. She believes herself to be infinitely innocent, benign, and altruistic. In her own eyes, she is consummately loving and lovable, free of any malice towards others, feeling nothing but good will for all. Furthermore, Ruth reinforces these illusions with pride. She is proud of her absolute innocence and all its manifestations.

But we have seen that regardless of her unconscious pretenses, Ruth is far from free of Vindictiveness. Despite her repressions, she still expresses her Vindictiveness toward others with great skill and finesse. That she expresses it obliquely does not alter its character. Ruth is essentially vindictive, and her pretenses cannot change that.

But her Fantastic Self's innocence is all that Ruth is. Having long ago foregone her aggressive independence, should Ruth lose her innocence, she would lose her self.

Harold and Carl eventually come to terms with their expressions of Vindictiveness. But Ruth can never face hers. To Harold and Carl, evidence of the true nature and origins of their Vindictiveness threatens their pride. But to Ruth, it threatens her very existence.

In order to survive, the Synpathic Type must develop a system of defenses designed to protect her illusions of innocence from her own expressions of Vindictiveness.

Passive Withdrawal

The first way Synpathic Ruth devises to protect her illusions from the effects of her Vindictiveness is to evade it through Passive Withdrawal from other people. First of all, she avoids contact with those who especially stimulate her Vindictiveness. She unconsciously seeks only people who seldom, even inadvertently, threaten her illusions.

Surely it is normal to want to associate with people one likes and avoid people one does not. But Ruth's criteria for liking and disliking are colored by her need to evade expressions of her own Vindictiveness. For example, she may withdraw from people who seem happy and content, who are well regarded by others, who have developed personal skills she would aspire to, regardless of their likable qualities. She may withdraw from friendly and gregarious people, those of a higher economic or social status, or those who are physically attractive and take special care of themselves and their appearance. Her criteria for choosing companions are not based on people's generally likable qualities, but rather on cherishing her own illusions. She must evade anyone who, just because they possess enviable qualities, stir up her resentments.

Obviously, such choices are not easy to find. She can always discover something about someone to resent. Even though she may choose associates on the basis of her perceived superiority, she becomes resentful once she learns of their hidden assets. As a result, she must eventually evade close contact with virtually everyone.

Second, she avoids real intimacy. She not only minimizes the quantity of her relationships, she minimizes their quality. Since intimacy automatically involves self-disclosure she must keep her relationships superficial in order to blind herself to her associates' hidden assets and conceal what she considers to be her own shortcomings.

As a consequence, she rarely takes anyone else very seriously. How they affect her may be of paramount importance, but as fellow human beings they do not count. She cannot face other people with honesty and clarity, assessing their qualities and deficiencies with fairness, or sensing their inner hopes and desires with equanimity. Nor can she expose herself to them. She must keep her emotional distance, even when some intimacy would normally be the rule.

It may dismay Ruth's family, spouse, children, or closest friends to learn that she actually has not the slightest genuine interest in them or any real knowledge of their own inner feelings, their needs, their hopes for the future.

Of course, she can show some commonly accepted signs of sympathy, despite her withdrawal. This is especially true in situations relatively free of threats to her illusions. When she is well and her friend is sick; when she is securely married and her friend is undergoing a traumatic divorce; when she comes to a party with a handsome escort and her friend comes alone; when she enjoys relative wealth or status and her friend does not; in all these instances she can suddenly find closeness, sympathy, and depth.

But generally, she must maintain her distance. Any situation that threatens her illusions can automatically elicit her Vindictiveness. And her Vindictiveness, however expressed, is the greatest of all possible threats to her innocence.

Finally, and most importantly, she must deprive herself of her own needs for contact with other people. She must withdraw from them, even while she desperately needs them, in order to escape the humiliation they cause her. She may learn to withdraw very early in life, never giving them a chance to humiliate her. The one who hides her Vindictiveness behind a cloak of isolation or social shyness for a lifetime is a familiar type.

The consequences of passive withdrawal seriously alter our outward picture of the Synpathic Type Suicide. But though it camouflages her need to validate her innocence through contact with other people, her passive withdrawal is necessary. Otherwise, the inevitable humiliation, repressed rage, Vindictiveness and all its expressions, will exact their terrible toll.

INTERNALIZING

The second, even more self-destructive way the Synpathic Type protects her illusions of innocence from expressions of Vindictiveness is to displace it by Internalizing it. She unconsciously introjects it, turning it back against herself. Her illusions of innocence escape injury, and other people escape its fury, but she does not. She actually becomes vindictive towards herself.

On the surface, internalized Vindictiveness looks like expression of Self-Hatred. But they differ in a very important respect. Self-Hatred originates from the Suicide's inability to live up to the criteria of the Fantastic Self. Its expressions are directed solely at the Suicide. It is nourished by unfulfilled inner dictates, self-accusations, self-contempt, self-defeat, and self-punishment. Self-Hatred and its expressions relate entirely to the Suicide's Empirical Self.

On the other hand, Vindictiveness originates with other people failing to confirm the Suicide's Fantastic Self. Its expressions are originally aimed against other people. It is nourished by their frustrating her claims, by their denying her accusations, by their ignoring her contempt, and by their surviving her retaliation. Vindictiveness and its expressions relate entirely to other people.

So when Ruth internalizes her Vindictiveness, she not only turns it against herself, she puts herself at other people's mercy. The more they provoke her Vindictiveness, the more she grows vindictive toward herself. However, since other people cannot avoid provoking it, Ruth suffers intensely from internalizing it.

The effects of internalized Vindictiveness range from relatively mild but chronic discontent with herself to an occasional self-murderous rage. Overall, she suffers chronic and intense anxiety on its account. By not understanding its origins, she is helpless in the face of it. Yet it is so automatic she is rarely ever free of it. Someone inadvertently arouses her Vindictiveness, and she unconsciously takes it out on herself.

Consequently, internalized Vindictiveness lies behind Ruth's paranoid suspiciousness. Since she experiences its pain as resulting from other people's actions, she has every reason to suspect them. They are out to hurt her. There is no one she can trust.

Furthermore, because of internalized Vindictiveness, she generally feels that life has dealt her a losing hand and everyone else is a winner. She cannot help but see herself as a loser, regardless of her actual assets and achievements. She focuses on the disparities of her past, present, and future, and contrasts them with the apparent good fortunes of others.

Often, she concentrates her general feelings on some specific example. She may look to some past condition such as the poverty of her youth, the cruelty of a parent, the good fortune of a favored sibling, the belief that she was a weak, homely, or sickly child. She may focus on past psychic, physical, or sexual abuse.

On account of internalized Vindictiveness, she sees these past conditions or events as irrevocable proof of her own despicableness. The poignancy of her situation is great. She converts her rage against others for past and current wrongs into rage against herself.

Although she might have valid reasons for believing she was wronged in the past—and she very often does—her internalized Vindictiveness prevents her from dealing with it.

But on top of past wrongs, both real and imagined, she continues to incur more humiliation every day. Her internalized rage builds and builds until she feels she will explode. The resulting anxiety grows beyond her control. She feels like a bundle of raw nerve endings, that she is stripped of her skin, that just a soft touch or a passing wisp of a breeze can cause her unbearable pain.

She looks about her and sees others going their ways. She feels so alien and apart. She cannot get near them for fear of that one more hurt that will do her in.

On account of internalized Vindictiveness, such lonely survival may be all Ruth can maintain. Although she protects her innocence by internalizing her Vindictiveness, she does so at tremendous risk and expense to herself. But it is worth the price to her. At least, it is worth it to her Innocent Fantastic Self.

SURROGATE SACRIFICES

Lonely survival may be all the internalizing her Vindictiveness allows her, but Ruth threatens even her survival by making Surrogate Sacrifices to it. Surrogate Sacrifices closely resemble the Token Concessions the Antipathic Suicide makes to placate his hateful tyrant within. Only here, Ruth's behavior again is unfortunately intertwined with other people. Instead of hurting herself to relieve Self-Hatred, she hurts herself to get back at them. Ruth makes herself a sacrificial lamb to her Vindictiveness towards other people. And, once again, she unconsciously puts herself at their mercy.

On account of surrogate sacrifices, she may go through all the familiar tactics of harming and denying herself. These range from mild self-denials, through accidents, illness, and self-torture, to abortive suicide attempts. Her motives may be thinly veiled behind unfortunate circumstances, situations apparently out of her control, unaccountable disasters. But two factors are always present.

One, her unconscious goal is to hurt someone else by hurting herself. And, two, although she suffers on account of the injuries, her internalized Vindictiveness is obviously relieved.

Perhaps the most tragic aspect of surrogate sacrifices is that they can become an unconscious pattern aimed exclusively at herself. The objects of her unconscious Vindictiveness rarely suffer from them at all. She is the only one hurt.

Ruth may even be expressing unconscious Vindictiveness against a long-dead parent, a rival sibling whom she hasn't seen for years, an old lover who has long ago forgotten their encounter. This phenomenon points out the irrational nature of surrogate sacrifices. Ruth becomes other people's surrogate, and she injures herself accordingly.

Those close to her usually sense what is going on. If they are vindictive towards her—which they often grow to be—they quickly learn how easily to inflict pain on her. All they have to do is elicit her Vindictiveness, and she injures herself just for them. If they genuinely care about her, they get caught in a terrible double bind. They cannot avoid eventually arousing her Vindictiveness, thereby causing her to hurt herself. As a result, they often feel blackmailed into trying to satisfy all her unconscious expressions of Vindictiveness.

They try to adhere to her claims, however unfair. They try to concede her accusations, however unfounded. They try to submit to her contempt, however cruel. They even try to absorb her vindictive retaliation without complaints—all in the futile hope of preventing her from hurting herself.

The situation can be fraught with danger. Everyone involved, including Ruth, may grow keenly aware of the trap. Yet no one seems to know how to get out of it. Indeed, she actually does blackmail those around her with open or subtle threats of harm to herself. They cannot help but fail her. She simply must escalate her threats, whether other people try to appease them or not. Her one and only answer is the ultimate weapon. She can hurt them the most by committing suicide.

Part V

THE DESPAIR OF BEING ALIVE

Chapter 15

ORIGINS OF HOPELESSNESS

Hopelessness results from the despair contingent with the existential impossibility of the Suicide's Fantastic Self. For although the Suicide creates his Fantastic Self partially to compensate for his inhibition from the mainstream of worldly life, he endows it with unworldly attributes. Believing himself to be the impossible, he automatically incurs a profound and pervasive despair. He despairs of his Fantastic Self ever becoming a reality.

Yet despite his Fantastic Self's impossibility, his real Empirical Self is founded on it. This only compounds his despair. For having fixed on one of his Fantastic Self's impossible attributes, he molds his real Empirical Self accordingly. Not only is all that he unconsciously believes himself to be not possible; but its impossibility renders futile all that he really is.

The rational element within the Suicide often senses this awesome dilemma. His entire existence sometimes seems an unsolvable puzzle. He knows something, but he knows not what. He fears something, but he cannot put a finger on it. He senses something amiss, but he cannot quite piece it together.

He can make phenomenal efforts to force himself into being what he unconsciously believes himself to be, but he finds himself far short of his impossible goal. Other people can pamper his illusions, but they cannot confirm his secret convictions. His life goes on, but his unconscious mission in it is doomed from the start.

Fierce and sudden pain seemingly comes from out of nowhere. For no apparent reason, he feels angry, hurt, guilty, bewildered, insulted. He grows inexplicably hostile, mysteriously grieves, struggles with the vacillations of erratic feelings. The sources of his distress are nebulous, yet the pain is sometimes overwhelming. He tries to escape it; resolves to live with it. Yet it often seems unbearable.

Without apparent cause, he flails out at others, discovering himself suddenly hostile, hysterical, enraged. Other people seem cruel, heartless, inconsiderate. They are utterly contemptible and without understanding. He resolves to fight them to the bitter end. He tries to surrender to them. He decides resolutely to keep his distance. He needs other people, but he cannot bear the anger, frustration, or misery they cause him.

He objectively examines his life and sees that he may be in the center of a family, or a religious, civic, social, business, or professional group. But he still feels alien and apart. As an outsider to life, looking in on those actually living it, the few moments when he truly feels a part of life are fleeting. They pass through his experience leaving trailing wisps of memories he cannot grip and which cannot grip him.

He is gripped, however, by existential despair. And it holds him a virtual prisoner. He struggles to loosen its viselike hold on him, trying to shield himself from it. He resorts to anything to avoid it. He plunges into frenzied activity. He sinks into suffering self-pity. He retreats into ascetic detachment. But his despair clings to him like a leech. He feels haunted by it even when he stays active or preoccupied. He comes face to face with it when he is idle and alone. A terrifying dread grips him that he may not actually exist.

The normal joys and adversities of life can overwhelm the Suicide, for they each constitute a test of his existence. Every life experience contains the critical elements of an existential trial. From the trivial to the profound, they all carry the same ponderous weight, each experience inevitably challenging the Suicide's very existence. Behind each one lies his existential despair.

Existential Impossibility of the Fantastic Self

Whether aware of it or not, the Suicide lives in a constant state of existential despair simply because of the existential impossibility of his

Fantastic Self. Since his Fantastic Self is but a figment of his imagination, there is no reality to it.

But his despair would not necessarily ensue if he did not so glorify his Fantastic Self that he makes it the only thing that counts. Ordinary things, ordinary situations, ordinary other people, his ordinary self are all utterly insignificant. Being absolutely powerful, absolutely benign, absolutely detached is all that really matters. Indeed, just his experiencing this sense of ordinary mediocrity regarding himself and his environment can cast him into the depths of conscious despair.

To be sure, his existence—indeed, all existence—is mediocre compared with the absolute attributes of his Fantastic Self. For underneath his conscious despair gapes the impossibility of his unconscious Fantastic Self's absoluteness.

Finally, just because of the imaginary absoluteness of his Fantastic Self, there is no real phenomenological self. There is only, from his unconscious point of view, a metaphysical self. For the self he believes he is, is not his real self of flesh, blood, and bone. The self he believes he is is a metaphysical self who comes, like a trailing cloud of glory, from the Absolute.

FUTILITY OF THE EMPIRICAL SELF

The Suicide's Empirical Self is his true being as he, other people, and his environment empirically experience him in everyday life. But it, too, provides him cause for despair because he founds it on his impossible Fantastic Self. Harold would not drive for power, control, and mastery of life if he did not found his Empirical Self on his Omnipotent Fantastic Self. Ruth would not feel altruistic, compliant, and infinitely deserving if she did not found her Empirical Self on her Innocent Fantastic Self. Carl would not seek freedom, objectivity, and detachment if he did not found his Empirical Self on his Transcendent Fantastic Self. All that the Suicide strives for is founded on an illusion.

Even his choice of attribute becomes cause for despair. His adolescent resolution does provide him the appearance of unity, identity, and functional utility. But the resolution, itself, is an artificial one. For even though the Suicide manages to repress two of his Fantastic Self's attributes, he cannot eliminate them. And even though he fixates one of them, he cannot manifest it.

Moreover, the Suicide's empirical characteristics are also founded in despair. Harold would not become hostile, arrogant, and rigid if his secret goals were not impossible. Ruth would not feel abused, inadequate, and deprived if her beliefs about herself were not futile. Carl could not incur ambivalence, detachment, and inertia if his mission in life lay within the realm of reality. But, beyond that, these characteristics themselves add to the Suicide's despair. Harold's behavior blocks his own progress. Ruth's feelings interfere with her gaining satisfaction. Carl's remoteness denies him his real existence. The Suicide's empirical characteristics invariably exacerbate the despair from which they stem.

Finally, the Suicide's despair derives from his intrinsic alienation. Inhibited from the course of organic life by his lack of spontaneity, each type tries to offset his alienation a different way. Harold tries to resolve his by moving against life, other people, and his own inner processes. Ruth tries to resolve hers by moving towards them. Carl paradoxically tries to alleviate his by moving away. But each type's efforts end as futile by virtue of the impossible attributes of the Fantastic Self they are designed to sustain.

The Suicide consequently experiences his life as an abstract thing, completely separate from him. He often talks about life impersonally, as though it had nothing to do with his existence. And because he experiences it as an abstraction apart from himself, he despairs of ever being the motivating force in his own life. He can experience it as though he is a leaf in the wind, a puppet on a string, a cog in the wheel, unable to determine or even influence the directions life seems to take him.

Along with his feeling out of control of his own life, comes a despairing lack of responsibility for it. He finds it virtually impossible to face his condition with clear recognition. He cannot fairly assess his personal assets and liabilities. He will not squarely attack his real problems with real solutions in mind. He dare not make decisions and act on them with the willingness personally and solely to bear the consequences. As a result, his life has no intrinsic value for him. Experiencing life as an abstraction apart from himself and over which he has no control or responsibility, he relates to life rather than actually living it.

The Suicide despairs of ever having a life he can call his own. Mysteriously feeling like a sojourner in this world, he sinks further into existential Hopelessness. Unaware that he even believes he is his Fantastic Self, let alone recognizing its impossibility, he founds his Empirical Self upon it. And the despair inherent in this move generates deeper existential Hopelessness.[1]

REPRESSION OF HOPELESSNESS

The Suicide can only live in existential Hopelessness. Given the impossible premise of his entire existence, it cannot be otherwise. Since he cannot escape Hopelessness, he must express it in his everyday life.

But the Suicide cannot express his Hopelessness in its absolute state for integral reasons. First, should he do this, he would have no option but to end his existence. Secondly, should he experience his Hopelessness in its absolute state, he would have no real existence to end. He must repress his Hopelessness in order to exist.

But even though repressed, his absolute Hopelessness underlies the entire course of his existence. For he can only repress it, he cannot expel or expend it. He goes about his life, but his unconscious Hopelessness is expressed at his every turn.

Chapter 16

EXPRESSIONS OF HOPELESSNESS

The Suicide's state of existential Hopelessness remains unconscious. Of course, he may experience feelings of hopeless despair from time to time. In fact, his conscious hopeless feelings can grow pervasive, rendering him pessimistic, gloomy, and despondent. But regardless of how pervasive his conscious hopeless feelings, they differ from his profound and unconscious state of existential Hopelessness in a crucial respect.

His conscious feelings of hopelessness grow directly out of unmet mundane goals. These goals can be realistic or relatively idealistic, practical or impractical, feasible or infeasible. But regardless of their degree of feasibility, they are real goals made in real life.

On the other hand, his unconscious state of Hopelessness grows directly out of his conviction that he is his supramundane Fantastic Self. Since being his Fantastic Self is existentially impossible, he automatically lives in a state of existential Hopelessness. And since his conviction in his Fantastic Self remains unconscious, so does its resultant state of existential Hopelessness.

This fine but essential distinction affects the Suicide's expressions of unconscious Hopelessness in two major ways. One, he is unaware that they arise from his existential state of unconscious Hopelessness. And, two, he sometimes believes that he consciously feels hopeless on their account.

But as with many other phenomena of the Suicide Syndrome the true sequence is the reverse of what appears. The Suicide's Abstract Values, Chronic Discontent, and Hopeless Resignation *express* his state of unconscious Hopelessness, rather than *cause* it.

ABSTRACT VALUES

The primary way the Suicide expresses his unconscious Hopelessness in his everyday life is through a system of Abstract Values. Since mundane life has no intrinsic value to him, he must impart his own system of values to it. And since he relates to life as an abstraction apart from himself, those values he imparts to it are necessarily abstract.

Like his inner dictates and external claims, his abstract values may appear deeply rooted and sincere. But on close examination, their spurious nature comes to light. It first appears in his values' irrational idealization. He gives no rational consideration to the real ways of the world or of the possibility of his values ever becoming a reality.

Their hopeless origins also appear in his values' transcendence. His values are simply not of this world. They are not grounded in the mundane character of worldly conflicts and confluence. Instead, his values possess a transcendental quality, completely out of context of ordinary life.

Lastly, their hopelessness appears in their artificiality. The Suicide need not incorporate his values into his own attitudes and behavior. His believing in them is enough. But he usually expects other people to live up to them. More importantly, he fully expects them of life itself.

This unconscious hypocrisy stresses the abstract quality of his value system. And it renders his values disastrous to him. Although he must formulate his values on the basis of real life experience, he hopelessly applies them to life in the abstract.

For example, he formulates such values as rightness, fairness, and justice on the basis of real experience. People, individually and collectively, can be right, fair, and just in their treatment of each other. But the Suicide extracts such values from reality and applies them to life in the abstract. And he blinds himself to the essential distinction. As a result, he fully expects life, in the abstract, to be right, fair, and just—especially to him.

Just as he charges himself with living up to his inner dictates, and other people with satisfying his external claims, he charges life in the abstract with the fulfillment of his value system. But he does not simply expect life to adhere to such values as rightness, fairness, and justice. What he really expects of life is for it to adhere to his own conviction that he is his Fantastic Self. The inevitable failure of life to adhere to all his abstract values causes him additional and profound despair. His despair automatically generates additional Hopelessness, further enriching the soil from which his abstract values spring.

Each Suicide formulates his values generally in accordance with type. In the process, he usually borrows values from outside sources. Yet he invariably interprets this borrowed material in his own way, to suit his purposes, and in the light of his own needs.

For instance, the identical religious, philosophic, or political creed entails one set of values to Harold, a radically different brand to Ruth, and still another to Carl. Each of them selects, extrapolates, and interprets only what and how he wants from borrowed value systems, tailoring them to suit himself.

Each type also experiences his value system in his own way. As he does with virtually everything else in the syndrome, Harold identifies with his. And as he does with his inner dictates and external claims, Antipathic Harold designs his abstract values to substantiate his idealization of power, aggressiveness, and the mastery of life.

For example, Harold values self-reliance. He believes everyone should have to carry his own weight. Everyone, Harold believes, should have to compete on his own account and earn his own way through life. But to point out the spurious nature of Harold's values, he believes that he deserves recognition now for future potential. He believes rewards, status, and success should come his way on the merits of who and what he believes himself to be.

Although Harold usually exempts himself from his own value system, he does not hesitate to impose it on everyone else. He believes his standards to be those of the world—his values, universal. Despite any pretenses he should bother to make, Harold really believes that might makes right. And since he believes he possesses infinite powers, he cannot see how he could ever be wrong.

Harold's values always reflect and complement his empirical hostility, arrogance, and rigidity. He values competition, competence, and perseverance. And the more he values them, the more hostile, arrogant, and rigid he becomes.

In contrast, Synpathic Ruth bases her value system on universal love, goodness, and understanding. But she would be hard-pressed to say exactly why. Ruth passively accepts her values, rather than consciously formulating them from moral, spiritual, or intellectual concepts. And since she enmeshes herself in her feelings, she experiences her values as feelings. Ask Ruth what she thinks about values. She will tell you what she feels.

Since Ruth only feels her values, there is no need for her to put them into practice. To Ruth, just feeling her values is proof enough she has them. But like Harold, Ruth imposes her values on life in the abstract. She fully expects life, in the abstract, to treat her with love, goodness, and understanding. When life inevitably fails her, Ruth is shattered. She has been so good! Why won't life be good to her?

Failing to see the inherent fallacy in the bargain she strikes with life, Ruth feels deeply deprived of her just desserts. She sinks into bitter despair, bringing her old passive-aggressive tactics into the fray. She gets back at life by proving herself inadequate to it. Consequently, Ruth ends up feeling abused by life.

While Harold automatically identifies with his values and Ruth passively accepts hers, Apathic Carl devotes deep and serious thought to the formation of his value system. But despite his time and efforts, his values inevitably reflect his particular idealizations. And despite his conscientious sincerity, his values become even more spurious than Harold's or Ruth's. Whereas Harold and Ruth impose their values on life in the abstract, Carl actually values abstract life, itself.

Fundamentally, virtually nothing about real living means anything to Carl. He tentatively ventures into the thick of things from time to time. But he always holds back a part of himself. Carl cannot be wholehearted about any mundane value. He always saves the core of himself for the abstract.

Because of his ambivalences, Carl sometimes appears to adopt a value system similar to Harold's or Ruth's. He even tries to combine the two, with always confusing, and often disastrous results. At times, we can hear him voicing the work ethic with almost as much gusto as Harold. Later, we can hear him speaking softly about his love for mankind, like Ruth. But in neither case does Carl appear as blatantly hypocritical as Harold or as Ruth. Carl's aloof and tempered manner prevents his commiting too obvious a travesty of the values he professes.

But regardless of appearances, Carl does not really buy the values he often says he chooses. In fact, if you were to try to pin Carl down, you would have a difficult time deciding what he really does care about. And so would Carl. The reason his value system is so hard to pin down is that he has no values applicable to the mundane course of life. What values Carl really endorses have an ethereal quality about them. They all echo the one thing Carl values most: a brand of existence so transcendent it could only be abstract.

The value system each Suicide endorses inherently reflects the results of his repressions, fixation, and idealization. But the disastrous move they each make is to impose these abstract values on real life. Inevitably, life fails to fulfill them. And life's failure drives the Suicide into the depths of despair. Consequently, he must strike back. And he strikes back at life by growing chronically discontented with it.

CHRONIC DISCONTENT

The second way the Suicide expresses Hopelessness is through Chronic Discontent. His chronic discontent often appears as a pervasive dissatisfaction with himself. Although he feels dissatisfied with himself in just about everything, he usually concentrates it on those aspects of himself beyond his power to change. Added to his self-contempt, his chronic discontent virtually guarantees that nothing he can ever do or be can bring a lasting contentment.

The same holds true for those around him. On top of the vindictive contempt in which he holds other people simply because they are a part of his life, they are never quite right for him. Regardless of their assets, he is never content with them.

Naturally, he is rarely content with his situation in life. Everything would be all right, he believes, if only he could change his circumstances. His list of dissatisfactions could go on, ad nauseum. Whatever his situation happens to be, he feels discontented with it.

He idealizes everything in life that he does not have. This is especially true if it is completely out of reach. The more unavailable, the more he desires it. This hopeless idealization of the unavailable often appears as the root of his chronic discontent. But like so many other dynamics of the syndrome, the sequence is just the opposite of what appears. If whatever he desires were available, he would automatically become dissatisfied with it, too.

His chronic discontent also appears in his pervasive restlessness.

Never content with himself, those around him, or his situation in life, he always quests for greener pastures. Though he usually knows from experience that each new turn inevitably brings further dissatisfaction, he secretly believes the next one will prove to be the exception. While his quest may be manifested simply as passive longing for change, his passivity in no way diminishes his pervasive restlessness.

Finally, chronic discontent with his life leads to his utter contempt for it. He begins to hate his life and all it holds. Nothing it offers brings lasting satisfaction. Everything worthwhile is always out of reach.

In his heart, Antipathic Harold knows that ultimate mastery will always lie just beyond his grasp. Yet it is the only thing that could make life worthwhile. But it is not his fault victory eludes him. It is because life is so despicable. Although Harold glorifies the law of the jungle, he accuses life of being only a dog-eat-dog existence. To Harold, life is no damn good. And he rarely refrains from saying so.

Of course, such good as life does have to offer Harold is not good enough for him. His rigid inflexibility prevents him from enjoying many of its gifts. Because of his arrogance, he denies himself small pleasures in the simpler things. In the end, Harold feels that he is too good for life.

Synpathic Ruth feels victimized by life. Ruth believes life has dealt her a losing hand and everyone else a winning one. She rarely acknowledges that everyone else must also overcome obstacles, deal with everyday problems, incur disappointment, frustration, and grief. She is the only one who must undergo any of life's turmoil. But even if other people are confronted by such difficulties, theirs are never so difficult as hers. Besides, other people are better equipped to solve or absorb their difficulties. Ruth believes life deprives her of such strengths.

She often wonders if she can make it through just one more day. Overwhelmed by life, Ruth cannot take firm charge of it. As a result, the good that life does offer is unavailable to her. Life abuses Ruth by depriving her of everything she expects from it. Most of all, it deprives her of the means of getting its goods for herself.

Consequently, Ruth turns to other people as the only source of the good things in life. But as we have seen, here too she winds up feeling abused, inadequate, and deprived. As her real and imagined disappointments accumulate, she grows increasingly discontent. Ruth feels victimized by life and she can see no change in sight.

Apathic Carl never gives his life a reasonable chance. The values he imposes on it are so hopelessly abstract there is no possibility for even partial fulfillment. His expectations are so esoteric, no chance for satisfaction exists. His alienation is so pronounced, he never actually enters into life. Carl expresses his discontent with life by never genuinely living it.

Perhaps the most disturbing element in life to Carl is its mundane practicality. Although he pictures himself the pragmatist, his logic, in truth, is an esoteric one. Life never falls into the theoretical pattern he designs for it. In his infinite wisdom, Carl knows everything there is to know about how life could be. But from his alien remoteness, he knows very little about the way life really is.

Carl tries his best to stay detached from any kind of involvement. But because of his ambivalence and chronic discontent, he keeps getting himself involved. His sporadic forays into mundane affairs inevitably end as disasters. When his ambitions surface, he plunges in and fights with the best of them, but he invariably decides competition is not for him. It costs too much of his cherished freedom for him to stay in there and fight. When his needs for other people surface, he becomes almost as loving and compliant as Ruth. But, again, he eventually decides the benefits are not worth the expense. It takes too much away from himself for him to stay very close to anyone.

But his ambivalences do not operate only in respect to his repressed attributes. They operate in his comprehensive relation with life in the abstract. Carl actually experiences the course of his existence as his moving in and out of life. He may even sometimes say to himself, "I'm losing touch with life. I must get back to it."

But to get back into life, Carl must overcome his characteristic inertia. Although he usually finds the going much easier than the getting started, he rarely has the energy or desire left to sustain it. He eventually decides he wants no more of it. His ambivalent needs to the contrary, what he needs most is his transcendence. Blind to the futility of that mission, he turns on life in the style he knows best. He expresses his contempt for life by further detaching himself from it. Growing increasingly remote, he reduces his needs to the barest, only to feel more discontented with life on account of its barrenness.

Because of unconscious Hopelessness, life is despicable to Harold, cruel to Ruth, and not worth the time and effort to Carl. Failing to see that his chronic discontent stems from his unconscious Hopelessness, the Suicide keeps its origins tightly under wraps. He believes he grows hopeless because life itself is so despicable, cruel, and barren.

His chronic discontent actually does deepen the despair from which it originates. Contempt for life adds more grist to the mill. Rather than discharge his unconscious Hopelessness, his chronic discontent ironically exacerbates it. He inevitably sinks into hopeless resignation.

HOPELESS RESIGNATION

Hopeless Resignation is the third way the Suicide expresses Hopelessness. We usually think of resignation as a condition inherent to later life. The hopes and dreams of youth begin to pale in the light of middle years. We almost expect people to become resigned to the fact that much they hoped and dreamed for themselves will never come about.

Yet such resignation is not necessarily inevitable. To be sure, the normal course of life entails disappointments, frustrations, and grief, providing more than ample cause for occasional discouragement. But all this differs radically from the comprehensive and profound Hopeless Resignation resulting from the Suicide Syndrome.

In the first place, it differs temporally. Hopeless resignation can occur in the syndrome at any age, not just in later years. The student who abandons his humanistic goals and resigns himself to a job in his father's brokerage; the young woman who forsakes her faith and trust in mutuality with others and resigns herself to a life of lonely isolation; the child who unwittingly judges everyone else on the basis of his mother's hysterical egocentricity and resigns himself to a painful private world of autistic withdrawal, all serve as obvious examples.

In the second place, hopeless resignation differs existentially. It entails a move radically different from simply coming to terms with the realities of life. On the contrary, it entails an unconscious refusal to come to such terms.

For the Suicide to come to terms with the reality of life requires him to come to terms with his convictions in his Fantastic Self and its impossibility. In the absence of that bold stroke, he must necessarily resign from life, not to it.

This brings us to the third way in which hopeless resignation differs from normal disappointment or discouragement. It differs ontologically. Even though the Suicide may consciously experience himself as discouraged or disillusioned by the realities of life, he unconsciously experiences his Fantastic Self as transcendent to it. As a result, the Suicide becomes resigned without necessarily showing the outward signs of profound disappointment or discouragement.

Finally, hopeless resignation differs from normal disappointment in its inevitability. Regardless of the real life fortunes of the Suicide, because of his convictions in his Fantastic Self, he must necessarily resign from life. But since the entire process comes about unconsciously, he may never be aware of it. Nevertheless, his hopeless resignation manifests profound consequences.

Antipathic Harold seems less aggressive, a little more willing to comply with others. He begins to show some affection. He may even allow himself some obvious dependency. Synpathic Ruth may appear to have learned that she really must rely on herself for some things in life. Her work habits may improve. She may seem to stiffen up a bit. She starts to take things more in stride, to take better care of herself. Apathic Carl appears to seek something and someone a little more reliable. He may actually settle down to work, get married, accumulate some possessions, make a few commitments. Family and friends might observe that each of them has finally come to terms with life.

But the insightful ones among them may grow more concerned. They may see that along with his settling down he loses a certain sparkle in his eyes, a spring to his gait, a spirit in his voice. Situations that once brought exquisite ecstasy or abject despair cause little more than a few moments of concern. His reactions become less discernible. His personality seems flat.

Harold may still muster up some hot and heavy anger, but his wife and co-workers say his bark is worse than his bite. Instead of a driving, charging, determined achiever, he turns into an almost lovable cantankerous moralist.

No longer does the great romance hold forth its promise of mysterious delights to Ruth. She may now turn to the soaps, gothic novels, reveries of what might have been. She has a harder glint to her eye now; a renewed determination not to trust other people so completely or to look to them for everything her heart desires.

Carl's emotions begin to surface more consistently, but in a more moderate way. When his repressed aggressiveness appears, he simply finds a comfortable job, compromising with goals and working conditions. He settles for less than total detachment and missionary zeal. As his repressed need for others surfaces, it appears merely a genial sociability. A comfortable alliance, a handful of friends, even a common hobby or a trivial pastime may now attract his interest.

In many ways, all this appears as though the Suicide has arrived at some mature resolution of all his previous difficulties. As a matter of fact, if he could come face to face with his Fantastic Self, eventually ridding himself of it, then his outward behavior might very much resemble his behavior now.

But resignation is not resolution. With resignation, he does not come face to face with his Fantastic Self, eventually dispensing with it. He merely gives up the hope of ever being his Fantastic Self in this life. All his apparent constructive moves forward on account of resignation are actually regressive moves backwards. He does not become resigned to the reality of life. He becomes resigned to its Hopelessness.

However, he more than resigns himself to his fate. He actually resigns from his life. His compromises with reality are merely his way of serving out his allotted time. In fact, he often seems to be doing time, like a convict serving a life sentence. He may feel like a tired actor, playing out the last few performances of a long but mediocre run.

But behind the resignation hides his implacable Fantastic Self. Only his Empirical Self resigns from life. His Fantastic Self has an imaginary life of its own. While his mortal self plays out the hopeless performance, his immortal self waits impatiently in the wings for the final curtain to fall.

Chapter 17

DEFENSES TO HOPELESSNESS

Even though the Suicide represses his Hopelessness, he expresses it in every facet of his life. It underlies his Abstract Values. Since life has no intrinsic value to him, he imparts his own system of values to it. But since he relates to life as an abstraction apart from himself, those values he imparts to it are necessarily abstract. The inevitable failure of life to fulfill the values he imposes upon it brings him to the brink of utter despair, deepening his Hopelessness.

He strikes back at life by growing discontented with it. His Chronic Discontent shows in his dissatisfaction with himself, those around him, and his situation in the course of his life. Always aspiring to the impossible and unavailable, he despairs of ever finding a lasting contentment. His Hopelessness becomes more engulfing.

Finally, he sinks into Hopeless Resignation. But he does not simply resign himself to the reality of life. He unconsciously resigns from it. But only his Empirical Self resigns from life. His imaginary Fantastic Self has an eternal life of its own. He may go through the motions of serving out his allotted time, but his Fantastic Self feverishly craves the day of its eventual actualization.

To be sure, much devastation is wrought by expressions of Hopelessness from Antipathic Harold and Synpathic Ruth. But Hopelessness challenges the very essence of Apathic Carl's existence. How can Carl, who unconsciously believes he transcends mundane life, face the fact that he grows hopeless while submerged in its very coils? Carl must either capitulate to his Hopelessness or employ defenses protecting his transcendence from it.

STOIC DETACHMENT

The first way the Apathic Suicide defends his transcendence from his expressions of Hopelessness is to evade them through Stoic Detachment. Since anything in mundane life can stir up Carl's despair, thereby generating his Hopelessness, he must evade everything he perceives as mundane. His stoic detachment seems to defend and confirm his transcendence, but at great cost. It negates the possibility of his genuinely experiencing a real life.

Carl's stoic detachment somewhat changes the appearance of the Apathic Type Suicide as we have seen it thus far. Carl's stoicism is essentially an existential one. By this stratagem, he can appear to be participating in a wide range of mundane activities with gusto and zeal. But because of the existential quality of his stoicism, just appearing to participate is exactly how he engages. Regardless of how involved Carl outwardly appears, inside he holds himself stoically detached.

But Carl does not often bother with appearances. To stave off any chance of triggering his despair, he tries to evade everything that could possibly remind him that he is really a part of mundane life. Although his stoicism may allow him a cursory interest in "higher" endeavors—art, science, religion, philosophy—he must stoically evade any involvement with more earthly aims.

Further, Carl must shun any genuine and active strivings, especially on his own behalf. He might appear fanatic in his zeal for an esoteric cause, but only when he sees the cause as an end in itself. From his stoic point of view, art really is for art's sake and science "value-free."

Even when Carl does appear to get involved in mundane things, he must do so from an ethereal perspective. He enters politics for universal freedom, religion for universal good, education for universal improvement, social research for the universal advancement of humankind. Real actions shared with real people for real goals are far too mundane for Carl's stoicism.

But to be sure of his stoic detachment, he usually shuns interest or involvement of any kind. He stoically rejects work, ambition, setting goals, making even the most innocuous plans for the future. He often holds money and material possessions in disdain. What money he might obtain, he spends with reckless abandon. What material possessions he might accumulate, he neglects with casual indifference. The exception occurs when he invests in articles possessing of aesthetic value, such as fine scientific instruments or mechanical devices, works of art, books, or antiques.

His stoic detachment virtually destroys his already tenuous relations with other people. Ties that bind, roots that hold fast, plans that limit possibilities, all taste of bitter despair to him. While Carl can appear friendly and gregarious in a crowd of relative strangers or intimate in transient moments, inside he holds himself separate and aloof.

For even in general terms, Carl must stoically evade anything that even smacks of consanguinity or conventionality. Membership in the most loosely organized group, affinity with the most nebulous association, identification with the haziest popular custom, endorsement of the obscurest moral code, accepted ethic, or conventional ideal, must all be anathema to him.

Finally, to effect his stoic detachment, Carl must keep his experience of his own existence thin and desultory. His stoicism not only denies him the fruits of his own endeavors and the gratifications of relating to others. It denies him the actual experience of being alive.

But regardless of how much it cost him in real terms, Apathic Carl must embrace his stoic detachment. Anything less than absolute rejection of mundane life can automatically plunge him into the depths of utter despair. Then, the inevitable Hopelessness and all its expressions can bring him crashing down from his transcendent heights.

GENERALIZING

The second, more potentially destructive way the Apathic Suicide defends against his expressions of Hopelessness is by Generalizing it. He unconsciously displaces his own Hopelessness onto life in general. He then believes that it is not just his life that is hopeless. Life in general is hopeless.

The effects of Carl's generalizing his Hopelessness are devastating and profound. Certainly, to believe the course of one's own life is hopeless entails serious ramifications, as we have seen. The abstract values, chronic discontent, and hopeless resignation that unconscious Hopelessness promote take an awesome toll.

But to generalize this Hopelessness to take in all of life as a process only compounds its expressions. Furthermore, it renders the unconscious Hopelessness more inaccessible to possible alleviation.

No one—not even Carl—could consciously believe his life in particular is absolutely hopeless in a world of other people whose lives are not. If they can find hope, so can he. However, once he generalizes his Hopelessness onto life as a process, this becomes a moot point. Now, all life—his and everyone else's—is hopeless. Carl loses any chance for finding an incentive to discover just a modicum of hope for his own.

While generalizing his Hopelessness is an unconscious maneuver, its effects permeate Carl's everyday life. Since other people are hopeless, there is surely no reason for him to take a genuine interest in them. Their most earnest endeavors, their highest goals, their sincerest feelings are but satirical exercises in futility to him.

Of course, social institutions and all they stand for are hopeless, too. The conventions of social life—marriage, kinship, child-rearing, loyalty, love, hate, and revenge—are hollow and futile gambits in the hopeless game of life.

Finally, existence itself is hopeless. It has no meaning; no purpose; no redeeming features. In the face of the Hopelessness of existence Carl turns ascetic, mystic, or philosophic. He automatically becomes metaphysical in his outlook. Things actually concerning him— if anything actually does—are just not grounded in the reality of mundane life.

These consequences of his generalized Hopelessness underlie Carl's paranoid suspicions of the outside world. Just as Harold's externalized Self-Hatred and Ruth's internalized Vindictiveness render them fearful, hostile, and suspicious, Carl's generalized Hopelessness has a similar effect on him. But unlike Harold and Ruth who usually focus their paranoid behavior and feelings on specific threats, however numerous, Carl tends to generalize his.

Since he sees life in general as hopeless, Carl lives in utter dread of being dragged down into it. And since he sees any contact with mundane life as possibly dragging him down into it, he must keep a wary eye on everything and everyone to guard against the calamity.

He suspects any move in his direction made by other people as a possible move to drag him down. It matters little whether other people approach him with genuine warmth and friendship or with veiled or open hostility. Carl must eye them with the same degree of suspicion. In fact, hostile approaches can be less threatening than congenial ones. Carl knows he can escape from a fight. In the case of affability, he is not too sure. But in either encounter, what Carl dreads most is for him to get caught in the thick of things.

He extends this dread into the world in general. Social institutions, government agencies, the law and authority, political organizations, popular conventions of any kind are all equally suspect to him. While he may manage a vague affiliation with some others of his ilk, any other kind of contact causes him immediately to suspect the motives behind it.

He may carry his suspiciousness to agoraphobic dimensions. He may choose a hermit's life. He may become a vagrant on the run, a derelict in the streets. He may isolate himself in a private world of his own with only his illusions for company. He may minimize his needs to the barest, grasping for any means, however meager, scarcely to keep himself alive. Such marginal survival may be all his generalized Hopelessness will allow him. But he can forfeit even that in favor of Nihilism.

Nihilism

The third and most destructive way the Apathic Suicide defends against his Hopelessness is to compromise with it. In order to maintain his illusion of transcendence he allies himself with his generalized Hopelessness, and he strikes out at life itself through Nihilism.

The Apathic Type's Nihilism corresponds to the Antipathic Type's Token Concessions and the Synpathic Type's Surrogate Sacrifices. Through his nihilism, he purchases a temporary peace. He salvages his illusions of transcendence from the depths of despair by aiming to destroy life itself.

From the outside his nihilism must look insanely irrational. But from his Fantastic Self's point of view, we can see that it makes a great deal of sense. From his Fantastic Self's point of view, mundane life is the enemy. It tells Carl he is real. He tries to evade the Hopelessness of his situation through stoic detachment. But it cannot loosen his chains. He displaces his futility onto life in general. But generalizing his Hopelessness only adds to his own. He has but one way left to protect his transcendence. His Fantastic Self must either destroy mundane life or be destroyed by it.

Often to his own dismay, and always to other people's, Carl periodically goes about unconsciously demolishing almost everything in his private world which he experiences as tying him to it. As with token concessions and surrogate sacrifices, timing is of the essence to Carl's nihilism. Just when everything seems to be going great for him—at least from other people's perspective—is the very time his nihilism breaks loose.

But things going great from other people's perspective unconsciously means the very opposite to Carl. Accomplishment in work, success in interpersonal relations, integration into the social milieu, all represent the very antithesis of his Transcendent Fantastic Self. The more Carl involves himself with mundane life, the greater his need to destroy it.

Because of his ambivalences he can destroy his targets in both aggressive and passive ways. He can strike with vicious and devastating hostility. He can nullify with oblique but decisive indifference. But in either case, whether he actively destroys something of real value to him or passively procrastinates it away, he gains a temporary contentment from the loss.

His unconscious nihilism can eventually dominate his existence. He can set out to destroy every sign of life around him. He can strike out at symbols of social life—government, economic institutions, civil order. He can move against those in his immediate environment—their joy, their hopes, their plans for the future. Finally, he can aim at his own inherent vitality—his health, his safety, his very own existence. Ironically, this is exactly what his existential Hopelessness aims at. Only through the termination of his Empirical Self's mundane existence can his Transcendent Fantastic Self ascend.

Part VI

THE SUICIDAL LIFESTYLE

Chapter 18

SUICIDAL THINKING

Unconscious Self-Hatred, Vindictiveness, and Hopelessness motivate him towards suicide. But on account of his defenses against them, the Suicide survives. Their expressions take a terrible toll on his life. By his defenses he fares little better. Through a balance between them, however, the Suicide can attain a certain degree of what we customarily call normalcy. This is especially true in light of the sweeping prevalence of the syndrome. The Suicide can observe that his precarious and tenuous stability differs little from the lives of most other people around him.

The entire process growing out of his conviction that he is his Fantastic Self—his empirical personality characteristics, his suicidal motivations, their expressions and defenses—results in a comprehensive style of life completely dominated by the strictures of the syndrome. It encompasses his thinking, his feelings, his behavior, his sexuality, his interpersonal relations, and his social systems. Since this style of life is founded on and dominated by the Suicide Syndrome, it therefore constitutes a Suicidal Lifestyle.

Regardless of its prevalence, the Suicidal Lifestyle is rarely a happy one. Certainly, it may hold periods of relative equilibrium and tranquility, even moments of joy. But the destructiveness of the syndrome eventually wins out, if not with prolonged and abject unhappiness, then through chronic, debilitating, and insidious forms of unrecognized and therefore generally accepted self-destructiveness.

The Suicide Syndrome upon which this suicidal lifestyle is based is essentially an intrapsychic process. As we have seen, cultural, interpersonal, and existential factors do perform important functions. This is especially true with respect to conditions leading to early formulations and the drama of later manifestations. But these other factors must still be experienced by the Suicide as his sentient self: They must be intrapsychically experienced and interpreted by him.

Ultimately, how the Suicide fashions his social systems, how he relates to other people, how he behaves, and how he feels all are contingent with exactly what and how he thinks.[1] And fundamental to the Suicide's thinking is his unconscious conviction that he is his Fantastic Self.

The confusion, inner conflict, and distortion of reality resulting from its influence are so profound that they often appear to be the grounds for his unhappiness or his motivations for committing suicide. But these complications result from the Suicide Syndrome. They do not cause it.

PERCEPTIONS

The Suicide's unconscious conviction and the process growing out of it dominate his perceptions. They dictate how he perceives, what he perceives, and the way he perceives it.[2]

Central to his perceptual processes is the dichotomy inherent in his belief that he is his Fantastic Self. Since he unconsciously believes he is his noumenal Fantastic Self, he tends to perceive his phenomenal Empirical Self as an organism other than the real—and only—he. Consequently, he perceives his physical organism as though it were a possession, a thing apart from him. And the vague notion of "self" he consciously perceives is not the "self" he unconsciously believes he is.

This abstract notion of possessing a self other than him punctuates his conversation. "I get so mad at myself," he says when frustrated. It would be easy to dismiss such references as figures of speech without inherent significance, but Freud long ago proved the contrary. The Suicide's perception of his Empirical Self originates from his identification with his unconscious Fantastic Self.

He extends this unconscious dichotomy to his perceptions of his existence. He sometimes becomes consciously confused as to who really exists. Is it he? Is it the self he possesses? To be sure, this implicit dichotomy defies existential reality. But it is so much a part of his perceptual process he cannot shake its illusion. Such an illusion could only derive from his illusion in his Fantastic Self.

Harold, the Antipathic Type, believes he is Omnipotent. Naturally, he believes he perceives everything there is to perceive. To make certain that he does, Harold concentrates on every minute detail, failing to perceive the whole.

In the absence of proof of his infallible perception, Harold falls back on his arrogance. What he perceives, and only what he perceives could be important. Whatever he might miss is trivial. Because of his rigidity, he cannot perceive changes or variations, nor shift his point of view. Blinded by his arrogance and rigidity, Harold grows hostile with other people who—as he thinks—pretend to perceive things he cannot perceive.

Synpathic Ruth, on the other hand, is blinded by her innocent naiveté. It obscures her view of the realities of her situation, of the rights, feelings, and behavior of other people, and especially of her own. While Ruth can get a very sensitive overall feel of things, she cannot perceive their details nor their underlying systems. Her perceptions are far more global than Harold's, but they are superficial and impressionistic, lacking fine focus and discrimination.

Ruth's impressionistic perceptions of the ways of the world ensue in the light of her feelings. She feels abused, inadequate, and deprived, and she views the world accordingly. Ruth feels abused by those realistic aspects of the world she can perceive. She feels inadequate on account of those which elude her. And she feels deprived by the superficiality of her own perceptions of them.

Apathic Carl, who believes he is transcendent, naturally perceives the world from afar. From his distant perspective he captures neither the fine details of Harold's view nor the impressionistic feel of things which is Ruth's. But Carl's detachment does provide him a general perception of underlying systems neither Harold nor Ruth can perceive.

Yet on account of Carl's ambivalences, he is never quite sure of what he perceives. Unlike Harold who never doubts the accuracy of his perceptions and Ruth whose perceptions are determined by her feelings, Carl's perceptions are highly speculative. He views life like a spectator, catching glimpses of an overriding system here, a universal meaning there, cosmic truths everywhere. But his farsightedness blinds him to the exigencies of his immediate situation, especially his own drifting inertia.

We might assume that the commonality of human senses would assure uniformity in our perceptions. But within the context of the Suicide Syndrome and the lifestyle it promotes, such an assumption proves to be a grave and sometimes fatal error. Yet the Suicide has nothing more than what he perceives to build into his conceptions.

CONCEPTIONS

The Suicide formulates his conceptions by combining his perceptions with his expressions of Self-Hatred, Vindictiveness, and Hopelessness. His unconscious belief that he is his Fantastic Self provides their foundation. The resulting formulations determine his conscious self-concept, his concepts of others, and his concepts of the world in general.

Normally, the Suicide's conscious self-concept differs radically from his unconscious self-concept. His unconscious self-concept—that is, his Fantastic Self—is absolute, eternal, and infinite. His conscious self-concept is relative, temporal, and finite. His unconscious self-concept can know no bounds of reality. His conscious self-concept is tempered by his perceptions of reality, however distorted. His unconscious self-concept comprises everything he unconsciously believes he is. His conscious self-concept comprises what he wishfully thinks he can be. These distinctions are sharp in theory but obscure in everyday life. For while its illusion may never enter his consciousness, the Suicide forms his conscious self-concept as though he really were his Fantastic Self.

In formulating his conscious self-concept, he automatically omits the characteristics of the repressed attributes of his Fantastic Self and emphasizes his fixated one. Antipathic Harold consciously conceives himself a strong and masterful person, never helpless. He may secretly accuse himself of impotence or indecisiveness, but only because he conceives himself otherwise.

Synpathic Ruth conceives herself as a nice, sensitive, and lovable person, never hostile or indifferent. Of course, she may openly accuse herself of acting hateful or aloof. But she only acts that way as an understandable consequence of other people's behavior, not because that is the kind of person she is.

Apathic Carl conceives of himself as a pragmatic, impartial, and independent person, never irrational or demanding. He may off-handedly accuse himself of having prejudices or expectations, but because of other people's irrationality or life's eternal folly.

All three types endow themselves with an abundant intelligence, even though they might keep it well disguised. And they all believe they have exceptional reasoning and will power, even though they might accuse themselves of occasional lapses.

Because of the pervasive power of his expressions of Self-Hatred, Vindictiveness, and Hopelessness, the Suicide must incorporate them into his conscious self-concept. But because he believes he is either omnipotent, innocent, or transcendent, he carefully but unconsciously chooses which expressions to include and which to exclude.

In formulating his conscious self-concept, Harold always includes his expressions of Vindictiveness and Hopelessness which demonstrate his omnipotence. But Harold excludes his expressions of Self-Hatred from his conscious self-concept precisely because they challenge his omnipotence. He cannot admit to having irrational inner dictates to which his omnipotent self must adhere. He is the kind of person who only does what he wants to do. And as far as defeating and punishing himself, that is out of the question. Whatever adversity happens to Harold is always someone else's fault.

Ruth follows the same rules in formulating her conscious self-concept. She includes her expressions of Self-Hatred and Hopelessness which have the added value of demonstrating her innocence. But she always omits any genuine consideration of her Vindictiveness which would challenge it. She is not the kind of person who makes exploitative claims on others or who wants to control or condemn them. She only wishes they would love her and be as nice and as selfless as she. Nor is she the kind of person who would senselessly attack others. She cannot help being inadequate, tired, depressed, or hysterically agitated because of their callous acts or because of conditions obviously beyond her control.

Carl uses the same selective process in formulating his conscious self-concept. He includes his expressions of Self-Hatred and Vindictiveness, although obliquely, but he excludes his expressions of Hopelessness which challenge his transcendence. He is not the kind of person who concocts irrational values and projects them onto life in the abstract. Nor is he one who would feel discontented with himself or the course of his life. And, to be sure, there is no need for him to become resigned to a life he transcends.

The same rules govern the Suicide's concepts of other people. He formulates these from the same perceptual view and by utilizing the same selective expressions as with his conscious self-concept.

Harold generally conceives other people as weak, corrupt, and perverse, deserving of his hostility. They are the ones to blame for life's futility. They may try to raise themselves above their lowly condition, but their efforts are invariably paltry or comic.

To Ruth, other people are selfish and uncaring. She tries to understand them, even tries to help them. But they never appreciate her. They may sometimes pretend to have high moral standards or to care about her. But no sooner does she begin to believe in them than they prove her right in the first place.

Carl conceives of other people as ignorant, parasitic, and misguided. He may sometimes lower himself by lending them the benefits of his wisdom, guidance, or affection. But to no avail. They foolishly go their futile ways like a herd of sheep.

Finally, the Suicide builds his general concepts along the same structural formula. His concepts of social institutions, religion, art, science, morality, law, indeed of existence itself, all follow the same general pattern. There may be some apparent deviations now and then, but only in areas subjectively unimportant to him.

The aggregate effect of the Suicide's conceptual process mediates his concepts of consensual reality. For his conscious self-concept, his concepts of other people, and his general concepts all follow the same design. He founds them on his unconscious conviction in his Fantastic Self. He incorporates his fixed attribute into them. He necessarily utilizes his one-sided perceptions in the process. And he unconsciously includes or excludes certain expressions in accordance with the strictures of his role.

RATIONALIZATIONS

The Suicide's concepts often conflict with consensual reality. But since he formulates them in the light of his own perceptions, they present little or no conflict to him. Of course, he recognizes that other people's concepts are not always like his. He reconciles this discrepancy in characteristic ways. Harold knows he is right and other people are wrong. Ruth feels abused when people disagree with her. Carl attributes the differences to the ways of the world, provided they do not interfere with him.

However, on account of his defenses, the Suicide faces other, far more profound conflicts with reality, not so easily reconciled. As we know, the defenses employed by each type derive from different contingencies, but they share a common process. Each type employs defenses utilizing evasion, displacement, and compromise. And because of the inherent contradictions in his defenses, the Suicide must make apparent sense out of them.

He makes apparent sense out of his defenses by devising rationalizations for them. His rationalizations conflict with reality in proportion to the severity of the defenses requiring them. As a rule, each succeeding level of defense requires proportionately more fatuous rationalizations.

His first level of defense, evasion, generates intrapsychic conflict. His compulsiveness drives him, but his evasions hold him back. In addition, his evasions ironically contradict the unconscious convictions they are designed to protect. The Suicide must rationalize this contradiction away.

Antipathic Harold employs Checks and Avoidances to evade his expressions of Self-Hatred. He avoids anything causing him shame and thereby stimulating his Self-Hatred, and he puts a check on his own active strivings to evade the possibility of a shameful defeat. Yet the debilitating effects of his own evasions ironically contradict his imagined omnipotence. Harold must rationalize this contradiction away. Harold's rationalizations are often transparent, but they make good sense to him. "I wouldn't have the headaches of being president of this company," he says, "for all the money in the world." But as he says it, Harold secretly believes he should not just be company President, but undisputed leader of the world.

Synpathic Ruth employs Passive Withdrawal to evade her expressions of Vindictiveness. Yet the isolating effects of her withdrawal ironically contradict her imagined innocence. If Ruth is infinitely altruistic, lovable, and benign, why does she have to withdraw? Ruth rationalizes her withdrawal by innocently blaming other people for it. "Men are all alike," she says. "They only want one thing and then they're through with you." Or, "Women friends are all alike. Turn your back on them and they can't wait to stab you in it." Ruth's rationalizations are nearly always stated in the innocent or impersonal "you." But all the while she really believes the very personal "I" should be adored like the Virgin Mother.

Apathic Carl employs Stoic Detachment to evade his expressions of Hopelessness. Carl stoically detaches himself from anything in mundane life stimulating his despair and thereby his Hopelessness.

But Carl's stoic detachment automatically contradicts his imagined transcendence of mundane life simply by virtue of the fact that he must evade it. Carl rationalizes the contradiction away by philosophizing about it. "That's the way the cookie crumbles," he says. Or, "The anxiety and nausea of the human condition are the existential dilemmas contingent with the intrinsic absurdity of mankind's being-in-his-world." But behind his rough or misty euphemisms, Carl really believes he is out of this world.

This intrapsychic conflict often surfaces into the Suicide's awareness. He sometimes grows painfully aware of the contradicting discrepancies it contains. What the Suicide really believes and what he believes he believes lie at opposite poles. And he suffers extreme mental anguish on this account.

His more destructive second level of defense, displacement, generates more fatuous rationalizations—in fact, paranoid thinking.

By displacing his Self-Hatred, Harold Externalizes it onto other people. But by externalizing his Self-Hatred, Harold ironically contradicts his imagined omnipotence. If Harold were really omnipotent why would he have to hate others? Harold rationalizes the contradiction away by automatically believing that other people are out to get him. He suspects his wife of trying to prove him impotent, his children of trying to make him out a fool, his employer of trying to degrade him, his co-workers of trying to undermine his job status, even total strangers of trying to show him up as weak or ridiculous.

Displacing her Vindictiveness, Ruth Internalizes it against herself. But Ruth's internalized Vindictiveness contradicts her imagined innocence. If she is innocent, why must she make herself suffer? Ruth rationalizes the contradiction away by believing others seek to humiliate her and cause her pain. She suspects her husband or lover of affairs with other women, her children of wishing her away, her friends of trying to steal her man, her co-workers of trying to win favor over her with the boss, even complete strangers of trying to debase her.

Displacing his Hopelessness, Carl Generalizes it onto mundane life. But by generalizing his Hopelessness, Carl ironically contradicts his imagined transcendence. If mundane life is hopeless, why does transcendent Carl bother to live? Carl rationalizes the contradiction away by becoming suspicious of everything and everyone for trying to drag him down into mundane life's Hopelessness. Other people, intimacy, work, institutions, laws, moral codes, indeed existence itself, are all suspect.

The rationalizations required by the Suicide's displacement defenses virtually force him to think in paranoid ways. And he usually finds confirmation of his paranoid thinking in everyday life. Harold's suspicious hostility invariably turns people against him. Ruth's alienates the very people closest to her. Carl's gets him into trouble with the forces in life he most fears.

This confirmation of the Suicide's suspicions contains a doubly injurious effect. It not only reinforces his paranoid rationalizations. It also motivates him to escalate his unconscious illusions into his awareness. Harold must begin consciously to believe he really is omnipotent in order to be able to defend against his enemies. Ruth must begin consciously to believe she really is innocent in order to keep her tormentors at bay. Carl must begin consciously to believe he really is transcendent in order to escape the infinite perils of life. This escalation of his particular illusions, coupled with the contradictions inherent in his most destructive defenses, forces him to make rationalizations encroaching on the very borderline of reality.

The Suicide's third and most destructive level of defense against his suicidal motivations is to make compromises with them. Harold makes Token Concessions to placate his hateful tyrant within. Ruth makes Surrogate Sacrifices to quell her vindictive rage against others. Carl employs self-destructive Nihilism to offset his existential hopelessness. But in order to make sense out of these apparently senseless acts, the Suicide must invent rationalizations explaining them.

His rationalizations do sometimes seem to make sense, especially if they are not examined too closely. He lays the blame on coincidence, unavoidable circumstances, bad luck, poor health, etcetera. He may even admit to carelessness, rebelliousness, procrastination, or neglect. Such explanations convey an aura of general acceptance. Life does have its hazards, and he is, after all, only human.

But as his illusions begin to escalate, his rationalizations take on a distinctly different complexion. Now there is some inexplicable power forcing him to act. His spouse is trying to poison him. Society is out to destroy him. He receives thought waves through the ether telling him what he must do.

As his Fantastic Self rises into his consciousness, his body becomes a useless bag of bones, full of garbage or excrement. He is a numen from outer space, a cosmic spirit, an immaterial universal intelligence. He is the omnipotent Napoleon, the innocent Mother Mary, the transcendent Son of God.[3]

It matters little whether his body lives or dies. In fact, the sooner he is rid of it, the better off he will be. His body's death is but an infini-

tesimally miniscule occurrence in the cosmic order. Of course, his suicide can occur contingent with such rationalizations. The more unrealistic his rationalizations, the higher its probability. Combined with
other consequences of the Suicidal Lifestyle, this kind of thinking can
appear to cause his suicide.

But his perceptions, conceptions, and rationalizations are consequences of the Suicide Syndrome. They are not the real cause of suicide.

RATIONALIZATIONS OF IMMORTALITY

All Suicides must rationalize to a large extent. Most, however, do
not escalate their defenses to the level of consciously believing themselves to be Napoleon. But every Suicide does entertain one essential
rationalization, regardless of any others. This rationalization is required to support his unconscious belief in the immortality of his Fantastic Self.

The Suicide's unconscious conviction of the immortality of his
Fantastic Self is not the same as common intellectual, philosophical, or
religious concepts of immortality. Certainly historic or popular concepts can serve as conscious rationalizations for his unconscious belief.
They usually do. But whether the Suicide consciously professes a belief in immortality or not, he is unconsciously but unequivocably convinced of his personal immortality simply by virtue of his belief that
he is his immortal Fantastic Self.

The Suicide's conviction of his personal immortality often shows
in his ontological concept of death. It has been said that people who
attempt suicide do not consciously expect to die. This is not usually
the case. The obvious exceptions are children or those Suicides whose
rationalizations have taken them well beyond contact with consensual
reality.

To the contrary, most Suicides are consciously convinced they really will die should they commit suicide. But they unconsciously conceive of death as another state of their existence.

This ontological paradox lies at the very heart of suicidal behavior. And its importance to the understanding of suicide cannot be
overstressed. It surfaces in such innocuous-sounding concepts as, "I
just want to be dead," or "I just want to be free of this pain once and
for all." The Suicide invariably fails to see the existential contradiction

inherent to this kind of thinking. One cannot "be," "find peace," "be free of pain," should one cease to exist.

When this unconscious contradiction begins to surface into the Suicide's awareness, he experiences it as an inexplicable puzzle. He knows he will die should he actually commit suicide; he mysteriously feels that he won't. The contradiction causes him no little consternation. And it always contributes to the profound ambivalence the Suicide experiences in such crises. He must either take the fatal plunge, ignoring the contradiction and leaving its resolution up to chance,[4] or he must rationalize the contradiction away.

Such rationalizations often take the form of one or more of the popularly held beliefs in immortality. But since these beliefs are normally also endorsed by religious systems, he runs into religious taboos against suicide. He then tries to rationalize these away. He may endorse a concept of immortality but reject the admonitions accompanying it, or may make himself a one-time exception to the prohibitions. He may interpret his impending suicide as an admirable act of martyrdom, thereby escaping the taboos.

On the other hand, should he reject the more popular religious beliefs in immortality, he either endorses a more or less esoteric belief from a distant culture or he tries to originate one of his own. But here, too, he runs into difficulty. Since the topic of human immortality has been with us so long, it is virtually impossible for the Suicide to invent a new concept or endorse one that has not been cast in serious doubt. He may profess to out-of-body states, the transmigration of souls, or a vague belief in immortality which remains undefined.

But regardless of which theory he settles on, what the Suicide is really convinced of is his exclusive personal immortality. Indeed, he tends to reject—or at least question—popular notions of universal human immortality, simply because of their diluting effect on his convictions of the uniqueness of his own. For it is the Suicide's immortality, and his immortality alone, of which he is unconsciously convinced. And such a conviction could only stem from his belief that he is his immortal Fantastic Self. Even when he acknowledges the possibility of other people's immortality, in any form, he interprets it in terms of his own.

Once again, we return to the basic logic of the Suicide Syndrome. Only the Suicide's Empirical Self must live and must die in ordinary mundane ways. His omnipotent, innocent, and transcendent Fantastic Self is immortal.

Chapter 19

SUICIDAL FEELINGS

Many Suicides look to their feelings for grounds for their suicidal impulses. The emotions the Suicide usually points to, however, are *consequences* of the Suicide Syndrome. They do not originate with his congenital composition, nor invade him from out of the blue. How and what the Suicide feels, and when, all derive from the syndrome.

The Suicide often points to his feelings as reasons for his suicidal impulses because the affectual content of the Suicidal Lifestyle is turbulent indeed. Beyond the obvious emotional disturbances growing out of Self-Hatred, Vindictiveness, and Hopelessness, the syndrome generates anxiety, fears, and insecurity. It causes emotional suffering, underlies depression, produces feelings of guilt, ensures lack of motivation, and warrants boredom and shallow living.

All these emotions can grow so intense, it is easy to see why the Suicide believes them to be grounds for his suicidal impulses. But regardless of his rationalizations otherwise, they result from the syndrome in all its complexity. They are not the grounds for suicide.

ANXIETY, FEARS, AND INSECURITY

Anxiety is quite possibly the most painful affect human beings can experience. Yet while the Suicidal Lifestyle automatically generates massive anxiety, the Suicide paradoxically clings to it, and to the conscious fears and feelings of insecurity it in turn generates, as a means of bolstering his defenses. Even though his anxiety causes him exquisite pain, he clings to it.

The Suicide Syndrome and the anxiety it generates both derive from imagination. Genuine fear results from the autonomic reaction to a real threat, while anxiety results from an imagined threat or from a real threat to an imagined existence. Since the Suicide believes he is his imaginary Fantastic Self, anything he perceives to be a threat to his Fantastic Self automatically generates anxiety. Given the impossibility of his Fantastic Self and the constant threat reality therefore presents to it, anxiety characterizes the Suicide Syndrome.

The Suicide often experiences massive attacks of general anxiety. Although superficially inexplicable, they can usually be traced to some unconsciously perceived threat to his imaginary Fantastic Self or to any of the self-destructive consequences growing out of such a threat. Since it makes little sense to feel anxious for no obvious reason, the Suicide often converts such anxiety into more tangible fears, phobias, or feelings of insecurity. He may then repress his awareness even of these, unconsciously tailoring his behavior accordingly.

This is especially true of the Antipathic Type. Harold cannot admit to being afraid of anything. Consequently, he falls back on his customary defenses. Harold tailors much of his behavior towards reducing his fears, at the same time, condemning himself for being so defensive. This generates further anxiety and further need to defend against it.

Synpathic Ruth, on the other hand, adorns herself in fears, phobias, and feelings of insecurity. Although she may outwardly try to free herself from them, she inwardly clings to them as undeniable evidence of her innocent vulnerability. For this reason, anxiety and all its conscious manifestations hold special value to Ruth. If she had no reason to be afraid, then she would not be so vulnerably innocent.

Although threats to Ruth's imaginary innocence serve as the major source of anxiety, her defenses to Vindictiveness provide still more. Unconsciously knowing that as she grows more vindictive, she will only take it out on herself, Ruth has good reason to fear anything which might evoke her Vindictiveness. Yet anything can arouse it that Ruth interprets as rejection, humiliation, or exposure.

Consequently, Ruth grows paraphobic, developing a variety of conscious fears for a variety of ostensible reasons. For example, the risks of rejection in a close relationship, humiliation in public, or appearing foolish can paralyze her with fear. Of course, her fears, phobias, and feelings of insecurity eventually become functional. Through them she can further express her unconscious Vindictiveness by virtue of the services from others required to accommodate them.

Apathic Carl tries to transcend his fears. But the more he ignores them, the greater they grow. Carl must maintain his illusion of transcendence, thus keeping him in constant dread of falling into the pits of reality. Any degree of genuine fear reminds him of his essential humanity, compounding his dilemma. For this reason Carl attempts to maintain his illusion of transcendence by reacting to real and identifiable mundane threats with free-floating anxiety.

This has serious ramifications. For even in the case of a genuine threat, Carl tries to deny its reality by resorting to free-floating anxiety. As a consequence, free-floating anxiety attains a functional value for Carl, enabling him to transcend the reality of his actual fears. Carl never fears anything; he is always anxious.

Anxiety and all its attendant fears, phobias, and feelings of insecurity, possess functional value to each type of Suicide. Yet the pain of his anxiety can grow so great, he may feel driven towards suicide in order to escape it. However, escape from anxiety is never the cause of suicide. Instead, acute and pervasive anxiety results from the Suicide Syndrome.

EMOTIONAL SUFFERING

The Suicide suffers from the pain of his anxiety. But he also suffers on many other accounts. He may not recognize the depths and severity of his suffering. Even though he might present an outward picture of self-pity, in truth, he usually feels little, if any, genuine sympathy for his suffering Empirical Self.

Yet even to the degree that he recognizes the severity of his suffering, he may decide he wants no more of it. Failing to see any other way to rid himself of it, he turns to suicide as the only way out. But suicide never results from emotional suffering. To the contrary, his emotional suffering results from the Suicide Syndrome.

Emotional suffering is usually most obvious with the Synpathic Type. Submerged in her feelings, Ruth openly suffers, and she does not hesitate to let other people know about it. Clearly, most of her suffering derives from repressed rage and internalized Vindictiveness. At the same time, she uses her suffering to express the very Vindictiveness against which she defends. By suffering, she can feel superior to the insensitive people around her. Although Synpathic Ruth, far more than the other two types, points to her suffering as reasons for suicide, she also, far more than the others, makes her suffering subjectively valuable to her. The more Ruth suffers, the more innocent she must be.

Antipathic Harold suffers also. Like Ruth's defenses to Vindictiveness, Harold's defenses to Self-Hatred cost him dearly. But unlike Ruth, he rarely allows himself to experience his suffering, let alone display it to others. It sometimes surfaces as a smoldering anger aimed at life itself. Harold even externalizes the suffering he incurs by his defenses. He makes other people suffer on account of him, for omnipotent Harold could never suffer.

Apathic Carl suffers, too. But like Harold, he will not let himself feel it. In accordance with his transcendental principles, Carl makes himself oblivious to his own pain. Other people can observe his life and wonder how he can bear it, but Carl does not know what they are talking about. Only ordinary people suffer, and he is above their lot.

Each Suicide suffers on account of the complex processes of the Syndrome. Ruth wallows in her suffering, using it to further her claim to innocence. Harold projects his onto other people to testify to his omnipotence. Carl tries to make himself immune to his in order to demonstrate his transcendence. But suicide does not result from emotional suffering. The Suicide's suffering results from the Suicide Syndrome. But only his hapless Empirical Self incurs all the suffering. His innocent, omnipotent, and transcendent Fantastic Self remains unscathed.

DEPRESSION

Conventional wisdom often links depression with suicide. But conventional wisdom usually misinterprets the connection. Suicide does not directly result from depression. Depression results from the Suicide Syndrome.

Depression results from the syndrome on two accounts. It results directly from expressions of unconscious suicidal motivations, and also from defenses against them. On the first account, depression is an obvious consequence of the self-destructiveness of the syndrome. On the second, it paradoxically functions as a means for the Suicide to stay alive, if only in a depressed state.

Depression functions as a means for the Suicide to stay alive because it acts as a substitute for actual suicide. In this respect, depression must be distinguished from anxiety reactions and emotional suffering. Although it may be mixed with these, depression is distinctly different from them. It is, in fact, a kind of affectual suicide. The depressed Suicide cannot function normally. He cannot eat, cannot sleep, cannot work, cannot make love, and most of all, cannot feel. In a sense, he executes a partial suicide. He may even say, "I just feel dead."

Because depression serves as a substitute suicide, the depressed Suicide is in little danger of doing the real thing as long as he remains depressed. Only when his depression begins to lift does he become dangerously suicidal. This dynamic often confuses friends and relatives. "He was very depressed a few weeks ago," they may say after a suicide attempt, "but then he seemed to get better. Now this. Why?"

Because the Antipathic Type moves against his own feelings, Harold is particularly subject to deep and prolonged depression. The best way he can move against his feelings is to depress them completely. Yet the effects of pervasive depression threaten Harold's pride in his omnipotence. Periodically, he fights it off with spells of manic activity. But his activity invariably leads him into obstacles causing him shame, thus eliciting his suicidal Self-Hatred. Harold must then retreat back into his depression to keep himself alive. Consequently, Harold becomes subjected to virtually endless cycles of pervasive low-grade depression broken up by short spells of manic activity.

Because the Synpathic Type is enmeshed in her feelings, Ruth often confuses her anxiety attacks and emotional suffering with depression. Ruth rarely incurs depression all by itself. Engulfed by her feelings, she finds it almost impossible to depress them. She can sit and cry, lock herself up from the world, and call her behaviors depression. But the intensity of her emotions—a far cry from genuine depression—attests to her anxiety and functional suffering.

However, when Ruth does incur depression, it nearly always results from surrogate sacrifices. Nothing could represent a greater sacrifice to Ruth than for her to forego her ability to feel. But at the same time, she can be so overwhelmed by her feelings that she must depress them in order to survive. Thus Ruth's depressions assume the same functions as Harold's, although they originate from a different source. Ruth becomes depressed to defend against her suicidal motivations.

It is almost impossible for Apathic Carl to know when he is depressed. Having lost touch with his inner feelings, Carl can only identify what he feels, and when, by assessing his visible reactions. Sometimes Carl peruses his overt behavior and casually concludes that he must be depressed. But despite his inner detachment, he is also subject to depression. His depressions usually derive from his nihilism, functioning as a defense against his suicidal Hopelessness. Carl experiences his depressions as a kind of placid nausea. By growing depressed, he aims to destroy all signs of life, especially those represented by his emotions.

In all cases, the immediate suicidal danger associated with depression comes not from the depression itself but derives instead from superficial attempts to relieve it. Although depression most certainly may precede actual suicide, suicide never results directly from depression. Instead, depression functions as a defense against actual suicide. The superficial relief of depression in lieu of alleviating the complex process underlying it ironically deprives the Suicide of his defenses, thereby exposing him to the full force of his real suicidal motivations.

GUILT, STRESS, AND STRAIN

Suicides often say they feel guilty or complain of the burden of overwhelming stress, even becoming convinced they deserve to die because they are so guilty. On the other hand, they might see suicide as the only way left to escape their guilty feelings or to remove the burden of stress they cannot seem to alleviate in any other way.

Feeling guilty or feeling under unbearable stress and strain can certainly bring about great inner distress. However, these feelings do not constitute grounds for suicide. Instead, they result from the Suicide Syndrome.

Whenever a Suicide says he feels guilty, we must look at what he believes he is guilty of. Very few Suicides are really guilty of anything in the true sense of the word. It is the rare Suicide who has committed horrendous crimes against humanity. The worst that most can come up with is their having possibly mistreated friends or family. Indeed, very few of those who say they feel guilty can provide real evidence of offenses. Where, then, do the Suicide's feelings of guilt come from? Why does he believe—usually with convincing sincerity—he is so terribly guilty?

The Suicide's guilty feelings stem directly from the complexities of the syndrome. And, regardless of his convincing sincerity, what he usually identifies as his guilt is really not genuine guilt at all.

We have already seen how the Suicide's tyrannical Fantastic Self accuses and condemns his hapless Empirical Self to a judgment of infinite guilt. But what is his Empirical Self guilty of? On one level, he is guilty of not living up to his impossible inner dictates. But on a deeper level, he is no less than infinitely guilty for not actually *being* his Fantastic Self.

But more importantly, the Suicide usually experiences his shame, humiliation, and despair as guilt. And he inherently fails to see this fundamental distinction. Genuine guilt can only arise from real harm done to others, and not always then. His willingness to make restitution to relieve his guilt is the true test of its genuineness. If he refuses to make amends for his offense or if he claims it is beyond restitution, then guilt is not the issue. It rarely is.

On the other hand, shame, humiliation, and despair are all fundamental consequences of the syndrome. We have seen that shame derives from the Suicide's failure actually to be his Fantastic Self, humiliation from other people's failure to validate his Fantastic Self, and despair from his Fantastic Self's existential impossibility. Furthermore, all his expressions of Self-Hatred, Vindictiveness, and Hopelessness and all his defenses against them continue to add to the shame, humiliation, and despair from which they stem.

Instead of allowing himself to experience these affects in their true form—which would point out their irrational grounds—the Suicide experiences them as "guilt." Harold feels guilty for not working hard enough, Ruth feels guilty for not being able to please everyone, Carl feels guilty for allowing people to involve him. But none of these feelings are genuine guilt. They are shame, humiliation, and despair.

The stress and strain the Suicide experiences derive from similar grounds. They also result directly from the complexities of the syndrome, although the Suicide may experience them as issuing from the outside world. Harold's work is too demanding. Ruth's spouse is too critical. Carl's life is too boring. Furthermore, they may each feel "guilty" for resenting all of this and for wanting escape.

But of course, all this results from the complexities growing out of the Suicide's conviction that he is his omnipotent, innocent, and transcendent Fantastic Self. As long as he clings to this conviction he will continue to experience what he identifies as feelings of guilt, stress, and strain.

LACK OF MOTIVATION

The Suicide sometimes believes he gets depressed or feels guilty because of his lack of motivation. The insatiable criteria of his Fantastic Self are a major source of this feeling. But beyond the insatiability of his Fantastic Self, a pervasive lack of motivation results from other complexities of the syndrome.

Antipathic Harold's inner dictates, in particular, would certainly seem to motivate him. They tell him that he must be strong, always strive to get ahead. But because his inner dictates derive from his Fantastic Self, Harold does not intrinsically experience the motivation they seem to inspire. Inside, Harold rarely feels he wants to do anything, or that he should. Caught in this terrible double bind, Harold falls back on his defenses in order to maintain his illusion of omnipotence.

But Harold's defenses ironically contribute to his lack of motivation. His checks and avoidances, externalizations, and token concessions hold him back in every way. So even though Antipathic Harold may appear the most motivated, he also suffers the most from his lack of genuine motivation.

On the other hand, Synpathic Ruth's innocence inherently works against what our society customarily calls motivation. But knowing Ruth's secret goal in life, we see her inner dictates drive her as powerfully as Harold's drive him. Still, for the same reasons, Ruth never feels genuinely motivated. And Ruth also defeats herself and condemns herself for not feeling sufficiently motivated to attain her impossible goals.

Ruth's vindictive claims also contribute to her lack of motivation. Feeling herself infinitely good and deserving and needing to substantiate this by obtaining self-satisfaction from others, Ruth cannot allow herself to be motivated towards obtaining satisfaction. In this respect, genuine motivation actually contradicts Ruth's illusion of being infinitely deserving. As a consequence, Ruth seldom feels she wants to strive for anything, only that she deserves it. Finally, although Ruth's expressions of Vindictiveness block her motivation, her unconscious defenses against them fail to overcome the block. To the contrary, her defensive withdrawal, internalizations, and surrogate sacrifices only bolster it.

Like Harold and Ruth, Apathic Carl's expressions of Self-Hatred and Vindictiveness block his motivations. But unlike them, his goals lie beyond worldly achievement or close personal relations. But even Carl's motivation toward his esoteric goals is thwarted in the face of his Hopelessness. His values are so abstract, no real motivation can be derived from them. His discontent is so pervasive, he has nothing real to strive for. His resignation is so complete, no wish or want could disrupt it. Resigned from life, Carl can never find his cherished freedom from it. He blinds himself to the obvious by means of his defenses. Stoically detached in a generally hopeless world, Carl's nihilism denies him any sustained motivation.

The Suicide's Fantastic Self lies entrenched at the roots of his lack of motivation. Its insatiability ensures that he could never be motivated enough. Expressions of Self-Hatred, Vindictiveness, and Hopelessness growing out of his convictions block any chance for real motivation. His particular defenses against them finally bolt the door. Lack of motivation is inherent to the syndrome. As long as he believes he is his Fantastic Self, the Suicide can never be genuinely motivated.

SHALLOW LIVING

Anxious, suffering, and depressed, and divested of any genuine motivation to change, the Suicide shapes his life within the Suicidal Lifestyle. Imprisoned by his defenses, he settles down behind them into a routine resignation. Stripped of his intrinsic vitality and alienated from the essence of his nature, he patterns his consciousness along the desultory strictures of his role.

Here he finds his life devoid of any real meaning. Having repressed his awareness of his awesome suicidal motivations beyond the walls of his defenses, he focuses on the boring vacuity, the utter meaninglessness of his shallow life. Shallow living results from the Suicide Syndrome on manifold accounts. Fundamental to all is the Suicide's unconscious abandonment of his intrinsic vitality in favor of his pursuit of a private illusion. The complex system growing out of this fundamental move resists his reversal of it. His unconscious suicidal motivations, their expressions, and the defenses he maintains against them, dictate the conscious content of his life. This whole structure, by virtue of its being founded on a shallow illusion, automatically renders his everyday life meaningless.

The shallowness of the Suicide's everyday life appears in its superficiality. Because of his unconscious Self-Hatred, he cannot face himself with sincere recognition, nor value himself for his genuine worth. Because of his unconscious Vindictiveness, he cannot truly empathize with others, nor establish genuine mutual relations. Because of his unconscious Hopelessness, he cannot value his life for what it really is, nor plunge himself into its depths.

Lacking the motivation to devote his life to his deeper intrinsic selfhood, he subjects himself to the superficial strictures of his type, the customs and conventions of his society, and the symbolic superficialities prescribed by his personal and social role. His superficial behavior often takes the form of banal "games."[5] Harold plays winner games, Ruth plays loser games, and Carl plays bystander games. The pay-off to Harold's games consists of superficial demonstration of his omnipotence; to Ruth's, the demonstration of her innocence; to Carl's, his transcendence. Their superficiality naturally makes them banal, and their repetitiveness renders them shallow.

The shallowness of the Suicidal Lifestyle also appears in its narrow scope. The Suicide has a vested interest in keeping his life narrow, limited, and confined. Harold must limit his private world to that which he believes he can control. Ruth limits hers to that on which she can depend. And Carl confines it to that which will not hinder him.

Each may wander now and then, breaking out of the unseen bonds restricting him. But he eventually retreats or draws his new-found experience back into his narrow world. Harold may uncharacteristically venture into the arts, academia, or the social services. But sooner or later he rejects them as counterfeit, or tries to take them over by attaining the leadership role.

Ruth may experiment with starting a business or professional career of her own, or assuming leadership of a social organization. But her business fails unless she finds someone to instruct her every step of the way. Her leadership role leads to organizational chaos as she grows dependent on those she is supposed to lead.

Carl may recklessly plunge into a highly competitive business venture or marriage into a large and gregarious family. But no sooner does he leap than he tries to extricate himself. He either retreats from the venture, back into his solitude, or he sufficiently alienates his new customers, friends, or family to nullify the move.

Finally, the shallowness of the Suicidal Lifestyle appears in its stultifying uniformity. The Suicide either limits his experiences to those conforming to his role, or he injects the pattern of his role into every nonconforming experience. In religion, Harold invariably takes a fundamentalist conservative stand, advocating accepted dogma except when it conflicts with his aggressive ways. Ruth finds universal love and compassion in the same dogma where Harold finds a jealous and punishing God. And, in the same dogma, Carl sees spiritual freedom and the transcendence of the human soul.

The Suicide injects this kind of uniformity into all facets of his life, down to the most trivial details. It shows in his choice of literature, art, music, and world events. It is reflected by his heroes, opinions, and attitudes. It appears in his material possessions and his attitudes about them, even in the kind of clothes he wears.

Yet, all the while, he chafes under the shallow boredom of his life. He flails about seeking meaningful experiences while he nullifies their variety with his own redundancy. Unconsciously making his life narrow and limited, he consciously suffers under the restrictions. He may turn to the idea of suicide just to give some meaning and depth to his life.

But suicide never results from shallow living. Like all his suicidal feelings, shallow living results from the Suicide Syndrome. Just like his anxiety, depression, emotional suffering, guilt, stress and strain, and lack of motivation, shallow living derives from the Suicide's real motivations to self-destruction and his unconscious defenses against them.

Chapter 20

SUICIDAL BEHAVIORS

The Suicidal Lifestyle also determines the Suicide's behavior. The combined effects of his defenses and expressions not only influence his feelings. They determine his actions. Although he may believe he behaves the way he does because he wants to, he has little, if any, conscious volition in the matter.

In the first place, he simply must behave in accordance with his fixed attribute. Harold's behavior must express his omnipotent aggressiveness; Ruth's, her innocent benignity; Carl's, his transcendent detachment. Although his defenses sometimes appear to damper or disguise it, his overall behavior inevitably reflects his fixed attribute.

In the second place, his repressed attributes inhibit him. Try as he may, Harold cannot express deep and sincere compassion. Nor can he break free of the bonds holding him captive to his need to control. Despite her determination otherwise, Ruth cannot break down her taboos against genuine independent assertiveness. She may even seek outside help or training in her attempts, but just the fact that she must rely on others to help or instruct her indicates her inherent blocks to independent assertiveness. Regardless of Carl's am-

173

bivalences, he cannot sustain even the appearance of aggressiveness or closeness with others for long. He may move in and out of apparent assertiveness or intimacy, but his dictates against them always win out in the end. Even though each of them may desperately try, he can no more sustain behavior contrary to his repressions than he can act contrary to his fixation.

In the third place, the expressions of his secondary suicidal motivations tend to characterize his behavior. Harold's behavior must exhibit the specific expressions of unconscious Vindictiveness and Hopelessness. Ruth's must exhibit expressions of Self-Hatred and Hopelessness. And Carl's must exhibit expressions of Self-Hatred and Vindictiveness.

Lastly, the Suicide's behavior is shaped by his defenses against the expressions of his primary suicidal motivation. Harold must tailor his behavior to defend against expressions of Self-Hatred. Ruth must tailor hers to defend against expressions of Vindictiveness; and Carl his, to defend against expressions of Hopelessness. Regardless of the price, each of them must behave in accordance with his defenses in order to survive.

All these factors combine to control the Suicide's every act. Blind to these unconscious factors controlling him, the Suicide focuses on their effects. And their effects are devastating, indeed. They combine to induce him into alcoholism or other addictions. They cause him to incur accidents or illnesses and to seek superfluous surgery. On their account, he suffers chronic failure and misfortune. Because of them, he gets into trouble with the law or other authority. They can even impel him towards unconsciously deciding when and how to die.

Their effects are so devastating, it is easy to see why he often points to these effects as the cause of his suicidal impulses, rather than the other way around. But regardless of his conscious beliefs otherwise, his behavior results from his suicidal motivations. It does not cause them.

ALCOHOLISM AND OTHER DRUG ABUSE

Because of their inherent destructiveness, alcoholism and other substance abuse are frequently incorporated into the Suicidal Lifestyle. Although alcohol is the more prevalent, other popular addictive substances are heroin, cocaine, PCP, amphetamines, barbiturates, and tranquilizers. It would be redundant to describe here the destructiveness wrought by such addictions. It is a familiar tale. Obviously, it is this very destructiveness which holds forth the greatest unconscious attraction to the Suicide.

Substance addictions can grow to dominate, or at least pervasively influence, the Suicide's everyday life. The addiction itself can grow to such paramount importance that the Suicide points to it as his motivation to suicide.

The attractions of an addiction like alcoholism are threefold. Most obviously, alcohol narcotizes the Suicide against other facets of the Suicidal Lifestyle. Through alcohol, the Suicide can temporarily quell his anxieties, relieve his emotional suffering, hold a depression at bay, forget his lack of motivation.

Secondly, the Suicide can express his unconscious suicidal motivations through alcohol, simply by virtue of its inherent destructiveness. What better way for him to express his unconscious Self-Hatred than to destroy himself with alcohol? How could he more effectively express his Vindictiveness than to inflict on those about him the consequences of his addiction? What better way can he find to express his Hopelessness than to drown his life in drink? It perfectly fits his token concessions, surrogate sacrifices, and nihilism.

Such an addiction appears perfectly suited to all the many complex dynamics of the Suicide Syndrome. Its availability and convenience are difficult for the Suicide to resist. One of its main attractions is the nature of addiction, itself. By succumbing to it, the Suicide can disown his own self-destructiveness.

Antipathic Harold rarely admits to an addiction. He sees it as a weakness. Despite the obvious, he claims he drinks only because he wants to. He may even view his drinking as a sign of strength. Harold drinks hard, like a real man should. His drinking symbolizes the rough-and-ready character of his manhood. It goes with the normal stress of his competitive pursuits. It illustrates his tough disregard for the petty risks weaker folks fear in respect to hard drinking.

Synpathic Ruth innocently slips into an addiction. Her innocent fall illustrates her role as victim. Ruth always feels driven to alcohol, drugs, or tranquilizers by the harsh cruelty of other people or the overwhelming cruelty of life. Although she may try to hide her addiction for a while, she must eventually display it to other people to show them how much she suffers from it on account of them. Ruth ends feeling victimized by her own addiction. Innocent to the end, she cannot *help* being addicted.

Apathic Carl just drifts into addiction. It draws him like a magnet. He is especially attracted to mind-expanding psychotropic drugs for obvious reasons. But alcohol helps Carl express his nausea with the world. What better way can he find to express his disgust for life than to wallow in alcoholic nausea every morning?

Alcohol and other substance addictions fit the Suicide Syndrome as though they were tailored for it. In obvious and subtle ways, they mesh with all its suicidal motivations and defenses. This is why attempts to alleviate the addiction itself without alleviation of the syndrome usually prove unproductive.

TROUBLE WITH THE LAW AND OTHER AUTHORITY

The Suicide oftens gets into trouble with the law and other authority. His conflicts with authority arise on a variety of accounts. Basic to them all is his unconscious conviction in his Fantastic Self. How can mundane authority dictate to him what his Fantastic Self can or cannot do? Furthermore, positions of authority hold a magical attraction to the Harolds of our world. And once in the seat of power, the Antipathic never fails to exert it over anyone even remotely in conflict with it.

But the character of those in authority and the nature of authoritarianism aside, the Suicide has an unconscious vested interest in getting into trouble with it. His troubles can become chronic, characterizing the course of his life. Living outside the law, he unconsciously projects the entire complexity of his suicidal motivations onto his authoritative enemy. He deploys the powers of authority to destroy himself.

Most Suicides steer clear of chronic lawlessness. But when trouble does occur, it nearly always arrives via the strictures of the Suicide's role. Whether chronically or just occasionally in trouble, he erroneously points to his conflicts with authority as the cause of his suicidal impulses. Often, just the prospect of impending trouble will suffice.

But trouble with the law and other authority arises from his suicidal motivations. It also plays in the hand of his most destructive defenses. And, of course, capital punishment or a glorious shoot-out looms as the Suicide's ultimate reward.

Because of his idealization of power, Antipathic Harold seems to revere authority. An exaggerated respect for law and order occupies a top rung on his ladder of abstract values. But as with most of Harold's values, he usually exempts himself. Harold reveres authority only as a concept and only from afar. Should authority or those wielding it challenge him, his arrogant hostility always comes into play. Then, the inevitable war is on.

For while Harold reveres authority as a concept, he feels little but contempt for those who actually wield it. And because of his hostility, competitiveness, quick temper, and characteristic disregard for the rights of others, Harold can easily run afoul of the law. One day Harold wakes up to find himself a criminal. But in his view, Harold is never a common criminal. Once pitted against the law and authority, he turns the conflict into a personal vendetta. He must prove himself omnipotent by proving authority to be stupid, inept, and impotent.

In his vendetta, he can defy the law face-to-face. He will try anything to show his contempt. But by taking on such superior odds, he is bound to lose: if not by actual arrest, trial, fine, or incarceration—where he shifts his vendetta to the prison yard—then at least by the debilitating effects of its menace. The defeat hits Harold where it hurts the most. It threatens his imagined omnipotence, consequently eliciting his unconscious Self-Hatred, which is the real motivation behind his suicidal impulses.

Synpathic Ruth's utter dread of power usually keeps her clear of trouble with authority. But her unconscious need to feel persecuted can draw her into it. Once Ruth does come into conflict with authority she must prove herself innocent by proving authority to be unjust, cruel, and heartless.

Ruth tries to achieve this by innocently getting herself into deeper trouble. Having learned her tactics through experience, authority may defer, hoping to let her off the hook. But once Ruth's innocence is challenged, she will go to any lengths to prove it. She intuitively knows that people in authority positions often have a more or less disguised sadistic streak, and she knows exactly how to provoke it.

Ruth then cries out in a fit of injured innocence. She addresses pleas for help to anyone around, begging to be saved from the clutches of unjust authority. Should authority relent, hoping to be rid of her, Ruth devises an added, always innocent, provocation as she departs, further eliciting authority's wrath. Ruth then grows increasingly suicidal with the aim of striking back at unjust authority by injuring herself.

Apathic Carl gets into trouble with the law and authority simply by trying to ignore it. Almost nothing represents a greater threat to his imagined transcendence than the laws, rules, and regulations governing the common folk. Although Carl may not challenge authority the way Harold does, or provoke it like Ruth, he will consciously or unconsciously defy it in oblique and often petty ways as a means of asserting his aloof independence.

When authority finally takes notice of Carl's practiced defiance, he defies it further by resorting to Epictetian stoicism. There is nothing law and authority can do to shake him. Heroically, Carl defies authority to destroy him, thus transcending his own suicidal impulses by inducing authority into doing the deed.

CHRONIC FAILURE AND MISFORTUNE

The Suicidal Lifestyle is often characterized by chronic failure and misfortune. Although the Suicide may superficially seem to achieve significant success free of serious misfortune, a closer examination reveals that his genuine accomplishments usually lie well below his actual potential and that he incurs many avoidable misfortunes.

This condition entails compound ramifications for the Suicide. Because of his conviction in his Fantastic Self, he believes himself capable of anything. Furthermore, he believes he should not be subjected to even the most unavoidable misfortunes. But his actual life not only fails to live up to his Fantastic Self's infinite potential. His actual life usually fails to fulfill even his genuine capacities.

As a consequence, the Suicide can become overwhelmed by failure and misfortune. He may feel that just one more reversal or disappointment will be the one to do him in. But suicide never directly results from failure or misfortune. Instead, chronic failure and misfortune result from the Suicide Syndrome.

In the first place, chronic failure and misfortune obviously result from the Suicide's expressions of unconscious suicidal motivations: Self-Hatred, Vindictiveness, and Hopelessness.

In the second place, his unconscious defenses further assure chronic failure and misfortune. Antipathic Harold's defenses to Self-Hatred inherently hold him back. Synpathic Ruth's defenses to Vindictiveness inevitably entail failure and misfortune. And Apathic Carl's defenses to Hopelessness serve him no better.

Finally, all the consequences of the Suicidal Lifestyle add to his failures and misfortune. His feelings resulting from the syndrome — anxiety, emotional suffering, depression, guilt, lack of motivation, and shallow living—all take their toll. His suicidal behaviors—alcoholism or other addiction, accidents and illnesses, trouble with the law and authority—do their part in courting disaster. In all, his suicidal motivations, his defenses against them, and the consequences of his suicidal lifestyle, aggregate to form a pervasive base for chronic failure and misfortune.

By ordinary standards, Harold's chances for conventional success and escaping undue misfortunes would seem rather good. His inner dictates drive him towards success, which he supremely values. He develops his skills for work and at defeating competition. His rigidity affords him dogged persistence and often infinite patience for detail.

But at the same time, because of his arrogance, real success, at least in his own eyes, lies always beyond Harold's grasp. All the manifold self-defeating dynamics of his role work against Harold's ever attaining a modicum of his genuine potential. Even should he attain some degree of visible success, it is never enough. He looks around for other fields to master. He may aspire to social status, pretentious cultural activities, politics, "old money" and aristocratic connections.

But regardless of his achievements, both real and pretentious, Harold still secretly counts himself a failure. Insatiable to the end, Harold cannot achieve enough or erect defenses strong enough to protect him from his own Self-Hatred. And because he cannot admit hating himself, anything he sees as a failure or potential failure on his part can trigger his suicidal impulses. But Harold's suicidal impulses originate in his Self-Hatred which in turn is precipitated by his failures and misfortunes.

Ruth's chances for conventional success lie in a vocation in which she can be of appreciable service to others. But since Ruth's goals rarely include conventional success except as a means of gaining other's affection or trying to live up to their expectations, success is not inherently important to her. Still, despite her vested inadequacies, her innate gifts and intelligence can raise her to some degree of achievement.

But Ruth cannot tolerate success in love or in work. Success for her in both is impossible. Ruth usually fails at love relationships, and any success in work situations virtually assures it. Should she begin to feel successful in her work, it immediately triggers her repressed arrogance and aggressiveness, thereby causing her to drive her mate or lover away.

Although success in service to others may satisfy her need to feel loved, eventually Ruth yearns for more impassioned fruit. She will toss away what worldly success she might attain for the slightest chance for romance. But the shining glory of romantic love inevitably pales in the light of her expectations of it.

With success in love and work beyond her reach, Ruth flounders in misfortune. In desperation she strains for any sign of progress, however meager. She settles for low-level employment. She involves herself with aggressive friends who invariably mistreat her. If she has children, she martyrs herself to what she sees as their welfare. She entangles herself in destructive romances with drunkards, bullies, and cheats.

Whereas Harold can be done in by his failures and misfortunes, Ruth uses hers to further her illusions of innocence and to express her unconscious Vindictiveness. Her failures and misfortunes elicit other people's sympathy, illustrate her unblemished innocence, and prove the despicableness of other people as compared to her.

Since success in work and relations with others can be anathema to Apathic Carl, his peculiar mark of achievement is to be free of them. But since he lives in a world governed by social and economic contingencies, Carl can never be so free. Thus Carl automatically incurs a failure of a very special kind. But he also fails in conventional ways. Not equipped with Harold's aggressiveness, he falters under competition. Lacking Ruth's eagerness to please, he blunders in social situations.

Yet competitive society demands his participation, if only for survival. So Carl sets his sights either on winning freedom from these demands through successful work or on balancing the ledger by minimizing his needs. In the first instance, he invariably fails to attain the degree of success necessary for the brand of freedom he seeks. In the second, his minimized needs cloak him in a pervasive ambiance of misfortune.

Although the Suicide may look to his chronic failure and misfortune as motivations for considering suicide, this is never the true story. Blind to his real motivations on account of his defenses, he concentrates on the consequences that those motivations and his defenses against them cause him. These are the sources of his failures and misfortunes. And these are the factors motivating him towards suicide.

ACCIDENTS AND ILLNESSES

Many reasons the Suicide gives for his problems and misfortunes center around his accidents and illnesses. He may even cite the resulting pain and disability as grounds for his suicidal impulses. But illness and disability are not grounds for suicide. A nonsuicidal person, however disabled, tenaciously clings to every moment of life up to his last breath.

Rather than provide grounds for suicide, multiple accidents and illnesses often result from the unconscious self-destructiveness of the syndrome. Evidence for the unconscious origins of many common illnesses such as gastric ulcers, hypertension, asthma, and arthritis is sufficient that we need not reiterate it here. However, while the so-called "will to live" is credited with saving many lives, the unconscious "will to die" is rarely blamed for life-threatening or terminal illness.

Yet researchers working with cancer patients have discovered that events in the course of some of these patients' lives in months prior to diagnosis are virtually identical to those precipitating suicide.[6] The world cancer and suicide rates apparently rise and fall in almost perfect unison.[7] And numerous studies have consistently confirmed the accident-proneness of people previously known to be highly suicidal.[8]

To be sure, modern life is full of hazards, and even the most vital person is subject to occasional infection or disease. But the connections between the Suicide Syndrome and accidents and illness are far too strong to be ignored. All the self-destructive expressions of the syndrome—Self-Hatred, Vindictiveness, and Hopelessness—contribute powerful motivations towards disabling accidents and critical illnesses.

The Suicide's defenses ironically also provide unconscious motivation for his accidents and illnesses. Token concessions, surrogate sacrifices, and nihilism all specifically aim at his physical pain or demise. The more destructive they are, the greater they suit his unconscious purpose. Although outwardly disturbed, inwardly the Suicide gains a lasting peace from critical or debilitating illnesses, near-fatal and disabling accidents, or lengthy and pervasive chronic conditions with no real abatement in sight.

Antipathic Harold's illnesses usually strike with unexpected severity. He can be the picture of robust health one day and a critical cardiac case the next. Because he believes he is omnipotent, he generally ignores routine health care. Yet at the same time, in order to illustrate his omnipotence, he must always appear as the epitome of health. For these reasons, Harold tends to ignore signs of impending illness and compulsively keeps them a secret.

For the same reasons, Harold's accidents are generally near-fatal ones. Constantly on guard against trivial mishaps which would challenge his omnipotence, Harold unconsciously sets about proving it by risking far more serious ones. After all, trivial mishaps would not prove a thing. But nothing could please Harold more than miraculously to walk away from or at the very least survive an accident everyone would expect to prove fatal.

Synpathic Ruth's illnesses are usually profuse and persistent. Unlike Harold, she can't wait to get a physician's attention and then tell everyone about it later—in detail. If Ruth does conceal her illness, she does so only for effect. The longer she keeps it a secret, the more shocked and sympathetic her listeners will be—and the more they will admire her for previously suffering in silence.

For the same reasons, Ruth is extremely accident-prone. Unlike Harold, minor mishaps serve her well. They prove how very fragile and helpless she is. Minor cuts, bruises, scrapes, strains, and breaks are her badges of courage—her decorations won on the field of battle with cruel and heartless life.

Finally, Ruth's accidents and illnesses function as excellent ways of expressing her unconscious vindictiveness. In addition to the obvious—the care, attention, and trouble other people must go to on account of her distress—others must also admire her and feel just a bit guilty for being healthy while she suffers. Naturally, the best way for Ruth to get hurt or sick is through the fault of others, either by innocently provoking their physical hostility, incurring an accident on their account, or falling ill while in service to them. Then she further retaliates by bravely carrying on, showing other people how much she suffers because of them.

As we would expect, Apathic Carl's accidents and illnesses are generally hopeless ones. Like Harold, he neglects routine care and signs of impending illness, but for different reasons. Carl transcends mundane impediments like getting sick. Like Ruth, his illnesses are often chronic and protracted, but again for different reasons. Chronic illness symbolizes Carl's disdain for functional living.

It is not really important to him whether he stays well or sick. He transcends all that. But staying sick does have its unconscious advantages. On the one hand, it enables Carl to escape all the other contingencies of life. On the other, it puts others at his service, tending his needs without obligation from him.

Carl's accidents have these same vague unconscious motives. He can get himself hurt in bizarre ways. He rarely takes undue risks like Harold, nor does he get injured by countless daily hazards like Ruth. Instead, Carl gets hurt by the senseless, irrational, and mundane world. He gets caught in the crossfire of other people's battles, laid waste by the grinding reality of the larger insentient world.

Finally, a diagnosis of terminal illness questions the very essence of the Suicide's fundamental but unconscious beliefs about himself. At this great moment of truth, his artificial repressions desert him. He is his Fantastic Self: Omnipotent, Innocent, and Transcendent. And —logically—he is immortal!

Regardless of the Suicide's rationalizations as to why he wants to end his life ahead of prognosis, the absolute attributes of his Fantastic Self and its immortality underlie them. He may claim he wants to avoid the pain, the expense, the "indignity" of a lengthy illness, or that he wants to spare his family. But knowing the dynamics of the syndrome, we can see that while his rationalizations may sound logical or noble, they are essentially ludicrous.

Behind the Suicide's illnesses and accidents parades his immortal Fantastic Self. Because he is omnipotent, he must be the one to decide when, how, and where. Because he is innocent, he cannot deserve to die except by his own will. Because he is transcendent, he will not succumb to an ordinary demise. And because he is immortal—like a death-row suicide cheating the vindictive State of its revenge—he believes that by his suicide he can even cheat death.

Hyper-Reaction to Casualty and Loss

Many misfortunes, accidents, and illnesses result from the Suicide Syndrome. But of course, many do not. Modern life has its hazards. Even the most vital person is subject to illness, the disabling effects of aging, and the inevitability of death.

Certainly, the casualties of life as a process can be upsetting. The loss of a loved one, the misfortunes of social and economic events, war, oppression, natural catastrophe, all take their toll. Grief, disappointment, and discouragement inevitably occur in the course of all human life, as even every child knows. But the Suicide often singles out the casualty and loss inherent in everyday life as his motivations for suicide. He may believe that he cannot, should not, or dare not go on living in the aftermath of his loss.

The Suicide's unconscious belief that he is his Fantastic Self lies at the bottom of his suicidal reaction to casualty and loss. He should not be subjected to even the most common—especially the most common?—kinds of calamity. His Fantastic Self lurks behind his belief that his loss, his particular tragedy is far worse than anyone else could possibly incur. It is so much worse that no one else could even understand its impact.

When we look at the Suicide's reaction to casualty and loss, we must also examine what such events mean to him from the viewpoint of his type. Any common casualty or loss automatically challenges Antipathic Harold's omnipotence. Nothing unfortunate should happen to him. Nothing affecting him should be beyond his control. Casualty and loss challenges Synpathic Ruth's innocence. She is infinitely good and deserving. Certainly she cannot deserve to lose a parent, spouse, or child to illness or accident, or to lose a valued status or possession to the misfortunes of fate. Casualty and loss challenges Apathic Carl's transcendence. He is above being subjected to mundane events, above having to experience grief or bereavement in the ordinary course of life.

Often, there is a suspension of belief in the reality of the event. The Suicide may deny that the event has really occurred, deny the way in which it really happened, or cling to a pseudo-grief reaction of extreme intensity, extending it almost indefinitely. In such instances, for him to stop grieving would constitute his unconscionable acceptance of the final reality of the event.

But in any case, the Suicide's refusal to accept the reality of the event always stems from his far more urgent need to believe he is his omnipotent, innocent, and transcendent Fantastic Self. When the Suicide says, "I can't believe this is happening," what he really means is, *I can't believe this is happening to me—to my Fantastic Self.*

Finally, because casualty or loss challenges the Suicide's most fundamental conviction that he is his Fantastic Self, all the other complexities of the syndrome are brought into play. Out comes shame, humiliation, and despair, and the unconscious Self-Hatred, Vindictiveness, and Hopelessness they respectively elicit. These must be expressed and, for the Suicide to survive, he must employ his characteristic defenses against them.

Consequently, in the face of casualty or loss, Harold employs all his defenses against Self-Hatred. When he incurs an unavoidable loss, he usually converts its threat to his imagined omnipotence into a secret satisfaction with its consequences, however dire they may be. Similarly, Ruth employs all her defenses against Vindictiveness. She often furthers her suffering by getting sick, hurt, or by depriving herself of recovery from the event. Likewise, Carl employs his defenses against

Hopelessness. He philosophically shrugs it off, spiritually rises above it, aesthetically finds beauty or a higher meaning in it, or he strikes back at life—usually a part of his own, or of those closest to him—to offset his despair.

In order to survive, each type of Suicide must employ his particular defense system against the challenge that casualty or loss presents to his illusions. Yet in the wake of a casualty or loss sufficient to overwhelm the strength of his defenses, the Suicide may resort to more deadly means. But casual events or losses, however tragic, cannot cause his suicide. His unconscious belief that he is his Fantastic Self and the systematic syndrome founded on it determine all his behaviors including his hyper-reaction to casualty and loss.

Chapter 21

SUICIDAL RELATIONS

The Suicide's interpersonal relations are an essential part of the Suicidal Lifestyle. For the syndrome not only defines his thinking, feelings, and behavior. It also determines the necessity, the character, and the nature of his relations to other people.

To be sure, the character and nature of his earliest relationships initiated his entry into the Suicide Syndrome. Shorn of his autonomy, empathy, and spontaneity mainly by the influence of others, he had little choice but to create his Fantastic Self and to become convinced of it. But his continued belief that he is his Fantastic Self in the face of its impossibility is his own doing. And that belief alone essentially determines how he relates to others.

All the complex ramifications of the Suicide's unconscious convictions influence these relationships. His choice of role automatically sets their tone. Harold, the Antipathic Type, automatically moves against other people. He is out to exert his power over them in order to manifest his omnipotence. Ruth, the Synpathic Type, automatically moves toward other people. She is out to win their love, to exploit and depend on them in order to manifest her innocence. Carl, the Apathic Type, automatically moves away from other people. He is out to ignore them, to depreciate their banality in order to manifest his transcendence.

Furthermore, the characteristics of the Suicide's Empirical Self shape his relations to other people. Antipathic Harold relates to others with hostility, arrogance, and rigidity. Synpathic Ruth feels abused, inadequate, and deprived by them. Apathic Carl can relate to others only through his ambivalence, detachment, and inertia. Regardless of what the real situation or other people's actions would normally call for, the Suicide's empirical characteristics prevail.

In addition, although aimed at himself, his expressions of Self-Hatred also affect his relations to other people. No matter what behavior would otherwise be appropriate, he simply must relate to others in accordance with his Inner Dictates, Self-Accusations and Self-Contempt, and his Self-Defeat and Self-Punishment.

Of course, his expressions of Vindictiveness are inherently aimed at disrupting his relations with other people. His External Claims are designed to control and exploit them. His Contempt for and Accusations against others prevail regardless of his shallow attempts at disguise. His Vindictive Retaliation establishes the law of talion as his customary way of relating to other people.

Even his expressions of Hopelessness, although existential in origin, necessarily lend a distinct slant to his relations to other people. His Abstract Values, Chronic Discontent, and Hopeless Resignation are not just aimed at his life in the abstract. They are also aimed at the people included in it.

Finally, the Suicide's defenses mold his relations to other people. Harold's defenses to Self-Hatred regulate how he responds to them. Ruth's defenses to Vindictiveness characterize her relations to them. And even Carl's defenses to Hopelessness bear on his relations to others.

All these complex processes of the Suicide Syndrome determine who the Suicide relates to, how he relates to them, and why his relations with them are invariably destructive. Indeed, the effects of the syndrome on the Suicide's sexual, close interpersonal, and broad social relations can grow so destructive, he may believe he grows suicidal on their account. However, the Suicide's conviction that he is his Fantastic Self, and the resulting complex syndrome make his relations to others destructive. They are the only true causes of his suicidal impulses.

Sexual Disturbances

No other area in everyday life is more susceptible to severe disturbances of the syndrome than the Suicide's sexuality. This is not just because his sexuality is usually intertwined with his otherwise discordant close relationships. Beyond that involvement, the Suicide's sexuality is vulnerable to serious disruption on its own account.

Social mores also enter the picture. Fluctuating morals and conventions often place conflicting premiums on variations in sexual behaviors. However, social values actually play a very limited role in the formulation of the Suicide's own personal value systems, feelings, and behavior. Each Suicide selects and interprets social mores for himself in strict accordance with his particular type. The same moral code means one thing to the Antipathic, another to the Synpathic, and still another to the Apathic Type.

But difficulties in close relations and social mores notwithstanding, sex in itself poses a profound and inherent dilemma to the Suicide. Indeed, it is this very dilemma that renders the Suicide's sexuality so vulnerable to disturbances. For sexuality embodies the very antithesis to the Suicide's unconscious convictions.

The Suicide's unconscious conviction that he is his Fantastic Self renders it impossible for him spontaneously to express natural sexuality. He is his Fantastic Self, omnipotent, innocent, and transcendent. There is no possibility for him wholly to surrender to the engulfing experience of sex. It inherently compromises his conviction in his Fantastic Self.

This compromising effect alone carries enough weight to inhibit the Suicide's natural sexuality. It triggers such complex ramifications that the Suicide often singles out his sexual conflicts as the root cause of all his problems, believing that if he could just get *them* resolved, everything else would fall into place. But there can be no genuine resolution between natural sexuality and his artificial Fantastic Self. Rather than resolve the conflict—and to abandon his conviction in his Fantastic Self—the Suicide attempts to incorporate sex into the complex process founded on it.

While each type may employ a variety of sexual behaviors, the Suicide's belief in his Fantastic Self and its fixed attribute always constitutes the underlying theme of his sexual behavior. In short, the Suicide utilizes sex in the service of his role.

Sex, to Antipathic Harold, is a power play. Indeed, the only way he may be able to participate is to keep his partner literally beneath him. Although he may become relatively adept at techniques—Harold will take his perfectionism to bed with him—his partner feels like an instrument on which he plays rather than a living, breathing colleague in joy.

Naturally, he deems his partner a sex object. Her fulfillment interests him only as proof of his potency. Never sensing the artificiality of his approach, Harold pictures himself the perfect lover, and being perfect, he sees no reason to change. He can rigidly adhere to a regularly scheduled, punctually performed, mechanically executed missionary position year in and year out.

Unconsciously, Harold has good reason to fear sex. But consciously, he loves the power and strength he can experience through it. He dreams not of ecstatic moments of sexual abandon. He dreams of helpless maidens crazed by their passions for him, laid waste by his instrument of power, decimated by his infinite potency.

For obvious reasons, Harold lives in utter dread of sexual impotence, a word and concept possessing special meaning to him. But, ironically, just because he utilizes sex to express power, he renders himself highly susceptible to various forms of real and imagined impotence.

First, Harold can never be as sexually potent as his illusions make him out to be. Secondly, just because he uses sex to conquer his partner—"opponent" would be better—he sets himself up for defeat. By making sex a contest, he strains the delicate psychophysiological mechanisms of masculine sexuality beyond their capacity, also bringing his partner's need to defeat him into the fray. Finally, just his exaggerated fear of failure is often enough psychically to abort the complex mechanisms of erection and ejaculation. So Harold calls upon himself the very thing he fears the most. To omnipotent Harold, sexual impotence constitutes the ultimate defeat.

In order to avoid even risking impotence, Antipathic Harold can become very antisexual. Sex is for animals, the lower classes, the weak. Hard work, manly competition, disciplined self-control are what really matter in life.

The Antipathic female deals with sex in much the same way and encounters many of the same problems. She is out to control or defeat others through sex. No man is ever man enough to make her come. No penis is big enough. No erection is hard enough or sustained enough to satisfy her. After conquering or defeating enough men, she may pursue women with the same goals in mind. She plays on the senses of the compliant and less experienced, never allowing them to do anything but rest at her breast.

Sex, to Synpathic Ruth, means love. But she believes that perfect love will make her into her perfect Fantastic Self. Ruth unconsciously charges sex with this same impossible mission. Hers is a search for the magic penis—one that will take charge of her, transport her to ecstasy, bring out all her hidden splendor. Through the offices of the magic penis, Ruth will be all she unconsciously believes herself to be. Yet at the same time that Ruth seeks affirmation of her secret convictions through sex, she encounters an inherent contradiction. Carnal sex contradicts Ruth's imagined innocence. Sex is inherently humiliating to Ruth.

Ruth may try to evade the humiliation by consciously or unconsciously denying herself sexual gratification, withdrawing into her inorgasmic self. Or she may actually lend herself to the humiliation, participating in sex for reasons other than itself, but feeling guilty, and debased.

Because she romanticizes sex, Ruth can feel as helplessly driven to sex as she feels helplessly driven to love. Her heart yearns for moments of glorious sensuality, rapturous romance, ravishing love. But none of this is ever really forthcoming, or at best, is never sustained. As a result, Ruth feels deprived of the love sex means to her.

Because she must consciously or unconsciously evade the humiliation sex causes her, Ruth can become passively asexual or at least inorgasmic. Her dreams of rapturous moments rarely come true for her. She draws her partner into her, wraps herself around him, thrills to his touch, then at the crucial moment fails to orgasm. Her failure automatically feeds her feelings of inadequacy in sex.

Finally, because Ruth experiences the humiliation sex entails for her, she can only participate for reasons other than her own fulfillment. She does it to please her partner, to gain his attention, affection, or to secure his fidelity. And because she must subject herself to it in the name of a higher cause, Ruth then feels abused by sex.

Endowing her partner with a magic penis, she resents him for his power over her. Subjecting herself to him in the service of a higher cause, she hates him for expecting it of her. Feeling inadequate in sex, she abstains, or harboring her resentments, she enhances her attractiveness and overtly or covertly prostitutes herself. Or she may render her physical appearance nondescript, unattractive, even rejecting, denying the sexual aspects of her femininity, exuding her unconscious resentment from every pore. Feeling deprived of love when she abstains, inadequate to sex when she does not, and abused in any case, Ruth ends up torn, confused, and overwhelmed by her own sexuality.

The male Synpathic encounters the same inner contradictions but with the added social contradictions contingent with his type. Despite his disguises, the Synpathic male inevitably ends up feeling used by sex. Like the female Synpathic, he may turn to others of his own gender to seek the impossible fulfillment he expects from sex and to express his thinly-veiled resentment of not realizing it with women.

But whether male or female, the Synpathic Type winds up feeling victimized by sex: if not victimized by the deprivation of gratifying sex and the love it subjectively entails, then victimized by having to be subjected to it in a cause other than itself. For orgasmic sexuality inherently contradicts Synpathic Innocence.

Harold uses sex to express his infinite powers. Ruth feels used by sex in her search for ultimate love. Correspondingly, Apathic Carl attempts to utilize sex in his quest for transcendence. Carl's main unconscious goal in expressing his sexuality is paradoxically to gain sexual release.

For this reason Carl can seem wholeheartedly to embrace his sexuality. In contrast to Harold and Ruth whose pretenses are transparent, Carl can usually keep his motives disguised. His need to gain orgasmic release from sexual tensions generally appears as a bona fide expression of genuine sexuality. But unless his partners are equally detached, they sense the sham. Should any of them attempt to impart any meaning to sex, she will soon find herself alone.

Although Carl utilizes sex as a release from sexual tension, it would be far better from his point of view not to have the tension at all. Since he believes he transcends mundane life, Carl secretly savors asceticism. He may romp through a succession of sexual partners, yet secretly dream of the day when he can turn his sexuality off.

Torn between expressing his sexuality and striving to transcend it, Carl drifts on his own sexual inertia. He may become a patron of the one-night-stand or slide into a sexual alliance of relative durability. He may visit a local prostitute for a weekly sexual release. Or like the biblical Onan he may satisfy himself with periodic masturbation. But however Carl might express his sexuality, he must remain detached from it. He observes his own sexuality as a spectator views a sporting event. He may see action, comedy, or pathos in it, but never experiences it as his own.

However, because of his ambivalences, Carl can temporarily lend sex meanings similar to those imparted by Harold and Ruth. In an aggressive mood, he can grow as hostile and overpowering as Harold, using sex to demean or defeat his partner. In a more compliant mood, he can grow as affectionate and receptive as Ruth, experiencing himself as being used to satisfy the needs of another. But in neither case does Carl really believe in the meanings he imparts to sex, or sustain them for long. For above all, Carl must have his freedom. He must be free of mundane meanings, of interpersonal contingencies, of worldly ties of any kind.

For this reason, Carl unconsciously resents his ties to his own sexuality. Harold fears sex because it challenges his imagined omnipotence, Ruth feels victimized by sex because it contradicts her imagined innocence. But Carl resents sex because it denies his imagined transcendence.

His resentment shows most clearly when he interprets the attitude of a potential partner as expecting sex from him. For nothing can intimidate Carl more than facing obligation. He may consciously or unconsciously employ virtually any tactic to avoid fulfilling it.

The male Apathic Type's unconscious resentment of sex can become focused on what he experiences as mundane sex with women. In a last ditch stand against his unconscious taboo against natural sexuality in general, he may see only heterosexual intercourse as depraved and dirty. Sex with other males—especially young and innocent males—is the pure and transcendent sex of the Olympian gods and their philosophers.

The female Apathic harbors the same resentments and employs much the same tactics. She can turn herself off in a situation of earthbound obligation. Imagining herself a Diana of the woods, she glorifies transcendental sexuality while feeling revulsion in the face of sexual reality. She, too, can turn to sexless caresses with members of her own gender in her attempt to transcend her natural sexuality.

But denial of sex in any form suits Apathic transcendence best. The Apathic may turn to spiritualism, asceticism, intellectualism, or alcoholism and other drugs to nullify sexuality. Alone, deep in an ascetic trance or drug-induced stupor, the Apathic at last finds release from mundane sex.

Blind to the basic contradiction between natural sexuality and his artificial Fantastic Self, the Suicide focuses on its consequences. He focuses on conflicts with social mores, impotency, inorgasmia. He is overcome with feelings of sexual inadequacy, deprivation, and unfulfillment. He flounders in sexual frustration, desperation, and guilt. He sinks into confusion, denial, and impossible yearnings. But all this merely symbolizes and at the same time derives from the Suicide's basic conflict with sex.

DISTURBANCES IN LOVE RELATIONS

The Suicide necessarily brings these sexual conflicts into his close interpersonal relations. However, these relationships are subject to severe disturbances by the complexities of the syndrome in their own right. The syndrome virtually dictates the necessity, the character, and the instability of the Suicide's love relations.

The needs, conflicts, and contradictions inherent in love relations seem to dominate the Suicidal Lifestyle, especially for the Synpathic Type. However, any Suicide, regardless of type, may come to believe events in connection with love relations the main cause of his suicidal impulses. But these disturbances are consequences of the Suicide Syndrome. They are not the cause of it.

Disturbances in love relations can be destructive for all types simply because, to the Suicide, being loved means no less than the absolute confirmation of his impossible Fantastic Self.

The Antipathic Type's futile search for omnipotence is especially vulnerable to the fortunes of fickle romance. Often, the more he succeeds in demonstrating his powers in other fields, the more susceptible to love's frustration he becomes. But whether sitting on an official dais or simply at the head of a family kitchen table, the Antipathic Type is extremely vulnerable to frustration in love.

What frustrates him most about love is his lack of power over it. While he normally seeks a Synpathic Type who is always eager to please, her automatic compliance cannot prove his omnipotence. A thousand women at his feet could not hold the attraction of the one girl who would have the temerity to reject him. Here lies a real challenge to his omnipotence, and he will paradoxically prostrate himself before her to overcome it. He will uncharacteristically subjugate himself to any indignity to capture her love. Of course, once conquered, she no longer holds this magical attraction for him, and he looks around for other loves to conquer.

For the Antipathic Type is constantly conquering new loves, either in reality or in the realm of his imagination. His need to prove his potency and powers is insatiable. Even should he settle into a convenient marriage or arrangement, he never loses his wandering eye. For love to Antipathic Harold means the continual confirmation of his Omnipotent Fantastic Self.

It is for this very reason that Harold needs a mate or lover. He needs her in order to have someone he can control. But her value to him extends well beyond her apparent willingness to try to satisfy his immediate demands. Her function in life must be to serve as a help-mate in manifesting his powers.

So while Harold normally picks a mate who will not challenge his powers, her characteristic limitations impair her capacity to fulfill the other functions he unconsciously assigns to her. Harold inherently fails to see the contradiction. How can anyone so innocent and benign actively help him manifest his omnipotence?

This impossible double bind virtually forces Harold's mate to walk a very narrow line. On the one hand, she must be careful never to challenge his powers. But on the other hand, she must try her best to help him exert them. Yet should she take too active a role it would implicate his lack of omnipotence, thus tilting the balance. The consequences are often confusing to them both. He keeps her powerless and supine, and then chafes at her lack of vitality. She follows his criticism and tries to take more responsibility, make herself more attractive, more sociable, and he then reacts to a perceived threat to his control.

In order to maintain any semblance of stability in their relationship, Harold and his mate must fall back on pretense. It is not absolutely necessary for Harold always to be in control, but it is absolutely necessary that he appear to be. His mate must never call attention to his inadequacies, nor openly challenge his mastery. She must never cross him, nor fail to shower him with accolades. She must guard against his children acting too independent, or openly defying him. They must act as though he is Absolute Monarch by the Grace of God, even though all of them—including Harold—may secretly perceive the sham.

Furthermore, Harold expects his mate to represent his powers, status, and prestige to the outside world. It matters little whether he is Chief Executive Officer of a large corporation or a welder in a steel mill. It is up to his mate to demonstrate to the world how powerful, successful, and competent he is. Even in adversity—should he lose his job, fail to make expected advances in his work, incur a business failure—she still must act as though he is master of the world.

But regardless of how well she may fulfill all these functions, in his heart Harold knows he deserves a better mate, one superior to everyone else's. He deserves a glamorous model, a perfect mother to his children, an exemplary homemaker, a successful career woman, a sex goddess. Even though all of this would threaten his own sense of control, he paradoxically believes he deserves and wants it.

Obviously, no one woman could satisfy all of Harold's criteria. To relieve his feelings of being cheated, he often supplements his primary relationship with real or imagined affairs with other women. But while Harold believes he deserves to supplement his primary relationship with others, his mate had better not try the same tactic, or even allow him to suspect she does. Because of Harold's suspiciousness, this is not easy. He stays on constant guard against sabotage from without and sedition from within.

Finally, because Harold's mate cannot validate his impossible omnipotence, he eventually rejects her. He may nominally stick with the alliance for various other reasons. Love relations rarely occupy a top priority with Harold. But, on the other hand, he might act on the rejection, discarding his mate in favor of another whom he perceives as more clearly reinforcing his illusions.

Although Harold automatically rejects his mate, whether he acts on it or not, her rejection of *him* can be his undoing. Rejection to Harold can mean a devastating blow to his illusions of omnipotence. It matters little whether or not he believes he loves her. The issue is his omnipotence, not love. Should her rejection catch Harold unprepared—and because of his arrogance it usually does—Harold can become extremely suicidal. But unlike Ruth and Carl, who also can become suicidal on account of rejection, Harold can also grow homicidal.

Homicide-suicide constitutes Harold's last-ditch attempt to manifest his omnipotence in the wake of its devastation by rejection. He destroys the person who rejects him while at the same time he destroys the weak and hated Empirical Self she rejects. Throughout it all, he remains his Omnipotent Fantastic Self.

The Synpathic Type normally makes love relations the central and most important aspect of her life. However, Ruth's goal to love and be loved is ironically frustrated by her incapacity for it. Bereft of genuine empathy with others, Ruth can only unconsciously fall back on gross demonstrations of its pretense.

Yet beyond that, all her empirical characteristics paradoxically work against her. Just as a matter of course, Ruth feels abused by love, inadequate to it, and deprived because she never gets enough of it.

Ruth feels abused, inadequate, and deprived by love because of what love inherently means to her. For to Synpathic Ruth, love means no less than the absolute confirmation of her Innocent Fantastic Self. This precondition alone renders it impossible for Ruth to attain her ideal love. But additional contradictory factors stand in her way even when a relatively satisfactory love relationship would be well within her grasp.

Because of her repressed aggressive independence, Ruth must choose an aggressive Antipathic Type or independent Apathic Type as a mate or lover. Yet the Antipathic abuses her with his hostility; the Apathic deprives her with his detachment. Each keeps her inadequate and one-down to him.

However, should either type attempt to appease her feelings by suppressing his own aggressive independence, Ruth reacts in an hysterical panic. If her mate is weak and dependent, who will she compliantly depend upon? Above all, Ruth must show the world that she deserves a strong and independent man. Therefore, just like Harold and his mate, Ruth and her mate must fall back on pretense in order to maintain any kind of stability. He must continue to assert his aggressive independence and continue to reap the benefits therefrom. But they must both pretend he is not that way in his relation to her.

But this pretense, too, has its contradictory ramifications. For Ruth can only love from a one-down position. Despite all her complaints of mistreatment, neglect, and subordination, it is absolutely necessary for Ruth to feel inferior to her mate. He must be brighter, more accomplished, more ambitious, of a higher social or economic status, work at a more respected vocation, be stronger and more attuned to the ways of the world than she. For Ruth not only believes she deserves a mate who is superior to everyone else's, but that only the love of an obviously superior person could possibly validate her innocence.

Yet at the same time Ruth unconsciously demands her mate's superiority, she consciously resents him for it. For even though she can only love from a subordinate position, she suffers from the comparison, feels insecure in the relationship, and—most paradoxically—blames her mate for the superiority she unconsciously demands he maintain.

Her resentment growing out of this contradiction only adds to her customary and unconscious expressions of passive Vindictiveness. She may usually just express it obliquely, but that does not diminish its potency. Her mate senses it, and he experiences it quite effectively.

The closer people get to Ruth, the more they experience her Vindictiveness. And since Ruth picks an Antipathic or Apathic partner, he usually retaliates. Even should he try to hold his retaliation in abeyance, Ruth will automatically escalate her provocations until he finally reacts. Ruth is a master at provoking the vindictive retaliation of even the most patient partner. And when it comes, she falls back into naive injured innocence. After all, being abused, inadequate, and deprived are the hallmarks of Ruth's imagined innocence.

It is for this very reason that Ruth will subject herself to all kinds of physical and emotional abuse. She will even tend to provoke it. For the more Ruth is battered, either physically or emotionally, the more innocent she must be. Even though other people might show dismay over her physical and emotional bruises, which Ruth invariably displays or at least tells about, she can see no way out. Nor does she unconsciously want to. She might impulsively flee to the protection of a friend's or relative's home, or to a shelter, but she eventually returns to the same or another abusing alliance.

Finally, Ruth will tolerate abuse rather than risk total rejection. For there is nothing more devastating to Ruth's illusions than being rejected by her mate or lover. In order to endure it at all, Ruth must exaggerate her role as victim to the extent that should the rejection precipitate a suicidal crisis—which is very likely—she must point to the one who rejects her as being responsible.

Ruth's fear of rejection is founded on her paralyzing fear of humiliation. For Ruth fears humiliation more than she fears death. Her fear of being humiliated renders her almost infinitely jealous. While Ruth usually talks of love in connection with her jealousy, the issue is not love, but humiliation. Her fear of being humiliated renders her suspicious of her mate's most innocuous contacts with other women. For only exclusive, absolute, and timeless love can even approximate confirmation of Ruth's illusions. And she will go to any lengths in her futile attempt to win it. She will cling to the most empty liaison in her quest for the perfect love. Indeed, the more unrewarding it appears to others, the more she must seem to cling.

All these contradictions make Synpathic Ruth's love relations tenuous, at best, from the start. But the final irony is yet to come. For while Ruth focuses her every effort on winning undying love, she paradoxically loses her feelings of love for her object once she becomes convinced she has finally won him to her. First, Ruth can only feel her brand of love from a subjugated position. But once her love object confesses his irrevocable love for her, he automatically forfeits the position of superiority. Ruth loses her awe for him, simply because he loves her. Now she sees all his faults and weaknesses, not as cherished idiosyncracies of her lord and master, but as magnified proofs of his utter contemptibleness.

Secondly, we know Ruth suppresses her open expressions of Vindictiveness partially to win the affection of others and to avoid their retaliation. But once her partner capitulates, Ruth feels safe. All her suppressed hostilities are triggered as a result of his capitulation. He surrenders his love and she responds with pent-up fury. She will make him pay for her past humiliations.

Thirdly, and most important, her partner's love cannot make Ruth over into her Fantastic Self. And this is what she has been secretly counting on all along. Unconsciously convinced that only through perfect love can she become her perfect Fantastic Self, Ruth discovers that her partner's love fails to fulfill this impossible promise. Thus, she must either turn against herself or turn against her partner, blaming him or his love.

Turning against herself, she unleashes all the power of her unconscious self-destructiveness. This is why the Synpathic Type often reacts to proposals, impending marriage, anniversaries, reunions, or any sign of apparent success in love with anxiety, depression, mysterious or sudden illness, or other indications of suicidal impulses.

Turning against her partner, she can make even Harold's invectives pale by comparison. Her partner is weak, devious, selfish, and cruel. He doesn't love her enough. He can't. Her range of accusations is limitless. Her hysterical rage, beyond control. But in the aftermath of her hysteria she is usually filled with remorse, puzzled over her own vituperativeness, and convinced that she really didn't mean it. All she really wants, she tells her mate, is to love and be loved.

Blind to the true nature of her impossible expectations, Ruth's futile search for the perfect love often ends as a futile search for the perfect man. She may flit from man to man in her Odyssey, or limit her search to her private world of fantasy, staying with a mediocre alliance. But in either case, Ruth's need for love to validate her illusions remains insatiable. In the face of its undeniable impossibility, she may finally turn to suicide in her futile attempt to confirm her Innocent Fantastic Self.

Love relations inherently contradict Apathic Carl's secret mission in life. While Harold's and Ruth's relationships suffer on account of their functional contradictions, Carl's can only survive despite this inherent one. However, Carl can maintain a relatively stable relationship provided he stumbles into a suitable partner under generally conducive conditions. But regardless of potential partner and circumstances, it always requires a considerable, albeit well-disguised, effort from him.

Valuing personal freedom and the absence of worldly ties as paramount, Carl views close and intimate relations from a perspective of aloof disdain. Detached from his own inner processes and from the conventional ways of the world, he has only his ambivalences to shake him from his detachment. But even should Carl aspire to a love relationship, he paradoxically looks to it for confirmation of his infinitely free and Transcendent Fantastic Self.

But despite his illusions and this inherent contradiction, Carl has need for a mate or lover, or at the very least an affectionate companion. In the first place, Carl can never be as self-sufficient as he believes he is. Although he tries to reduce his needs to a minimum, he still requires someone else to fill in the voids, compensate for his procrastination, attend to the mundane details of life he simply must evade.

In the second place, Carl cannot be so free as his illusions make him out to be. Indeed, he needs a mate or lover simply to help him sustain his illusions. Of course, he will not make overt demands on his mate on this account as Harold makes on his. But whereas Harold openly demands that his mate represent evidence of his omnipotence to the outside world, Carl secretly needs his mate to reflect his particular brand of transcendence.

In the third place, Carl cannot maintain his transcendental detachment—and still maintain his sanity—without ties to someone with two feet planted firmly on the ground. As the winds of his illusions carry him higher and higher into the intellectual, spiritual, or aesthetic ether, his mate or lover must hold fast to the other end of the string.

But at the same time that Carl needs a mate or lover, he has a vested interest in keeping his relations with her vague and void of serious commitment. In short, Carl needs the advantages of a love relationship, but he is repulsed by its usual concomitants.

Like Harold and Ruth, Carl and his mate must employ ample pretense to maintain any sort of stable relationship. It is not absolutely necessary for Carl to have his freedom, but it is absolutely necessary for it to seem that he does. He and his partner must both act as though he is not really dependent, not really committed, not really involved. They can maintain a relationship only if they pretend the relationship does not exist.

Moreover, just as Carl moves in and out of contact with the course of mundane life, he moves in and out of contact with his mate or companion. Should she get too close for comfort, he backs away. Even should his own drifting inertia put him in a situation where he feels that he is dependent upon his mate or unduly influenced by her, he reacts as though he is being imprisoned or violated. For Carl must have his private domain; his general need for privacy is insatiable. But beyond that, Carl must reserve his work, his interests, his few associates, even his own private places for just himself. He interprets a passing interest in any of them on the part of his mate as a gross and violent invasion.

We would expect that with all these contradictions, Carl's relationships would be turbulent, but this is not always so. Carl usually avoids conflict as he avoids closeness. It is not that he cannot fight; he just does not want to get that involved. He will tolerate a great deal of offensiveness with little more reaction than increased detachment.

That is, he will as long as he is able to sustain his illusions of freedom. But let his mate appear to obligate him, invade his private domain, make assumptions of his unwavering affection, act possessive or domineering to him, and she will get a taste of his more open hostility in ways she may not have seen before. He may silently endure for a while, but eventually he will strike. For Carl interprets any such moves as designed expressly for his entrapment. It makes little difference whether the move is aggressive or affectionate, Carl will react with the same degree of revulsion. His illusion of transcendence is at stake.

It is in this very cause that Carl will seek additional relationships. Harold seeks other women to validate his omnipotence. Ruth seeks other men to confirm her lovable innocence. Likewise, Carl wanders to demonstrate his transcendence. Encounters with other women, whether real or imagined, prove to Carl he still has his freedom.

He usually extends a similar license to his mate. Unlike Harold and Ruth whose suspicions render them jealous over any kind of contact, Carl seems oblivious to jealousy. But this is only so long as he is able to maintain his detachment. Should his mate confront him with real evidence of her infidelity, he will react. But as with Harold's and Ruth's jealousy, the issue is not love. From Carl's point of view, such sordid entanglements threaten his ascendancy.

In all these disturbances Carl's first impulse is simply to walk away. But before he departs, he may let his erstwhile partner feel the full force of his resentment. Even should the relationship result from Carl's own dependent inertia, he resents his partner for it. She is to blame for his having chafed under its restrictions, however few. She is to blame for his having made the commitment, however limited. She is to blame for his having invested in the alliance, however sparingly. She is to blame for everything.

It is of little importance whether it ends by Carl rejecting his mate or her rejecting him. Carl is still confronted by the same degree of despair in his ever being able to maintain a love relationship and still sustain his transcendence. He may try to fight off the Hopelessness his despair elicits by employing his customary defenses. Yet these, too, have their self-destructive effects. The aggregate consequences could be enough to do him in. But only his earthbound Empirical Self must contend with disturbances in love relations. His Transcendent Fantastic Self rises above all that.

FRIENDLESSNESS, LONELINESS, AND SOCIAL ALIENATION

With his true sexuality abated and his close interpersonal relationships in discord, the Suicide turns to other people in his social milieu. But instead of finding a deep sense of social mutuality with them, he encounters a virtually universal and impenetrable wall. Regardless of how many people he may have around him, the Suicide often experiences himself as friendless, lonely, and socially alienated.

Friendlessness, loneliness, and social alienation can loom very large in the Suicidal Lifestyle. The Suicide may conclude that unless he can find some friends on whom he can rely, some people with whom he can relate, some comradeship with others based on gratifying grounds, his life is not worth living. But friendlessness, loneliness, and social alienation are not causes of suicide. They are the consequences of the Suicide Syndrome and of its prevalence.

This absence of genuine social mutuality in his general relations is another reason his close interpersonal relations and their stability become so vitally important to him. He may secretly sense or openly acknowledge that if he did not have a mate or lover to call his own, he would have no one else with whom he could relate. But while the social destructiveness of the syndrome may remain in the background during periods of relative stability in the Suicide's close relationships, it burgeons into immediate and overwhelming importance should his close relationships break down. In the absence of close interpersonal ties, more general alliances become crucial.

However, regardless of how or when the Suicide experiences his social alienation, the syndrome guarantees its pervasiveness. Unaware of its true origins, the Suicide can only concentrate on its effects. He finds himself friendless, lonely, and alienated from other people and cannot comprehend why.

For example, he rarely takes cognizance of his own social prejudice, how it blocks congeniality in his social relations, and why he fails to question its grounds. Although without friends, he most likely cannot name a single real and accessible person with whom he would like to be close friends. Of course, he may express an offhand admiration or spurious curiosity in regard to some individual or group. But he always finds some rationalization for why he cannot initiate friendship.

He is equally unaware of his pervasive competitiveness and how it interferes with his social relations. Indeed, his desire for many friends often ironically stems from his need to win out over other people who would have fewer or less prestigious friends than he.

The Suicide's competitiveness in social relations is so all-pervasive, he normally just takes it for granted. If he grows cognizant of it at all, he ascribes it to human nature. But the brand of competitiveness growing out of the syndrome is very different from just looking after one's own best interests. To the contrary, it usually works against the Suicide's real best interests, especially in his ability to establish social relationships.

Antipathic Harold normally founds his few social relations on open competition such as work or sports. But he is not alone in bringing competition into his social relations. Ruth must be more attractive, have a more ardent mate or lover, get more love, attention, or material favors from spouse, family, or friends than her competitor. Carl, who seems to shun competition, becomes instantly competitive once close contact is made. He must be more esoteric, more intelligent, more knowledgeable, more philosophic about the ways of the world than anyone else. Harold's competitiveness may appear more obvious than Ruth's or Carl's, but not when we remember what they see as their individual mark of competitive superiority.

Most paradoxically, the Suicide can even point to his lack of friends to prove his competitive edge over others. Harold proves his superior powers by showing how other people are too weak and afraid to relate closely to him. Ruth proves her superior moral standards by pointing out her friendlessness among the selfish hedonists around her. Carl proves his superior self-sufficiency by discounting a need for friends.

Finally, the Suicide usually blinds himself to the artificiality of his relations to others. Harold needs to relate to other people solely to express his powers; Ruth, just to illustrate what a nice, likeable, and deserving person she is; Carl, to contrast his own wise and aloof self-sufficiency.

The Suicide's social relations must be founded on artificial grounds simply because he believes he is his Fantastic Self. For his unconscious convictions cause the Suicide to need far more than just real friends, congenial company, and social integration. What the Suicide really needs from his social relations is the absolute confirmation of his impossible Fantastic Self.

He may experience the pain of his friendlessness. He may suffer from isolation and loneliness. And he may experience the anxiety of social alienation. But the crux of the matter is, the Suicide cannot lower himself into genuine social mutuality. Despite the terrible consequences of his real situation, genuine social mutuality would constitute an even more terrible and unconscionable compromise to his belief that he is his Fantastic Self.

Chapter 22

SUICIDAL SOCIETIES

Lacking a deep sense of social mutuality with other people, the Suicide can only form general associations with them on the principles of the Suicide Syndrome. Such associations constitute Suicidal Societies.

A Suicidal Society is any social system founded on or dominated by the Suicide Syndrome. The unconscious goal of a suicidal society is the termination of its own existence. Its individual current members need not perish on account of its suicide, but it is essential to a suicidal society that it aim at its own extinction in the service of the logic of the syndrome.

Like any social system, a Suicidal Society is a relatively durable association of three or more people interacting within a set and organized structure. It has a social goal or product, projects a social image, and maintains social norms.[9] But unlike a social system which would function on the basis of human mutuality, a Suicidal Society functions on the basis of the Suicide Syndrome. This social syndrome parallels the individual syndrome in every important respect.

The social goal of the suicidal society is the manifestation of a Social Fantastic Self.[10] Its social image is the fixed and glorified attribute of its Social Fantastic Self. And it maintains social norms strictly and exclusively in support of its Social Fantastic Self.

CHARACTERISTICS OF THE SUICIDAL SOCIETY

The Social Fantastic Self lies at the very heart of the Suicidal Society. It comprises all the society unconsciously believes itself to be. Although the Social Fantastic Self is rationally impossible, this does not deter the loyal members of the society from their collective belief in it, nor the society from pursuing its impossible fulfillment.

Like the individual Suicide's Fantastic Self, the Social Fantastic Self is Omnipotent, Innocent, and Transcendent. Consequently, it is immortal. To the extent that the society cannot manifest its attributes in its system, it sees them as its potential. To the degree that outsiders fail to ratify its existence, the society blames their ignorance or hostility. To the measure that the course of its history fails to affirm it, the society looks to an inexplicable promise of the future.

All the Common Characteristics resulting from the Suicide Syndrome follow a society's adoption of the belief in its Social Fantastic Self. The society automatically becomes proud, with pride in its characteristics normally a praiseworthy endeavor of its constituents. It automatically becomes egocentric. As a social system, it believes itself to be the measure of all others, past, present, and future. It becomes narcissistic. Love of the system is an explicit duty of its members. It becomes perfectionistic. Nothing short of the ultimate satisfies it for long. It becomes compulsive. Its functioning and the interaction and behavior of its members must be aimed at manifesting the ideal. It becomes obsessive. Behind its every function lies the concept of the ideal. It becomes arrogantly superior. Other systems, inasmuch as they differ from it, are seen as inferior, evil, misled. And it becomes irrational. No amount of real evidence contradicting its impossible beliefs about itself can dissuade it for long.

Like the individual Suicide, the Suicidal Society represses two of its Social Fantastic Self's attributes and fixates and glorifies the remainder. But like the individual, the society's identity is rarely undiluted. This is especially true if it is a very large one, although one particular attribute always predominates. But in any case, the more comprehensive its fixation, the more cohesive the society becomes, regardless of size, and the more prone it is to immediate social suicide.

Furthermore, as does the individual, the Suicidal Society incurs shame, humiliation, and despair resulting from the impossibility of its Social Fantastic Self. These, in turn, respectively generate Self-Hatred, Vindictiveness, and Hopelessness. Although the society also represses the origins and nature of these motivations, it still must express them in its everyday social functions.

The specific ways each Suicidal Society expresses Self-Hatred, Vindictiveness, and Hopelessness, and the unconscious defenses each builds in regard to them, depends upon which attribute of the Social Fantastic Self it fixates and glorifies. As with individual Suicides, there are Antipathic, Synpathic, and Apathic Suicidal Societies.

THE ANTIPATHIC SOCIETY

The Antipathic society fixates and glorifies Omnipotence. Its principle underlying goal is to be the most powerful society that has ever existed. No amount of historical evidence regarding the fate of other such societies deters it from its impossible goal, as each Antipathic society secretly believes it will be the exception. It will attain immortality, thereby reigning over the world forever, by virtue of its omnipotence.

In its drive for ultimate power, the Antipathic society must constantly persevere. In its view, nothing could be more disastrous than for it to waver from its singular course. It must continually develop its strengths at any cost to its own best interest.

It capitalizes on the vitality, ingenuity, and human resources of its populace. It indiscriminately utilizes the material resources it may have under its control. It mobilizes its friends, allies, and sympathizers in its cause. It does anything it can in any way it can to manifest its omnipotence through economic, industrial, political, or military means.

Internally, the Antipathic society must strive for absolute overt or covert control over all its constituents. It effects its control over them in many interrelated ways. First of all, it effects its control through the education and training of its youth. Despite its pretenses otherwise —if it should bother to make them—it educates its youth to aspire to its goals, endorse its ideals, and to become eager workers at any level in its cause. Some may be taught to provide leadership, support, or amusement for the workers. But the primary function of Antipathic education is to produce a productive work force.

Secondly, the Antipathic society controls its constituents through a system of rewards and punishments. Those who possess the means of production or those who can induce others into being more productive are given the highest rewards. Most others who do not actively contribute to or epitomize the social goal of ultimate power are deprived or ostracized.

Thirdly, it controls its constituents by the establishment of a status hierarchy. Those constituents who more nearly approximate the ideal—who control others or who display political, economic, or brute strength, proven competitiveness, and the desire to defeat or manipulate others—occupy the higher status levels. Those who lack power over others or who demur from exercising it occupy the lower status levels.

Fourth, it controls its constituents by assigning them social roles designed to facilitate realization of the overall objective. Since the society indiscriminately views obvious signs of strength as most desirable, it assigns a more active competitive role to its physically stronger men and a more passive support role to women. In order to render the assignees more eager to accept their assignments, it encourages men to believe they are omnipotent and women to believe they are innocent, reinforcing the Antipathic Type for men and the Synpathic Type for women.

Fifth, it effects internal control over its constituents through the proliferation of social subsystems either reflecting the overall system's ideals and organization, or complementing it. Complementary subsystems are drawn into the support of the overall system. Contradictory subsystems are outlawed, ostracized, or ignored.

Sixth, it effects control over its constituents through folklore, mythology, and the idealization of folk heroes, both real and imaginary. Its heroes display strength, powers, and competitiveness. Its mythology focuses on the concepts of victory at any price. Its folklore deals with perseverance in the face of adversity and the inevitable defeat of those not so strong and self-reliant as the hero.

Finally, it effects its control through leadership. Its leadership must reflect the qualities of its folk heroes and the ideals of the society. The first requisite for its leaders is their apparent ability to render the society more powerful, more self-reliant, more industrious. The leader—usually an omnipotent male—must ostensibly reflect these very qualities, regardless of any other personal qualities he may or may not possess.

Externally, the Antipathic society strives for ultimate power and control over all other social systems. It may attempt to disguise its true motive behind a false humility, an apparent concern for the rights of others. But behind the pretenses, it is really out to win allies in opposition to a threatening competitor, to bring other societies under its own political, economic, or military control, to exploit their human or natural resources for its own use, or just to enhance its public image.

Antipathic societies call each other Powers. They call the larger and more militant among them Superpowers. They expend most of their time, resources, and energies competing with each other for power positions, manipulating threatening alliances, and intimidating each other into conflict.

Existentially, the Antipathic society sees its existence as a struggle of all against all. Logically, it had best not even appear appeasing, weak, or impotent. Its constituents dare not question the rationality of its stance or ideals. The Antipathic society is not kind to its dissenters, even though it may condemn other societies for the same attitudes. Social ostracism is the very best a dissenter can expect.

As a consequence, its constituents strain under the burden of its demands on them. They chafe under the exploitation of their human resources, suffer the misuse of their homeland, are often even willing to die in the service of the society's impossible ideals. Yet they rarely collectively question its idealization of omnipotence. Instead, they, as individuals, aspire to power positions, devote their lives to working for that end, and emulate the system by striving for ultimate control over each other. Some may wonder about the logic and humanity of the system, others may occasionally rebel. But within the Antipathic society, the idealization of omnipotence always wins out.

Obviously, the Antipathic society has but one way to go, as history has proven. It may live with its illusions for a while, but it can never sustain them. The Antipathic society must inevitably go to its own self-destruction by means of the very power it glorifies.

THE SYNPATHIC SOCIETY

The Synpathic society fixates and glorifies Innocence. Its ultimate goal is to manifest immortality for itself and its true adherents through infinite love, altruism, and benignity. Since genuine evidence of this brand of absolute and immortal innocence is impossible to come by in real life, the Synpathic society must place a paramount premium on simply believing in it. Consequently, this premium on pure faith characterizes the Synpathic society. This affords the Synpathic society total release from the confines of mundane rationality. It has no need to evade recognition of its own irrational beliefs as might the Antipathic society. To the contrary, it celebrates its irrationality through faith. Indeed, it seems the more irrational its beliefs, the greater the premium placed on them.

Its premium on pure faith also leads the Synpathic society into an obvious operational duplicity. For it is not really necessary for its adherents actually to put its principles into practice in everyday life. Just believing in them is paramount.

Moreover, this premium on pure faith allows the Synpathic society to ally or assimilate with other blatantly contradictory social systems. And because of its beliefs in its innocence, its shallow taboos on its own overt aggressiveness, and its not too secret admiration of omnipotence, the Synpathic society must usually form a symbiotic alliance with a more aggressive Antipathic society. The marriage—like that between Synpathic and Antipathic individuals—is punctuated by pretense, compromise, and hypocrisy. But the more aggressive host society does reinforce the Synpathic's innocence by lending material support, physical protection, and political deference to its beliefs. In turn, the more dependent Synpathic system spiritually supports the Antipathic's imagined omnipotence by reinforcing its external aggressiveness and internal control, premium on work, status hierarchy, and assigned social roles.

Finally, this premium on faith results in an irrational discount of human corporeal existence. Affairs of the flesh are not just depreciated, but ostensibly despised. In order for the system and its adherents to function in the real world, they must resort to some rather transparent pretenses.

First of all, the system develops a pretentious structure of practices and ceremonies aimed at disguising, sanctioning, or otherwise absolving the function of its fleshly or earthly qualities. Possible violation of the ritual then becomes the central issue.

Secondly, the system must endow its adherents with a dual nature. The fleshly component is despised, depreciated, or at best, ignored. The other becomes a conscious and ritualized glorification of the Fantastic Self. For this component is at once omnipotent, innocent, transcendent, and—naturally—immortal. It is indestructible, although it may be manipulated by outside evil forces. It is benign, although it may be punished on account of the acts of its correspondent. It is ethereal, although it may descend to mundane life rather than ascend from it. And it is eternal, although it may have good reason to wish it were not.

Thirdly, because of its conscious idealization of the Fantastic Self and its complementary depreciation of the flesh, the Synpathic society must invoke prohibitions against individually motivated suicide for its adherents. Without these prohibitions, the logic of the syndrome would automatically win out. For once an adherent accepts the tenets of the Synpathic society, suicide would be his only logical objective.

All these contradictions look most confusing to the objective observer of the Synpathic society. They may even become confusing to its adherents—but not when we remember the consequences stemming from its premium on pure faith. For should any of its adherents attempt to apply common sense or rationality to its precepts, the system condemns him, ostracizes him, or at best, simply pities him for his unconscionable loss of faith.

Internally, the Synpathic society controls its adherents in similar ways as the Antipathic controls its. But in contrast to the overt, often oppressive, control methods of the Antipathic, the modern Synpathic society's methods are usually more abstruse and covert. Characteristically, most adherents of the Synpathic society accept its control on faith, as though this were the order of things.

However, like the Antipathic, the Synpathic society controls its adherents through the indoctrination and education of its youth. It instills into its youth its own ideals, creed, and superiority of concept through the recitation of myths and parables gauged to their understanding and presented as fact. When even a child would question these, the system falls back on faith.

The Synpathic society also controls its adherents through a system of rewards and punishments. But in contrast to the Antipathic and in keeping with its benign altruism, these rewards and punishments are seldom overt. Those who strictly adhere to its control will be rewarded with the promise of eternal bliss. Those who do not will be eternally punished by some extrinsic but irresistible force.

The Synpathic society also controls its adherents through the employment of a status hierarchy and through the assignment of social roles. However, since the Synpathic society must usually exist as a subsystem within a more worldly Antipathic system, it normally endorses those statuses and social roles assigned to it. It thereby lends these assignments the weight of its endorsement on faith, regardless of how contradictory this may appear.

It also controls its adherents through the proliferation of subsystems closely reflecting the organization, function, and ideals of the main. Through these subsystems, the Synpathic society can be, and usually is, geographically dispersed within one or more contradictory systems.

The Synpathic society also controls its adherents through mythology, folklore, and the idealization of heroes. Innocence—often inexplicably rationalized as the power of innocence—is elevated to an absolute degree. Faith is invariably held to be supreme and is shown to win out over all possible contradictions to it, even death.

Finally, the Synpathic society controls its adherents through leadership. Its leaders are often endowed with ultimate, albeit altruistic, power over all its adherents. Since even this kind of power appears to conflict with innocence, it is usually derived from some outside force for which the leader is simply an altruistic spokesman.

Externally, the Synpathic society relates to outsiders and rival social systems with a holier-than-thou brand of moral superiority. It sees outsiders and other social systems, inasmuch as they differ from it, as barbaric or immoral. In short, like the Synpathic individual, the Synpathic society denies others what it sees as the best of being human, then condemns them for their inhumanity.

Existentially, the Synpathic society sees real existence in real life as a victimizing process. From its point of view there is little or no way human beings can get through organic life without being victimized by it. In fact, just being born into organic life is often seen as the ultimate contamination. Indeed, all the processes of empirical existence —birth, life, immutable death—automatically render the human condition base.

Of course, no one could even unconsciously sustain such a view of existence in real life without generating massive Vindictiveness against those who do not. For even though its dual interpretation of human nature and the meliorating effects of resignation allow it and its adherents to participate in real life, even to mount aggression against others with apparent immunity, the self-abnegation of the Synpathic society eventually takes its effect.

More important is the humiliation contingent with outsiders' failure to validate its superior brand of absolute innocence. Finding such validation only in the realm of metaphysical future possibilities, the Synpathic society must turn against all outsiders with Vindictiveness.

Even though the Synpathic society represses its Vindictiveness, it still must express it. It lodges external claims designed to gain material support, exceptions to worldly demands, universal deference to its concepts. It accuses outsiders of inherent evil and condemns them to eternal damnation. Finally, it retaliates against them in manifold passive but extremely effective ways.

But, such expressions of Vindictiveness contradict Synpathic innocence and the Synpathic society must employ defenses against them. It spiritually or actually withdraws from the ways of the world, harboring its resentments. It internalizes its Vindictiveness, castigating its adherents accordingly. Finally, it makes surrogate sacrifices, elevating martyrdom as the supreme expression of its own innocence.

But regardless of its defenses, the more withdrawn, self-castigating, and martyred the Synpathic society becomes, the more vindictive it grows toward outsiders. Eventually it must turn to suicide, the Synpathic's ultimate weapon against them.

THE APATHIC SOCIETY

The Apathic society fixates and glorifies Transcendence. It believes it intellectually, spiritually, or aesthetically transcends mundane life.

As we might suspect, Apathic societies are usually hard to find or difficult to identify. The Apathic revulsion against forming obvious ties renders his societies elusive, disguised, or dispersed. You might find a fairly cohesive Apathic system isolated atop some remote mountain range or sheltered from the rest of the world in a secluded countryside. But most Apathic societies are generally dispersed or relatively assimilated within the larger framework of other social systems.

The typical Apathic society coalesces around some intellectual, spiritual, aesthetic, scientific, or philosophic precept. Characteristically, each of its members envisions himself as fiercely independent, uniquely individualistic, and ultimately free from conformity. But, ironically, its membership is even more inclusive, more parochial, and more conforming than is the membership of either of the other two social types. Its members generally all look alike, dress alike, talk alike, and employ like pretenses with stultifying uniformity.

In its unconscious quest for absolute transcendence, the Apathic society views mundane pursuits with aloof disdain. But regardless of its illusions of aloof self-sufficiency, the Apathic society is rarely self-sustaining. Because of its taboos on mundane pursuits, it usually must depend on the resources of more worldly social systems for its own material sustenance. Of course, it is only right for a group with its superior calling to utilize the material resources generated by lesser beings.

For if the Apathic society has any goal at all, it must be a lofty one. To the Apathic society, nothing can ever measure up to the transcendental abstract. This superiority of the abstract over the concrete comes to characterize the Apathic society. Despite its overtures otherwise, the practical application of its precepts in everyday life is viewed as a demeaning contamination of them. The more abstract, the more esoteric, the more spiritual the precept, the less susceptible it is to mundane contamination and the more highly it is valued.

Thus, art really is for art's sake. Science is "value-free"—for the sake of pure knowledge. Principles are "on principle." Abstract concepts, as pure abstract concepts, reign supreme.

As a result of this premium on the abstract, each Apathic system develops its own abstract tautology. It has its own language, symbolic system, detached frame of reference, mysterious intellectual, spiritual, or aesthetic jargon. It usually looks down upon the vernacular and systems of expression of the more populous common folk with aloof disgust or patronizing amusement.

In this context, the Apathic society usually appears iconoclastic. The values, goals, and customs of its host system are normally viewed as lowly, degrading, and—the ultimate epithet—mundane. It often seems out to destroy, or at the very least depreciate, everything about more worldly systems differing from it.

However, regardless of how rebellious the Apathic society appears from without, it is vehemently intolerant of deviation within. While it may seem to tolerate rather wide variations in superficial things, no member may vary from or question its precepts or superiority of concept. Perhaps the greatest crime a member can commit is to apply the system's principles to mundane things or deal with them in mundane ways. Ridicule or ostracism is the very best such a rebel can expect.

To further emphasize its premium on the abstract, the Apathic society develops its own arcane methodology. Rigorous and ritualized adherence to the methodology becomes the main theme, not the real value of real things in real life. Polishing technique is far superior to gaining anything useful from it.

Finally, its premium on the abstract leads to depersonalization of its members. Its individual human beings merely meld into the abstract All. Discipline in technique, discipline in spirit, discipline in thought are paramount. The individual and subjective "I" must not just be denied, but obliterated.

All these self-contradictions render the Apathic society specious, hypocritical, and characterized by a submerged but pervasive duplicity. It demeans mundane pursuits, but it exploits the mundane produce of outsiders in support of itself. Its members each envisions himself a unique rebel, but he subjugates his individuality to the uniform depersonalization of the abstract. It appears iconoclastic, but it devises and venerates abstract icons of its own.

Internally, the Apathic society controls its membership in similar ways as the Antipathic and Synpathic. It educates its neophytes to uphold its ideals, submit to its discipline, adhere to its methodology, meld into its depersonalization. It rewards and punishes its members in accordance with their respective adherence to its complex rules of conduct and thought. It establishes a status hierarchy, elevating those who lay claim to having impersonally stumbled upon eternal truths to the higher statuses. It assigns those who still toy with mundane things to a lower classification. And it assigns its members social roles befitting their respective statuses.

It proliferates subsystems replicating the core. Each echoes its ideals, methodologies, statuses, and social roles. And it builds and promotes a massive collection of literature and mythology glorifying abstract notions or spirituality and their impersonal expression.

Finally, it controls through leadership. But, as you would expect, its leaders are merely spokesmen for the ideals which they impersonally represent.

Externally, the Apathic society relates to outsiders and other social systems with aloof superiority. The Apathic society will not usually attempt to overpower other social systems as would the Antipathic, or condemn them to damnation as would the Synpathic. Yet it can grow demeaning, rebellious, even violently nihilistic. But unless it finds support from other quarters in its offensive, it cannot sustain it. Apathic systems can and often do stimulate revolution within a larger social system, but invariably lack the power and perseverance to complete it.

Existentially, the Apathic society views its own existence with alien curiosity. For such pure detachment cannot be at home in a universe it believes it transcends. Thus, the Apathic society is confronted by the same existential riddle confronting the Apathic individual. It cannot possibly transcend the mundane existence it believes it transcends.

Consequently, the Apathic society is automatically rendered hopeless simply by virtue of its own existence. But Hopelessness while harbored in real existence contradicts its transcendence. Therefore, the Apathic society must employ the customary defenses against it.

By employing Stoic Detachment, it superficially participates in mundane life while maintaining its belief that it transcends it. By Generalizing its hopelessness, it views the processes of everyday life as exercises in futility. And by resorting to Nihilism, it unconsciously aims at destroying the mundane life it believes it transcends. But the more detached, disparaging, and nihilistic the Apathic society becomes, the more susceptible it grows to its own suicide through nihilistic acts or social disintegration.

SUICIDOGENIC FACTORS

The actualization of its Social Fantastic Self is the goal of every Suicidal Society, regardless of type. But since its actualization is impossible, it can only be metaphysically attempted through social suicide.

Nevertheless, just like the individual Suicide, the Suicidal Society can attain a level of relative equilibrium by striking a precarious balance between its suicidal motivations and its defenses against them. The Suicidal Society can even seem to approach its particular one-sided goal. It can prosper, flourish, even find periods of apparent advantage to the common weal.

However, even in such periods of stability, the Suicidal Society can be imminently dangerous to its suicidal constituents. It can become suicidogenic to some or to entire classes. A society becomes suicidogenic to its constituents by socially reinforcing their suicidal motivations and expressions but not reinforcing the specific defenses against them.

For example, white majority males have a higher rate of completed suicide in the United States than any other class of its constituents. This is because our society reinforces the process leading to Self-Hatred for all its males, but does not reinforce the specific defenses against them for the white majority male. On the other hand, he is expected by society to adhere to his illusions of omnipotence and to follow through on them in his everyday life.

In contrast, the completed suicide rate for minority Black and Hispanic males is dramatically lower. This is because our society coincidentally provides them with reinforcement of their defenses against Self-Hatred. Virtually insurmountable obstacles block all but the most exceptional minority male from expressing his imagined omnipotence in socially condoned ways. Witness the disproportionate prison population, the minority male murder rate, the self-destructive riots principally in minority neighborhoods.

Such Suicidogenic Factors can and do explain this and other variations in completed suicide rates. They even explain why white majority women have the highest rate of suicide attempts in our society. But it would be a serious mistake to focus only on them. For suicidogenic factors are not the root cause of individual suicides for several reasons.

In the first place, suicidogenic factors originate only in Suicidal Societies. And Suicidal Societies originate only in the Suicide Syndrome. Only a society that has already adopted belief in its Social Fantastic Self, with all the inevitable consequences, can reinforce the suicidal motivations of its constituents.

In the second place, it is impossible to interpret individual circumstances strictly on the basis of social phenomena. Look at highway accidents for comparison.[11] Certainly no one could argue that traffic accidents, especially deaths, could not be reduced by improved design of highways and vehicles, driver education programs, more stringent laws and enforcement. But no one could logically argue that these are the only, or even the main, factors involved in each particular accident. And so it is with the incidence of suicide.

Finally, all this is made moot by the simple fact that it is the Suicide's own unconscious convictions which render him susceptible to social suicidogenic factors. Although he may blame social pressures, this is a rationalization. It is his own suicidal motivations which goad him towards suicide.

For without his convictions that he is his omnipotent, innocent, and transcendent Fantastic Self, no society on earth could influence him to kill himself. This conviction, and this conviction alone, lies at the heart of his suicidal impulses.

Part VII

SUICIDAL CRISES

Chapter 23

ORIGINS OF SUICIDAL CRISES

Any situation in which the Suicide becomes motivated or feels driven to attempt the metaphysical actualization of his Fantastic Self constitutes a suicidal crisis. We ordinarily conceive of a crisis as a period of great disturbance to the status quo. But this is an overblown concept of the term. Our word "crisis" is derived from the Greek *krisis* meaning simply "to separate." A crisis is no more than coming upon a separation like a fork in the road ahead. A time of crisis obviously requires nothing more than a decision as to which way to go.

Therefore, every suicidal crisis involves an ultimate, albeit unconscious, decision. Shall the Suicide separate from real life and attempt the metaphysical actualization of his Fantastic Self? Or shall he continue to live, struggling with its real impossibility?

While this decision underlies the always present and harrowing ambivalence associated with a suicidal crisis, it is not exactly how the Suicide experiences his crisis. Since his belief in his Fantastic Self is unconscious, so is the threat of its metaphysical actualization. All the Suicide is usually aware of in a crisis is the ambivalence contingent with the exigencies of his real life situation.

However, each stage of development of the Suicide Syndrome involves factors precipitating suicidal crises peculiar to its own level of complexity. And later crises entail factors peculiar to the Suicide's particular role. But common to all suicidal crises is the Suicide's conviction that he is his Fantastic Self and the impossibility of its actualization in real life.

CHILDHOOD CRISES

Childhood suicidal crises result from the discrepancies between the compensatory value of the suicidal child's rudimentary Fantastic Self and the oppressive reality of his everyday existence. While the suicidal child has just barely escaped with his life from the crushing effects of the earlier contamination of his intrinsic responses, he does not escape with his autonomy, empathy, and spontaneity.

Objective observers of childhood suicidal crises can see that the suicidal child already experiences himself as inefficacious, unlovable, and inhibited from the mainstream of life. They can see that he is already overwhelmed by his feelings of insignificance, anxiety, and tension.

Eight-year-old Johnny Lear is IT in his family. The development of his intrinsic autonomy is no longer the question. He was forced to forfeit that comparatively early in his young life to the spurious demands of his Antipathic father. Nor is the development of his empathy an issue. His Synpathic mother's claims for his love, affection, and attention to her needs in lieu of her recognizing and unconditionally meeting his has dispensed with that. Nor can Johnny realize his spontaneity. The unleashed hostility of his older brother and sister, combined with the repressive conditions of the household, have seen to that.

Instead of expressing his autonomy, empathy, and spontaneity, Johnny desperately tries to survive by adapting to the contingencies of his environment. He desperately tries to meet his father's impossible demands, his mother's need for unlimited affection, and his older siblings' jealous desires to just have Johnny out of the way.

But the members of Johnny's family see the situation quite differently. They see Johnny as the source of their many problems. His difficulties at school are a continual source of embarrassment to his perfectionist father. His sad and despondent expression elicits his mother's guilty wrath. His sudden and inexplicable fits of helpless rage trigger his siblings' ridicule and reprisals.

With no real friends at school, nothing but adversary relations with his siblings, and little but condemnation from his parents, Johnny is alone with his fantasies. Here, he is Spiderman, Batman, and Robin. He is the Incredible Hulk, Superman, and all the other symbolizations of transcendental, benevolent omnipotence rolled up into one. He is the Great Avenger, godlike in his holy crusade for justice, sympathy for the oppressed, vengeance upon their oppressors. Yet all the while, Johnny experiences the pain of his apparent helplessness, the deprivation of his unlovableness, the frustration of his alienation.

His comic book collection, salvaged from his older brother's discards, is all he really has to call his own. Saturday afternoon, he watches through tears as his father burns the collection as Johnny's punishment for getting into more trouble at school. Early Sunday morning, his mother finds Johnny hanging from the shower rod, strangled by his father's favorite belt. On the medicine cabinet mirror, his enigmatic but carefully crayoned note.

YOU BURN ME UP

The dynamics of childhood suicide are not always so glaring. The processes involved in oppressive conditions can be very subtle. Nevertheless, three factors are always present.

One, the suicidal child has already forfeited the development of his intrinsic responses in favor of spurious strategies of survival contingent with his immediate environment. Two, he seeks compensation for the loss and its devastating effects by devising a crudely formed and rudimentary Fantastic Self. And three, he suffers immeasurably from the contrast between the two.

PREADOLESCENT CRISES

Preadolescent suicidal crises arise from failure sufficiently to repress the Fantastic Self. Precipitating factors are somewhat more obscure. Having accepted his familial and social role, the preadolescent Suicide must now become unconsciously convinced of his compensatory one. This is an internal process, and it usually takes place behind a relatively tranquil exterior. But the tranquility can be an ominous facade. A life-and-death struggle rages behind it.

Because of his normally dormant exterior, the preadolescent Suicide often seems the most inexplicable. In the aftermath, virtually no one can find an immediate explanation. Yet the violence of his act often reflects the violence of his internal struggle. The preadolescent, especially, may be prone to kill other people before he kills himself.

Ricky Hines, age twelve, sits sobbing at the family kitchen table, his father's shotgun nestled in his arms. His younger brother and older sister already lie dead in their rooms. His mother, the first to go, lies crumpled in a pool of blood in the living room. Ricky hears his father's car pull into the garage. He takes his position behind the kitchen door. As his father steps through the door Ricky says softly, "Daddy."

Ricky's father turns just in time to see both barrels of the shotgun blast in his face. Tearfully walking to the bathroom, Ricky reloads the gun on the way. With a single shot, he ends his own life.

Only after the police search Ricky's room do the clues to this tragedy begin to fall into place. There are notes in Ricky's desk, drawings in the back of his closet. They tell the story of his violent and terrible struggle within. They illustrate a far different picture of the externally quiet, well-mannered, and docile youth who regularly participated in evening prayers with his family.

It would be virtually impossible to isolate any single incident as precipitating Ricky's multiple-murder-suicide. But regardless of what precipitated Ricky's violence, it was there just waiting to be triggered. Having created his Fantastic Self, Ricky must either repress his belief in it or manifest it full force. Failing to repress it, he wreaks Samson-like destruction on the household around him.

ADOLESCENT CRISES

Adolescent suicidal crises result from interferences with negotiating a satisfactory Adolescent Resolution. Although this, too, is an internal process, external pressures on the adolescent greatly contribute to his difficulties in carrying out his selective repression, fixation, and idealization.

Having repressed his convictions in his Fantastic Self, the adolescent Suicide unconsciously attempts to manifest its attributes in his everyday life. Since it is impossible for him to express omnipotent power, innocent compliance, and transcendent detachment all at the same time, he must fixate and glorify one mode while repressing and despising the others. Interferences assuring his failure to carry this process to relative satisfaction can lead to a suicidal crisis.

Cliff Mayfield, a college freshman, inclines toward the Synpathic resolution. But pressures from his peers, social convention, and especially his father, push him toward the Antipathic. Cliff desperately tries to repress his aggressiveness and detachment. But at the same time, he incurs condemnation for his passivity and noncompetitiveness. Cliff clings to his idealizations of human love and mutual understanding. But society, his peers, and his father promote aggressive independence as ideals for which Cliff should strive.

Turning toward Antipathic aggressiveness on cue from his environment, Cliff not only incurs self-condemnation, but runs into open and undesirable competition from his peers and into unconscious but devastating competition from his father. Turning toward Apathic detachment, he not only encounters condemnation for his passive aloofness, but he suffers deprivation from the absence of closeness with others. Finally, moving back toward his favored Synpathic compliance, he eagerly tries to please his peers and his parents. But he ends displeasing them all simply by his eagerness to please them.

Since domination by others, especially his father, is the story of Cliff's life, he now has nowhere to go. He cannot express omnipotence, innocence, and transcendence simultaneously in mundane life. But he cannot find a way to repress any two of them and still survive. The resulting anxiety immobilizes him. Without his knowing why, suddenly everything seems to be falling apart.

Over the weekend, he tries his best to communicate his desperation to others. On Friday night, he calls home. His mother, sympathetic with his tears, still feels mysteriously repelled by her son's weakness. His father, utterly disgusted, accuses Cliff of being overdramatic. Cliff should learn to act like a man.

Saturday morning, Cliff talks to his roommate. He scoffs at Cliff's veiled allusions to suicide. How could Cliff be so dumb?

Saturday afternoon, he visits his old girlfriend. At first sympathetic, she becomes intimidated by Cliff's thinly disguised blackmail tactics in trying to win her back. She ends by telling him to get lost.

Growing more desperate by Sunday, Cliff calls the student crisis hotline. "Hey. Man. I hear you. We all get—you know—existentially alienated—you know—by all the shit in this world," the psychology student answering the telephone tells him.

Monday, Cliff cuts class. He spends the day at the library reading Schopenhauer and writing his Last Will and Testament. Twenty pages long, it tells of missed opportunities, misunderstandings, mistreatment. Everything he could call his own, he wills to someone in his life. Yet no one could miss the vindictive slant of his choices.

To his parents goes the double-knit leisure suit they gave him for his last birthday. "I've never worn it," he writes, "because I hate double-knit almost as much as I hate leisure suits. Next time," he continues, "give me jeans."

That night, Cliff jumps from his twelfth-story dormitory window.

POSTADOLESCENT CRISES

Postadolescent suicidal crises are precipitated by interferences with the Suicide establishing an effective defense system. Again, external pressures play a major part. The postadolescent is only slightly less susceptible to outside influences than is the adolescent.

Having artificially resolved the opposing attributes of his Fantastic Self during adolescence, the young Suicide must still contend with the suicidal motivations it inevitably generates. As he develops into adulthood he will begin to devise and employ the customary defenses against their expressions along with suitable rationalizations. But in the period immediately following his resolution, and prior to his developing effective defenses against his suicidal motivations, he is highly vulnerable to them.

Pam Baker, a young paralegal, negotiates her adolescent resolution with particular difficulty. But she does manage to fix on the Antipathic Role. She fixates omnipotent power, assertiveness, and competitiveness. She represses innocent compliance and transcendent detachment. Then Pam runs into trouble.

Societal and familial pressures work against her assertiveness. Pam's growing hostility, arrogance, and rigidity work against her establishing satisfactory relations with others. But, on top of all that, Pam encounters special difficulties in establishing a socially condoned sexual identity during her adolescent predicament. Pam ends with an added sexual confusion which taxes her ability to establish an effective defense system.

Homosexuality does not necessarily accompany the Antipathic role in females. Indeed, the two have little connection with each other. But because of other factors, Pam's heterosexuality never gets established. Pam runs into particular difficulties because our society is not very accepting of its Antipathic women. In addition, Pam gets continually rejected by vulnerable young men on account of her aggressiveness. And she continually rejects them on account of her own competitiveness. Finally, Pam settles on a pretty young friend, Joanne, as a lover.

But at the same time, Pam tries to establish a defense system generally based on her family's Fundamentalist Protestant ethic. In later, more experienced years, she might be able to rationalize the obvious conflict away. The rationalizations of the mature Suicide's defense system are marvelously flexible. But having just worked through her adolescent resolution with particular difficulties, Pam is not up to the task.

When Joanne begins to resolve her own identity problems, she abandons Pam in favor of a sympathetic young man. Having little or no defenses to reinforce her adolescent resolution, Pam falls apart. She goes to her parents' home for a weekend to seek solace. But instead of finding comfort, she encounters intractable rejection.

Both parents castigate Pam for her sinful ways. Her mother feigns a heart attack. Her father, seeking reinforcements, calls in their minister to help wash Pam of her sins. The neighbors, quickly learning of the scandal, don't want to "get caught in the middle."

Pam fights back, but the odds are against her. The collective condemnation, added to her own Self-Hatred, overcomes her. Sunday evening she returns to her city apartment and ingests a bottle of sleeping pills.

ADULT CRISES

Adult suicidal crises are precipitated by contradictions to the Suicide's Fantastic Self. The adult Suicide, having by now devised an elaborate system of defenses designed to protect him from his suicidal motivations, nevertheless remains infinitely vulnerable to them. Despite his defenses, his suicidal motivations remain as powerful as ever, just waiting to be triggered. Even though his defenses may lend him a superficial stasis, he treads his way through the course of his life like an infantryman through a minefield, unconsciously fearing each step of the way might expose him to the explosiveness of his own self-destructiveness.

However, the primary suicidal motivation for each type differs and corresponds to type. Each type has his own set of precipitating factors, reaction to crisis, and suicidal methodology. While these differences are extremely important, they are often confusing or obscured.

For instance, Harold, Ruth, or Carl may each incur a suicidal crisis precipitated by a similar event such as a loss, failure, or rejection. Yet each one's crisis is precipitated by radically different reasons. Furthermore, the complexities growing out of each of their reactions to crises compounds the confusion.

But as we shall see in the following chapters, common to all adult suicidal crises is the challenge reality presents to the fixed attribute of the Fantastic Self and the unconscious decision to attempt its metaphysical actualization through suicide.

LATE LIFE CRISES

Late life crises arise from contradictions to the immortality of the Suicide's Fantastic Self inherent in the debilitating effects of aging and the inexorable prospect of impending natural death.

As with the earlier childhood and adolescent crises, familial and social factors appear to play a more obvious part. But familial and social factors notwithstanding, the older Suicide's conviction in his immortal Fantastic Self and the process growing out of it are the real causes of his suicide.

Having survived repeated onslaughts on account of the syndrome on his organismic vitality, the aging Suicide must still face his natural physical decline and his inevitable demise. His more destructive defenses, dangerous before, can now spell his termination. In his weakened state, a token concession, surrogate sacrifice, or act of nihilism that might have brought him to the brink before, can now bring him to his end.

On top of that, our society does not treat its elderly too well. Many social systems reinforce suicidal impulses in their aging constituents. Cast out from the mainstream to a degree proportionate to his incapacity to contribute to or epitomize the social goal, the aging Suicide finds scant support for defending against his suicidal impulses.

Nevertheless, the suicidal impulses which he must defend against can originate only with the Suicide Syndrome. The elderly Suicide, just like all other Suicides, is self-destructive solely because of his belief that he is his Fantastic Self.

However, in late life crises, the immortality of his Fantastic Self plays a more prominent part. While the debilitating effects of aging and the proximity of natural death also challenge his omnipotence, innocence, and transcendence, these challenges pale in the light of that presented to his immortality on several accounts.

First, the aging Suicide can muster up a host of defensive rationalizations regarding most challenges to his omnipotence, innocence, or transcendence. He obviously has accumulated considerable experience and expertise at devising them. Secondly, the elderly Suicide can usually count on years of hopeless resignation having blunted or diffused his particular one-sided idealizations. While resignation does not cancel his unconscious convictions, its ameliorating effects tend to diffuse their active expressions. And thirdly, just because of his practiced rationalizations and the diffusing effects of his resignation, his Fantastic Self's immortality overshadows its omnipotence, innocence, and transcendence.

Yet while the Fantastic Self's immortality becomes the central issue in late life suicidal crises, traces of the Suicide's old fixed attribute still appear. In the end, regardless of the blunting effect of his advancing years, the Suicide still clings to signs of his primary motivation.

Rose Ashby walks to the dry cleaner's to pick up her old but finest dinner dress. Although shaken at the cost of having it cleaned, Rose tells the sympathetic girl behind the counter, "Don't worry. It doesn't matter. I won't be needing the money any more."

Walking through the streets of St. Petersburg, Florida, she still wishes it had been Miami. The west coast of the fountain of youth peninsula is not as warm as the east. If only Chet had left more insurance money, Rose could have afforded Miami. In St. Petersburg, Rose failed to unearth de Leon's promised fount.

Last week, she told the doctor she felt lonely and depressed. He said she should perk up. She had everything to live for. What does he know? Has he lost a husband like Chet, and his left breast to cancer all in one year? Has he suffered arthritis all his life? Were his ovaries so bad he had to undergo a hysterectomy? Did he have to suffer through menopause just to end up alone without family or friends? Does he have to live in a dungeon? Is his furniture worn, his carpet threadbare? What does he know? Might his every day be the last one for him?

As Rose turns into the walk to her white cinderblock apartment building, fat Mrs. Green asks if she is coming to the community center that evening. Who needs it? The social worker did say Rose should come. Since Rose was in such good health, she could help those not so well as she.

Help them do what? Finger-paint like little children? Make baskets like insane people? Sew? Who can see to sew? Besides, who would appreciate it? Who would thank her? Who could she tell about her troubles? Who cares?

When she told the doctor she couldn't sleep, he gave her the prescription but said that all elderly people have trouble sleeping. What does he know? Does he have a middle-aged daughter who can only think about her latest divorce, or grandchildren who only acknowledge her birthday check by the endorsement on the back? Are all his friends dead and gone? Is all the money from her dead husband's insurance used up? What does he know? Who could sleep in this dungeon?

Back in her apartment, Rose washes and sets her hair. It's good she has to do it herself. Look at this hair. So thin, so sparse, so frowsy. What would a hairdresser think?

Then make-up. Base. Rouge. Lipstick. Bright red. Perfume? No! No cheap perfume for Rose today. Remember the bottles of *Joy* Chet would buy for her? He always wanted her to have the best. He would boast that she had everything, and that she never had to work a day in her life for it.

"She doesn't have to lift her little finger," Chet would say, puffing on his cigar. Where is the *Joy* now? Dead and gone. With Chet. Rose manages a wry laugh at the play on words.

Slipping into her dinner dress, she looks into the dresser mirror. "It's good you can't see this face now, Chet. How old and ugly it looks."

Taking some lavender notepaper from the drawer, she stands at the dresser to write. Why didn't anyone warn her that growing old was like this? It is so unfair. But they don't care. People don't care about anyone except themselves.

Leaving the note on the dresser, she suddenly feels excited. Breathing hard now, she rushes to the sink—who could call a sink in the counter in the living room a kitchen?—and gets a glass of water.

Trying to relax, Rose arranges the folds in her skirt as she settles down on the chaise. Carefully sipping the water as she takes all the capsules so as to not smear her lipstick, Rose quietly begins to sob. After a lifetime of tears, these will be her last. Her note on the dresser is short, written to no one and to everyone.

You don't know what it is like
to have to grow old and die.

Chapter 24

ANTIPATHIC SELF-MURDER

Harold Roberts, our adult Antipathic Type Suicide, unconsciously believes he is omnipotent. In his lifelong attempt to manifest his Omnipotent Fantastic Self, Harold strives for power, mastery, and control over himself, other people, and life. But regardless of the scope of his real achievements, Harold obviously cannot achieve his imagined omnipotence. Instead, Harold becomes hostile, arrogant, and rigid.

But because Harold believes he is omnipotent, he cannot admit to any motivations beyond his conscious control. He must think he behaves, believes, and relates to others as he wants to. Consequently, Harold must identify with his unconscious expressions of Self-Hatred, Vindictiveness, and Hopelessness.

His unconscious expressions of Vindictiveness pose him little problem in this respect. Although he can never face their origins, in many ways their expressions reinforce his illusions of omnipotence quite well. It is only right for someone with his superior powers to lodge external claims against others, to voice his accusations and contempt for them, and to enforce his vindictive retaliation against them.

The same holds true for his unconscious expressions of Hopelessness. His abstract values reflect his idealization of power. His chronic discontent derives from his dog-eat-dog perspective of life. His resignation mirrors his belief in the survival of the fittest.

On the surface, even Harold's identification with his expressions of Self-Hatred seems to work. What we see as his Inner Dictates, he sees as self-discipline. What we see as his Self-Accusations and Self-Contempt, he sees as the voice of his conscience. What we see as his Self-Defeat and Self-Punishment, he sees as the law of the jungle.

However, the self-destructive consequences of these expressions are another matter. In order to maintain his illusions, Harold must blind himself to the consequences of his Self-Hatred by employing defenses against them. Through Checks and Avoidances, he evades challenges to his imagined omnipotence, thereby keeping his Self-Hatred at bay. By Externalizing, he displaces his own Self-Hatred onto others. By making Token Concessions to his hateful inner tyrant, he placates it.

Of course, Harold's defenses do take their toll. They grow increasingly destructive on their own account. But Harold can usually rationalize their self-destructiveness away. After all, in the perpetual heat of battle, almost any rationalization makes sense.

The inherent explosiveness of Antipathic Harold's condition becomes increasingly clear. Unable to manifest the impossible criteria of his Fantastic Self, he automatically grows to hate himself. He represses his Self-Hatred, but nevertheless must express it. He then must employ defenses against the consequences, however self-destructive his defenses may become. Finally, just because he cannot admit that he dances to the tune of his murderous tyrant within, he commits suicide on this account.

PRECIPITATING FACTORS

The Antipathic Type suicides primarily on account of Self-Hatred. Some Vindictiveness and Hopelessness also enter the picture, but their expressions are secondary. Harold customarily expresses them in all facets of his life, anyway. His suicide does not constitute an exception.

But because Harold cannot come to terms with his Self-Hatred, its expressions, and the necessity and nature of his defenses against it, he renders himself infinitely vulnerable to it. The power of his unconscious Self-Hatred expands to awesome proportions. No real threat to his real existence can measure up to the absolute existential terror Harold experiences in the face of his own Self-Hatred.

Indeed, Harold's Self-Hatred is so utterly terrifying and so ultimately self-destructive, just their potential for eliciting it lends the casualties of everyday life considerable power over him. Thus, the Suicide Syndrome hangs like a double-edged sword over Harold's very existence. In order to stay alive, he must constantly persevere towards manifesting his impossible omnipotence. At the same time, he must constantly guard against coming face-to-face with its impossibility.

Anything contradicting Harold's imagined omnipotence and breaking through his defenses, eliciting his Self-Hatred, can precipitate a suicidal crisis for him.

Of course, Harold faces actual contradictions to his omnipotence every day. But through his defenses, he can usually rationalize these contradictions away, convincing even the people around him. The Antipathic Type is so convinced of his rightness and so convincing in his expression of it, he has little difficulty in convincing others, too.

So when a suicidal crisis does arise it usually catches everyone, including Harold, by complete surprise. The last thing Harold and the people around him would ordinarily expect is for him to become suicidal. After all, suicide is for the weak not for the powerful, and fearless. But despite Harold's mastery, his unconscious defenses, and his convincing rationalizations, situations can arise for which he is not prepared.

First, the situation may contradict Harold's imagined omnipotence in a subjectively important area where he is accustomed to gaining spurious confirmation of it. As we know, Harold spends his life trying to gain confirmation of his illusions of omnipotence. A sudden or undeniable reversal, especially in such an area of importance, can precipitate his crisis.

Secondly, the situation may circumvent or come into conflict with his customary defenses. It may comprise a unique challenge to his omnipotence that he cannot evade through his customary Checks and Avoidances. Circumstances may somehow prevent him from fully Externalizing the Self-Hatred resulting from it. His Token Concessions may be too little or too late. The situation may be so laden with Self-Hatred, Harold just cannot muster sufficient defenses against it.

Thirdly, and most ironically, Harold may escalate his defenses to the level that they grow beyond his ability to rationalize. The debilitating consequence of his defenses could bring him such profound shame and arouse such massive amounts of additional Self-Hatred, he cannot find any more defenses to fight it off nor any more rationalizations left to explain it.

Any of these situations could precipitate a suicidal crisis in Harold. However, most crises are accumulative. An event of the first kind triggers Harold's defenses, a situation of the second kind prevents him from carrying his defenses out to satisfaction, and a condition of the third kind finally does him in. But regardless of how the Antipathic Type's suicidal crisis comes about, it always arrives through the complex ramifications of his Self-Hatred.

REACTION TO CRISIS

The saga of Harold's everyday life can be encapsulated in his reaction to a suicidal crisis. In his everyday life, Harold attempts to manifest his impossible omnipotence while, at the same time, he tries to defend against the Self-Hatred resulting from its impossibility. In a suicidal crisis, Harold pursues exactly the same goals. But once in a crisis, his pursuit becomes a battle between the forces of life and of death. Not surprisingly, Antipathic Harold fights for his life with all the fury he can muster.

In his furious attempt to regain his imagined omnipotence, Harold strikes out at everything and everyone in sight. And since his expressions of Vindictiveness and Hopelessness tend to reinforce his illusions of omnipotence, he automatically escalates all of them.

But at the same time Harold desperately tries to make his Empirical Self appear omnipotent to his Fantastic Self, he still must defend it from the consequences of his Self-Hatred, by escalating his defenses against Self-Hatred. By escalating his Checks and Avoidances, he tries to retreat from the field of battle; by escalating his Externalizing, he grows even more paranoid; by escalating his Token Concessions, he incurs additional losses.

Harold's vacillations between attempting to manifest his omnipotence and trying to defend against Self-Hatred can generate considerable confusion. In a suicidal crisis, Harold appears manic-depressive with overtones of paranoia. On the one hand, he is driven to manic excess in the futile attempt to manifest his omnipotence. Yet on the other hand, he must defensively depress his activities, feelings, and responses. With the added suspicions his externalizations bring forth, the normally self-controlled Harold becomes tossed about in a torrent of confusion.

His escalation of Vindictiveness and Hopelessness only add to the turmoil. How could the invincible *him* be drawn into suicidal impulses on account of Vindictiveness towards others? Discouragement and despair is for the weak, not the omnipotent. In the end, his escalated expressions of Vindictiveness and Hopelessness generate additional Self-Hatred by the shame that they cause him.

Finally, Harold's last-ditch attacks against other people and life can be very misleading regarding his true suicidal motivations. Because of these attacks it could be assumed that Harold originally aims his rage against other people and, in the absence of satisfaction, turns it against himself. But Harold merely strikes out at others as a means of forestalling the inevitable strike against himself. His Empirical Self desperately tries to prove his omnipotence to his murderous Fantastic Self before it is too late.

Should he succeed in making himself look sufficiently powerful, then his Fantastic Self might let him off the hook. But should the circumstantial evidence against his omnipotence outweigh his efforts to demonstrate it, then his Fantastic Self will strike.

Antipathic Harold's omnipotent and immortal Fantastic Self murders his impotent and hated Empirical Self.

SUICIDAL METHODOLOGY

Harold's suicide holds forth three false promises to him. One, suicide promises the ultimate expression of his unconscious Self-Hatred. Harold, in effect, murders himself in a fit of uncontrollable rage.

Two, suicide paradoxically promises him escape from having to face the existential terror of his unconscious Self-Hatred. Absolutely nothing he might face in life or in death could be so terrifying to him.

Three, suicide is the only way Harold can metaphysically actualize his Omnipotent Fantastic Self. Only by murdering his hated Empirical Self could Harold become his imaginary immortal Fantastic Self.

Because Harold's suicidal impulses are motivated by the Self-Hatred of which he is significantly unaware, they can sneak up on him completely unforeseen. The otherwise careful planner can make a sudden decision and carry it out before he even has a chance to be aware he made it; or he may come to a carefully considered decision and meticulously carry it out in minute detail.

In neither case is he aware of his true motivations. In the case of a sudden impulse, his true motivation does not have time to sink in. In the latter case, he usually preoccupies himself with the secondary vindictive and hopeless elements involved. With smiling satisfaction he mulls over how his demise will affect those who depend upon him— often planning his suicide to coincide with a situation when they will need him the most.

But whether Harold carefully plans his suicide or does it quickly and impulsively, he nearly always chooses a highly lethal method. When it comes to suicide, the Antipathic Type does not fool around with half-hearted measures. He rarely needs a second try. For that matter, he rarely gets a second chance.

Most often, his methodology lies somewhere between careful planning and sudden impulse. He may make detailed and meticulous plans including alternate times and methods. He may then lay his plans aside or hold them in abeyance, only to execute them suddenly, or follow still another unplanned but equally sure method, on impulse.

Because of his decisiveness, he seldom has time for a note. Moreover, he usually lacks the motivation to leave one. The last thing Harold wants is sympathy or understanding for his plight. And a note would only serve to humiliate him. He and only he knows what he has to do. And only he has the power to do it. After all, is he not his Omnipotent Fantastic Self?

HAROLD'S SUICIDE

With his usual lightning speed and irrevocable conclusiveness, Harold Roberts makes a decision. And, like all his decisions, this brings him a satisfying peace. He places the files in his attaché case and snaps it shut. Leaning back in his chair, he swivels it around to gaze out the window. He says to himself, "Done!"

From his twenty-fifth floor perspective, he surveys his domain. The river to his left echoes the city lights in shimmering reflections. Straight ahead, the central business district glows in the distance. To his right, headlights streak along the freeway. All his frenzied desperation of the last few days dissipates into the view. Now quietly and calmly, he feels the energy of the city below pumping new strength into his veins.

Without looking, he reaches behind him to the master panel on his chrome and rosewood desk. He dims the office lights.

"Done!" he repeats to himself. "Over and done with at last!" Without realizing it, he is standing. His chest expands. His head pushes high. Power surges through his body. His eyes glow with the brightness of the city lights below.

Again, hardly looking, he reaches back and grasps the attaché case from his desk. With one powerful swing, he spins and shatters the glass before him. The highly tempered glass crumbles into pop-cornlike pieces as in one continuous motion, he hurls himself out the window, attaché case in hand.

LOCAL DEVELOPER DIES FROM FALL

Harold A. Roberts, 49, a local real estate developer, died last night when he plunged from his twenty-fifth floor office window. Roberts, president of Harco Enterprises, and developer of East-Town Mall, Roberts Towers, and other local landmarks, apparently fell through his office window. . .

Marge Clevenger, private secretary to Harold Roberts, sits on the sofa in his office where she had sat so many times before. A large piece of plywood occupies a section of the glass wall across the room. Tears are forming in her eyes, again. She had cried uncontrollably early that morning after the shock of the call. Then, mechanically, she dressed and drove to the office to answer questions posed by the officers.

"Do you know of any reason Mr. Roberts would take his own life?"

"No!" Marge says. "No, I don't."

"We understand that there has been a problem with the government. Securities and Exchange Commission? Was Mr. Roberts depressed about that?"

"Not really. He is—was—accustomed to business problems. He knew that they didn't have—that their case was completely unfounded."

A few more questions. She wondered how many thousands of vague lies she had told for Harold Roberts in the eight years she had worked for him.

Now she was feeling the pain of it all. How could she have admired him and hated him so much at the same time? How could she have feared him, sensing all along how afraid he was behind that implacable front? How could she have felt so used by him, and still be willing for him to use her some more? How could she have listened to his stories of the past, his great moments of glory, all the while know-ing he painted such an idealized picture of it?

Looking into the chrome and glass étagere, she focuses on the brown leather holster holding his old carpenter tools. She remembers the stories of his carpenter years, his struggle to make foreman, his decision to start contracting on his own. Then, just a few years later, the bankruptcy.

"My world fell apart," he would say. "I lost my business, my wife, my friends, everything. That's the way it is with women. They stick with you till the goin' gets rough. Then, just when you finally need 'em, like they've always wanted you to do, they get goin'. What a dumb bitch she was," he would continue. "But believe me, she was plenty sorry later. Plenty sorry!"

Then, the real estate business. Again, the meteoric rise. As he would tell her about it, Marge would think, "He's talking like he took over the whole world, not just some little real estate company."

"She tried to tell me that she never wanted to leave," he would say, relating how his wife begged him to let her come back. "She said I drove her away. That she really loved me all along. Bullshit! Now that I was back in the green she loved me again. But don't worry. I told her just exactly what her love meant to me then. It wasn't worth the sweat off my balls. That's what."

Then, the divorce. How he humiliated her in court. Emotion-ally unstable, no skills, no ambition. "What difference did it make to him?" Marge would wonder when he recited the story. There was so little at stake. Why did he have to humiliate her?

Yet when he would say, "She got hers. She got hers, at last!" for some mysterious reason Marge would agree that his wife had de-served it all along.

How sheepish he looked when he told her he was getting married again.

"I met her at the club," he said as they sat together in his office af-ter Friday closing when the other employees were gone. "Her family is old-line establishment, landed pioneers of this great city."

She couldn't tell whether he was joking or not. He was so sarcastic most of the time, even about himself. Smiling, he said, " My mother used to talk about the Fairchilds. They have this big old mansion over on Hickory. Brought all the woodwork over from Europe, that kind of stuff. Isn't it something? Hal Roberts making that kind of connec-tion!"

"I hope that you will be very happy," she murmured.

"Happy? Christ, I've never been happy in my life," he laughed. "What the hell is happiness, anyway? You know what I always say, 'Happy people never get anywhere.'"

At home that night she thought about their conversation. A sudden but confusing sadness overcame her. How could she feel so very sorry for Harold, but at the same time admire him so? He accomplished so much, but then, there were his depressions.

Once, after she had visited her family over the weekend, he talked about his own parents. "My father was really strict when I was little. I'd get the hell beat out of me regularly, no matter what I did. One time—I don't know how old I was, ten or twelve, maybe—he started spanking me because I wouldn't say 'Sir' to him. It must have gone on for hours. I know that it seemed like forever to me. I couldn't help but cry, I was so goddamn mad, but I wasn't gonna call him 'Sir' no matter what he did.

"Well, I was crying. My mother was crying. Even my little sister was crying. But he just kept slamming away with his belt. Christ! I was stubborn, but I finally gave in. Then, he really rubbed it in on me. He kept asking if I was ever not gonna say 'Sir' to him again, and I had to keep sayin' over and over again, 'No, Sir. No, Sir. No, Sir.'"

He went on, "Mother said I was always stubborn, even when I was little. I must have been born that way. Well, I'll tell you what. I'm glad. It taught me to be a man. It was tough, but now I know that I can take anything. No one can ever get the best of me again. I wouldn't be where I am today," he would say, waving his arm as though his private domain encompassed the entire world, "if I hadn't learned to be a man."

Picking up the EastTown Mall brochure on the coffee table in front of her, Marge remembers the first time he told her about planning it. "The old Fairchild homestead land! A hundred and twenty acres! Over a million square feet of department stores and shops. What do you think of that?"

She couldn't tell him what she really thought. In a flash, she remembered him calling his new wife's family "landed pioneers" and, of course, she understood. She did manage to ask, "What do they—the Fairchilds—think of it?"

"Shit! They know that the old place has to go. Look where it sits," he said, waving his hand in the direction of the city map on the wall. "It would be a crime to let that valuable land go to waste, just for that old house. But I'll do something with the house when we tear it down. Maybe we can take some of that old European woodwork out of it and build a classy little gazebo inside the mall." He laughed. "Besides, I promised them I'd put up a bronze plaque. You know, 'Here stood the Fairchild Mansion, built in 1845, etcetera, etcetera, etcetera.'"

It took four years to get EastTown Mall completed. Four years of working night and day by everyone in the office. A few weeks before the Grand Opening, Harold said, "Well, it's done. It's over and done with now."

"Not quite," she replied. "There's still. . ."

"Oh, I don't mean EastTown," he said, "I mean Roberts Towers." To her puzzled look, he told her about the new twenty-five story office building he was planning and about the complicated and slightly shady real estate trust he planned to create to finance it.

"How can you say that a new project is over and done with, Harold? We haven't even finished the mall."

With a condescending look, he explained, "Look, Marge. It's the decision, the concept, the idea. That's what counts. The rest is just putting it into effect. That's nothing."

"Four years of working night and day is nothing," she repeated to herself as she cried herself to sleep that night. The next morning, she arrived at the office having decided to tell him she was through. There were roses on her desk. From him. She knew then she would never quit.

The Friday night after they moved into the new building, only three years later this time, she found him slumped in the new leather chair in his office. "Another depression," she thought.

Mixing him a drink, she tried to cheer him. "Roberts Towers! What do you think of that? And here you are, sitting on the top floor of your. . ."

"You know," he interrupted, "nothing I ever did was good enough for my parents. I'd make an 'A', and they'd want to know why not all 'A's. I'd make all 'A's, and they'd tell me how easy high school must have gotten. I'd study things outside of school, and they'd tell me, 'All work and no play makes Jack a dull boy!' I'd start playing around, and they'd say I was wasting my time."

"Most parents are like that," she said. "Mine are."

He continued, as though he hadn't heard her. "I sometimes wish that they could see me now, sitting here. But, do you know what they would say? 'Twenty-five stories? Shit. The building across town is forty.'"

"Most parents are like that," she repeated. "Mine are."

He looked up with fire in his eyes. "Who gives a shit about your parents? They wouldn't know an achievement if one hit them in the face."

She tried to talk back. "What do you mean? They're educated." She wondered how he always put her on the defensive. Not just her. Everyone.

He softened a little. "I know they're educated. That's not what I mean. Look, I'm just tired. Forget it."

She softened, too. He could always get her to soften. "Why are you doing this, Harold? I know what you're getting out of it financially, and it's not all that much, except on paper. What are you trying to do, impress your dead father?"

"Of course not," he replied. Then, after a pause, "I don't know, Marge. I've asked myself a thousand times, 'Why?' Sometimes I wish that I was still pounding six-penny nails then going home and fucking my old lady all night."

"You could do something you want to do. You already have a wife."

"Shit, Marge. Marianne and I haven't fucked in months. And not for months before that. Even then we 'made love.' You know Marianne."

Marge was incredulous. Not at what he was saying. She suspected that all along. But that he would admit it, even to her. For some reason, she wanted to cry. "But that's beside the point. I was talking about why you're. . ."

"Well, I don't know the answer to that. I know that there must be something wrong, but I don't know what. Besides, there's the SEC thing with the trust. You know they are trying to get me, and they just might succeed. The crazy part about it is that I knew it would come to this all along, but I went ahead."

Again, she was shocked he would admit it. "Do you think that maybe you could see a psychiatrist?"

"Are you serious? Those bastards are just a bunch of crazies!"

"Then what now?" she asked.

"I don't know, Marge. I don't know." He looked forlorn. "Why don't you go on home? There's nothing for you to do here."

A few weeks later, Harold began to look uncharacteristically disheveled. Then there were the auditors, the accountants, the attorneys, the investigators. An article appeared in the newspaper. It mentioned rumors of a pending indictment. Harold was staying at the office almost every night, staring out the window and drinking. One Sunday, he called Marge at home to ask where some correspondence was filed. Before hanging up, he said, "By the way, I guess you should know in case you need to locate me. I've moved out of the house. I'm staying at the Park Plaza Hotel."

Yesterday, he seemed in a panic. There was a horrifying look of fear in his eyes. She wanted to help him, to say something to him to make him feel better. But the words wouldn't come. Finally, she felt she could stand it no longer. At the close of the day, she went to his office. He was turned with his back to the door, looking out at the view. "I want to talk to you," she said.

He turned, and her heart sank. She had not known him ever to look this way before. Terror was in his eyes. "This man," she thought, "so strong, so determined. How could he be so afraid?"

"Is it the SEC investigation?"

"No," he answered, his voice flat and low. "I'm not worried about that. I can handle them. Even if they do find something, it would still be a long, drawn-out battle. They probably could never really get me on it." He turned back to face the window.

She strained to see his eyes, wishing he would turn around. "Then what is it? Is it Marianne? I've never seen you like this."

Without turning, he replied, his voice still flat and low, "No. It's not Marianne. She's never meant anything to me."

"Then for heaven's sake, Harold. What is it?"

"I don't know. I just don't know." His voice began to break. She could see his shoulders slump, his head bow. "I couldn't admit it to anyone but you, Marge, but I'm about to cave in, and I don't even know why." He was sobbing.

She took a step forward, "Is there anything I can do?"

He snickered sarcastically, "That's what Marianne asked. There's nothing she can do and there's nothing you can do. There's nothing anyone can do. Whatever it is, I have to do it myself."

"Harold." She spoke sharply, willing to take risks now. "Can't you for once admit that you need someone's help. Do you always have to be the one who. . ."

He wheeled about, pointing his finger straight at her eyes. "Listen to me," spitting his words out, "who the hell can I depend on? Sure you want to help. You want to preserve your job, right? Marianne wants to help. She doesn't want the holy Fairchild name dirtied, right? Everyone wants to help, but just to save their own damn necks.

"Well, I'll tell you. I don't need any help and I don't want any help. Not from you, and not from anyone else!" He swiveled his chair back to face the window.

She felt crushed. "I'm not trying to save my job, Harold. You know that. I'm concerned about you."

Slowly, he turned and rose from his chair. "Thank you. Yes, I do know that," he said, quite simply. He even smiled and hugged her. "But there's nothing you can do. Don't worry. Everything will be all right. I'm OK now."

A police officer is saying, "The security people want us to lock up. Everyone else is gone. Sorry, but you'll have to leave."

After looking around the room once more, she goes home.

Chapter 25

SYNPATHIC DEATH ON
THE ENEMY'S DOORSTEP

Ruth Parsons, our typical Synpathic Suicide, is unconsciously convinced she is Innocent. She unconsciously believes she is absolutely altruistic, ultimately benign, and infinitely deserving. She believes she cannot even know evil, let alone express it. Her ultimate, albeit unconscious, goal in life is to manifest her Innocent Fantastic Self.

Ruth seeks love to validate her innocence. Loving and being loved are all that really matter to Ruth. But since she must repress her aggressive independence in order to maintain her illusion of innocence, she loves through passive dependence. Yet regardless of how much she may or may not actually be loved, no amount of love can make Ruth into her impossible Fantastic Self. Instead of experiencing her actual Empirical Self as absolutely altruistic, ultimately benign, and infinitely deserving, Ruth ends up feeling abused, inadequate, and deprived.

Furthermore, since Ruth must repress her independent aggressiveness, what she feels and how she relates to others must derive from circumstances beyond her autonomous volition. As a result,

Ruth passively accepts her expressions of Self-Hatred, Vindictiveness, and Hopelessness.

Ruth's passive acceptance of her expressions of Self-Hatred cause her to feel more abused, inadequate, and deprived. Constantly putting herself down, she feels utterly worthless and unlovable. But all this is worth its price in order to reinforce her unconscious belief in her innocence.

Ruth's passive acceptance of her expressions of Hopelessness also escalates her feeling abused, inadequate, and deprived. She often wonders if she can make it through just one more day. But it is also worth its price to her. After all, the more abused, inadequate, and deprived she is, the more innocent she must be.

However, even though Ruth also passively accepts her unconscious expressions of Vindictiveness, she can never face their vindictive intent. Since she is innocent, she must be infinitely loving, understanding, and forgiving of others. Should Ruth get just a hint of her own need for vengeance, she always looks to other people or outside circumstances for its cause. For Ruth not only believes she is not vindictive. She unconsciously believes she inherently cannot be, even should she try.

But we have seen the true origins and nature of Ruth's Vindictiveness. We know she expresses it in many oblique ways even more effectively than Harold and Carl express theirs.

She stakes her External Claims passively but effectively. While she may seem merely to long for their satisfaction, underneath she really believes she deserves them. She displays her contempt for other people by denying them their humanity, then accusing them of being inhuman. Finally, she retaliates against other people in manifold passive but extremely potent ways.

While Ruth generally remains unaware that she expresses her Vindictiveness, other people do not. The closer people get to Ruth, the more they experience her Vindictiveness and the more they react accordingly. Consequently, pinning all her hopes on unlimited love to validate her imagined innocence, Ruth is invariably denied it.

To avoid the unbearable humiliation contingent with denial of her innocence, Ruth must resort to defenses against the consequences of her own Vindictiveness. She employs Passive Withdrawal, retreating from intimate contact to forestall the humiliation. She Internalizes her Vindictiveness, turning her rage against others back against herself. And she makes Surrogate Sacrifices, sacrificing her own well-being as surrogate for the persons she unconsciously rages against.

Ruth's defenses are extremely self-destructive. Passive withdrawal denies her close contact with those essential to her secret goals. Her internalized vindictiveness causes her additional suffering; her surrogate sacrifices take her to the brink of life's termination. But all of this is necessary to Ruth in order for her to maintain her illusion of innocence.

The terrible poignancy of Ruth's situation shows clearly through her defenses. Unable to gain the impossible affirmation of her Innocent Fantastic Self from other people, she grows infinitely vindictive of them. She represses her Vindictiveness but nevertheless must express it. She must then employ defenses protecting her illusions from the consequences of these expressions, regardless of how self-destructive her defenses grow. And, finally, just because her imagined innocence will not allow her to admit to her own Vindictiveness, she suicides on its account.

PRECIPITATING FACTORS

The Synpathic Type suicides primarily on account of Vindictiveness. Certainly, Self-Hatred and Hopelessness also enter the picture. Along with Ruth's defenses, their expressions characterize her everyday life. Her crises cannot depart from this pattern. So when a crisis does occur, it appears to derive from these other motivations, which is how Ruth invariably experiences it.

But regardless of appearances, just because Ruth cannot confront her own Vindictiveness, recognize its expressions, and dispense with her defenses against it, she suicides because of it. For the power of Ruth's Vindictiveness grows to terrifying proportions.

Indeed, Ruth's fear of her own Vindictiveness lies at the bottom of her helpless vulnerability. It renders her infinitely vulnerable to other people's way of relating to her and to the casual events of life. For anything contradicting Ruth's imagined innocence, humiliating her, and thereby eliciting her Vindictiveness, can precipitate a suicidal crisis.

Of course, situations contradicting Ruth's innocence arise every day. But Ruth can usually absorb these contradictions by virtue of her customary defenses. Even other people can become convinced of the unconscious pretenses her defenses allow her. Ruth appears so self-effacing that there is not a possibility she could harbor murderous wishes towards others. But there is usually little doubt about her murderous wishes towards herself. All her expressions of Self-Hatred and Hopelessness and all her defenses to Vindictiveness appear concert-edly aimed just at herself.

So when a suicidal crisis does arise, no one around is really sur-prised. Least of all, Ruth. The only element of surprise connected with Ruth's suicidal crisis would be that this time, she might really do it.

Just such a potentially lethal crisis can arise when other people or the casual events of life contradict Ruth's imagined innocence in an area where she is accustomed to believing they confirm it. Ruth spends her life trying to get other people to confirm her innocence through love, and often seems to succeed. A sudden rejection or loss of someone who usually reinforces her illusions, or any similar situa-tion can suffice. Sometimes, just the prospect of such events can be enough.

On the other hand, a situation may arise that conflicts with or cir-cumvents Ruth's customary defenses. She may not be able sufficiently to withdraw from its humiliating contingencies. Circumstances may interfere with her sufficiently internalizing the Vindictiveness result-ing from it. The ulterior motive of her surrogate sacrifice may be-come so evident that it loses its defensive effectiveness.

Finally, Ruth may escalate her defenses to the level that they ren-der her so miserable, lonely, and anxious that the situation paradoxi-cally challenges her innocence. How could anyone claiming to be as innocent as she, make herself suffer so?

Ruth's truly lethal crises are nearly always cumulative. She might foresee the prospect of a possible loss or rejection, react to the humili-ation with anxious hysteria, incur the actual rejection on account of her reaction, automatically escalate her defenses, encounter still fur-ther contradictions on account of the consequences to her defenses, and then become imminently suicidal as a result.

REACTION TO CRISIS

Throughout the process, Ruth remains generally unaware of her own vindictive intent. Instead of experiencing her Vindictive-ness, Ruth wallows in Self-Hatred and Hopelessness. And since their expressions tend to support her illusions of innocence, she uncon-sciously escalates them when her innocence is challenged.

The escalation of her expressions of Self-Hatred fuels the fires of

her self-destructiveness. The escalation of her expressions of Hopelessness serve her no better. Both cause her additional humiliation,
thereby increasing her Vindictiveness. For Ruth invariably compares
her condition with the lives of those around her. They don't suffer so
or seem to have such stringent rules of conduct they must follow.
They can assert themselves without having to worry about the consequences. They can be satisfied with themselves, and can enjoy life in
ways inherently denied her.

As Ruth's Vindictiveness keeps mounting, so must her defenses
against its expressions. Despite her need for other people, she must
withdraw further into herself. Despite the pain she already suffers,
she must internalize this added rage, causing herself still more suffering. Despite the losses she already incurs, she must add to them with
additional surrogate sacrifices.

Ruth's escalated expressions of Self-Hatred and Hopelessness
combined with her escalated defenses to Vindictiveness threaten her
very existence. The anxiety, emotional suffering, and hysterical panic
resulting from the combination can be overwhelming. But Ruth must
still cling to her illusions of innocence.

Just as Harold in a crisis must find some avenue to regain his
challenged omnipotence, Ruth must find some way to reconfirm her
innocence. But for Ruth to gain confirmation of her innocence, she
must turn to other people. Therefore, in a suicidal crisis, Ruth cries
out for help to anyone around.

All this lends much confusion to Ruth's suicidal crises in particular and to the conception of suicidal crises in general. Because the
Synpathic Type in a crisis has the need to elicit help from as many
people as will listen to her, she colors the beliefs about motivations to
suicide. Coupled with the distortions surrounding Antipathic and
Apathic crises, Ruth's public display of her particular reaction to crisis
makes it appear that all suicides are similarly motivated.

As we have seen, Harold makes his suicide a private affair. A few
people around him may see what is going on. His true motivations are
disguised by his increased hostility towards others in a crisis. Carl's crises are even more confusing and obscure. The Apathic Type makes
even his crisis difficult to identify, let alone the motivations behind it.
Furthermore, both Harold and Carl have a vested interest in keeping
their suicidal impulses well-disguised.

But the Ruths of the world dominate crisis hotlines and counsel-
or's offices. Rather than keeping her crisis private and disguised,
Ruth has a crucial vested interest in publicizing it. But it would be a

grave error, and one often committed, to generalize from the Synpathic Type's cries for help and the motivations behind them to the motivations for suicide in general.

To interpret all suicides as resulting from hostility toward others
turned back against the self would not merely miss the mark in terms
of Harold's and Carl's motivations. It would be a simplistic interpretation of Ruth's motivations as well.

For above all, Ruth must sustain her innocence. All her escalated
expressions of Self-Hatred and Hopelessness and defenses to Vindictiveness are aimed at this cardinal goal. And this is the underlying
goal of her cries for help. In order to maintain her innocence, Ruth
must lay her suicide on other people's doorstep.

SUICIDAL METHODOLOGY

Ruth's impetus to suicide is fueled by three almost irresistible attractions. First, suicide holds forth the lure of being the ultimate expression of her unconscious Vindictiveness. All her past expressions
are but insignificant preliminaries to this ultimate weapon against
others.

Second, suicide paradoxically offers her an escape from having
to face the true origins and power of her own Vindictiveness. The
greater her Vindictiveness grows, the stronger her impetus to escape
it through suicide.

Third, suicide is the only way her secretly vindictive Empirical
Self can metaphysically abdicate to her Innocent Fantastic Self. At
long last, her immortal true goodness will show.

But because Ruth's suicide is motivated by her repressed Vindictiveness, it is usually triggered by the actions of someone other than
herself. No one else can actually make her kill herself. But this is not
how Ruth usually experiences the dynamics. She can actually believe
someone else is making her commit suicide. And this belief serves as
her final expression of Vindictiveness. Ruth makes even her suicide
the fault of someone else.

However, Ruth rarely chooses an unquestionably lethal method.
Just as in other endeavors in life, the suicide attempts of the Synpathic
Type often prove inadequate. Because her method may fall far short
of actual death, she often just scars or incapacitates herself. Because
her attempts are of such low potential lethality, she reserves numerous opportunities to try and try again.

Consequently, Ruth can become an habitual suicide attempter. Eventually, even she may vaguely recognize the vindictive purpose of her abortive attempts. Often, she times them to have the most effect, being certain that the object of her rage finds her and saves her or, at least, is notified immediately by the person who does.

People may accuse her of only trying to get attention or to force them to give in to her demands. Obviously, there is a kernel of truth in both accusations. However, Ruth does run the risk of not being rescued in time. For example, she may overdose on barbiturates expecting her husband home at his usual time, only to have him arrive late. Her apparent abortive attempt could then turn into a genuine suicide.

If other people fail to get Ruth's vindictive message from her actions, they are bound to get it from her notes. Synpathic Types almost invariably write unconsciously well-calculated suicide notes. Indeed, the message conveyed in the note can be of such paramount importance, it overshadows the act. She may stage the whole event as a vehicle primarily designed to deliver the mail.

Synpathic notes usually contain references to how much better off everyone will be without her, how much she suffers, and how much unhappiness she innocently causes others. Even though she is innocent, everything paradoxically seems to be her fault. She does not understand all this, but she forgives other people for treating her so terribly, anyway. And she hopes they forgive her, even though she has never meant harm to anyone. Finally, as with all genuine suicide notes, hers contain an unmistakable air of inconclusiveness. Somehow, some way, the note conveys the idea that this is really not the end of her existence.

But even though Ruth may not see her suicide as her end, she lays it at other people's doorstep. She sincerely believes that someone else is out, if not actually to kill her, then intentionally to cause her suicide. As she swallows her pills or puts the razor to her wrist, she tells herself that this is what other people have wanted all along.

It may very well be what other people want by the time Ruth keeps inflicting on them the contingencies of her Vindictiveness. Other people's hostility plays right into her hand. The very best way of all for Ruth to suicide is for her to provoke someone else into doing it to her.

However, even if she cannot provoke someone else into killing her, they are to blame for her suicide. Infinitely virtuous to the end,

Synpathic Ruth's Innocent Fantastic Self survives, even if her hapless and suffering Empirical Self is no more.

RUTH'S SUICIDE

"I'll come by and get my things this evening," Ralph says. Ruth cannot believe it is happening. Here is her husband of only two years telling her he is getting a divorce. "I'm having the lawyer file tomorrow."

"But Ralph," Ruth pleads, "you said that we would be able to work things out."

Ralph walks to the door. "I'm not going through this all over again. You say 'work things out', but you don't do a damn thing toward making things any better between us. How are things gonna get better, Ruth? By magic? By the will of God? Dammit, Ruth, can't you see that the only way for things to get better is for us—and I mean both of us—to make them better?"

"Well, I'm willing," she pleads.

"You're always willing, Ruth, but dammit, you're never able. Dammit, Ruth, you just don't have the ability to make anything any better. Not for me. Not for us. Not even for yourself!"

"Well, I try. You know I try."

"How do you try? What do you do? You just sit there waiting for things to get better." Ralph calms himself. "Dammit, Ruth, I'm sorry. I don't mean to yell at you all the time. I just don't want to be married to you any more."

"Mad at Ruth, *again*," Ralph thinks to himself. All of her friends think she's such a sweet and innocuous person, but somehow, some way, she manages to make him furious by acting so innocent and abused all the time.

"Look, Ruth, I'll help with the car payments and I'll keep on paying the mortgage. But I just can't go on like this with you. I know you think I treat you terribly, but I don't know what I could do to make you happy anymore. I want a divorce and I'm going to get one."

Ruth walks over to Ralph, wiping her tears. "Just like that. Oh Ralph, why are you so mean to me? I *do* want our marriage to work," Ruth implores. "And here you are telling me that you just don't want to be married any more. Nothing that has gone before counts. Nothing that we've hoped for and dreamed for matters. I don't matter. My son, who loves you so much, doesn't matter. Nothing matters but that things are not just exactly perfect, the way you want them to be. How can you be so. . . ?"

His anger rising again, Ralph slaps the door behind him with his open hand, afraid to make a fist for fear he will hit Ruth instead. "Dammit, Ruth. Don't pull that 'my son' crap on me. Why in the hell do you think I've stuck it out as long as I have? I think the world of Joey. I don't know how he managed it, but at thirteen, that kid's more together than you'll ever be. Why in the hell don't you take lessons from your own little boy? He could teach you a thing or two about how to be a grown-up."

Ralph starts to open the door, then turns back to face Ruth. "I'm sorry, Ruth. Let's not bring Joey into this. I'd still like to take him on that camping trip I promised him. I'll call you later to make the arrangements."

"What do you mean 'take him on a camping trip'? You're not going to walk out on me and expect to still see Joey, are you? What are you trying to do to me? Are you trying to take Joey away from me too, so I'll be left with nothing? I think you like hurting me." Ruth is crying hard.

Her crying makes him angrier. "Don't start that, Ruth. I've had about all the tears I can take. That's about the only thing you ever do to try to change things. You cry and then you get hysterical and blame everything on me."

Opening the door, Ralph steps out. Looking back he says, "I'm sorry about the way things have worked out for you, Ruth." Anxious to get away from the confrontation, he hurries to his car leaving Ruth standing forlornly in the doorway.

Bewildered, Ruth closes the door and leans back against it. "He didn't even notice that I cleaned the kitchen," she says out loud. "How can he be so cold and uncaring. I feel so unhappy and all he cares about is himself. He never notices anything I do for him."

Remembering that Mr. Ross said she must call if she can't make it to work, she picks up the telephone to call. While dialing, she realizes it is too early. No one will be there yet. Besides, Mr. Ross will probably call her when he realizes she isn't at work. He knows what a hard time she is having. He even said to her just last week that he hoped she would be able to resolve her personal problems and not be bringing them to the job. He didn't go so far as to ask her if she wanted to talk about them, but he'd admitted being concerned. And, a supervisor is *supposed* to be supportive and human and caring. Not like Ralph.

Straightening her robe, she goes to the kitchen to fix some tea. She hears Joey stirring about upstairs.

"Hi, Mom." It's Joey, ready for school.

"Good morning, darling." She pulls Joey to her to kiss her on the cheek. "Do you want me to get you some breakfast?"

"What?" Joey asks, surprised, putting his books on the table.

"Do you want me to fix you some breakfast? I will if you want me to."

"No, thanks, Mom. I'll just get something at school like always." Seeing Ruth rummaging through his books, Joey impatiently asks, "What do you want, Mom?"

"I just wanted a piece of paper."

Still impatient, Joey removes two blank sheets from his notebook, hands them to Ruth, kisses her on the cheek, and leaves. Ruth finds a pen in the drawer and returns to the table to write.

> Dear Ralph,
>
> I know that you don't like for me to write notes to you, but when we talk, the words just won't come. There must be something terribly wrong with me that I cause everyone so much unhappiness. You have been so patient. I am a lucky girl to have you.
>
> I know that I must deserve it, but I just can't stand your criticism. It hurts me so much, I just want to slip off into nowhere. Why won't you believe me when I tell you that I love you? I do, more than you will ever know. I love Joey, too.
>
> I know that you don't really mean to hurt me. But when you hurt me, I just can't think or do anything else. I know that I'm not very good at some things, but I try. A person can be hurt only so much. People have hurt me so much in the past, I thought that you would be different. Why don't you believe me when I say things I really mean, like I love you? Maybe some day you will realize how much you hurt me.
>
> Love,
> Ruth

Folding the note, she puts it in the pocket of her robe. Suddenly, she feels frightened. Putting her cup into the sink, she goes upstairs to lie down. Thoughts keep running through her head. How could Ralph be so mean? He's no different than Pete. No different from any of the others.

Pete Peterson certainly fooled her. When she first met him, he seemed so strong, so kind, and generous. Just the thought of him would send thrills through her. But look how he turned out. No sooner were they married than he showed his true colors. He was mean, selfish, and hard. All the things he had said before were just lies. Like, when she first told him she was pregnant, he acted pleased and excited. He said they would get married, and that everything would be fine. Then, later, he accused her of getting pregnant just to trap him into marrying her. He never would have married her, otherwise. He was so weak and selfish, she couldn't understand how she could have been so fooled. She had thrown her life away, just for him. How could she have believed he really loved her?

All the other men were the same until she met Ralph. When she found him, she knew he was different. He was everything she had hoped Pete would be. Now, she is afraid she has been fooled again. "What's wrong with me," she wonders, as she reaches for the Valium, "That I keep getting fooled by men?" Taking two Valium, she cries herself to sleep.

The telephone awakens her. She picks up the receiver.

Mr. Ross is talking fast. She hears only a few words. ". . . been through this before . . . don't bother to come back . . . mail your check . . . tried to tell you last time . . . I'm sorry . . ."

As Ruth replaces the receiver, she tells herself, "Well, I didn't like that job, anyway. I only took it because Ralph made me." She dials Ralph's number.

"I was so upset this morning, I didn't go to work. Mr. Ross just called. Now, I've lost my job."

"Are you telling me," Ralph asks angrily, "that you lost your job because I upset you? That it's my fault?"

"I just said I was upset."

"Come on, Ruth, that's not what you meant."

Ruth is confused. Her heart is pounding. Why does he always have to pin her down? "I don't know what you mean. Only now, I don't know what Joey and I will do if you leave."

Ralph was getting angrier. "What do you mean, 'if I leave?' I'm leaving, whether you've lost your job or not."

"You didn't even notice," she replies.

"Notice what?"

"That I cleaned the kitchen."

"Dammit, Ruth, I'm telling you our whole marriage is over and you're telling me you cleaned the kitchen."

"But you're always criticizing me. You say I never do anything."

"Dammit, Ruth. Don't you understand? It's not important now. You haven't understood anything I've said for the last six months."

"I guess I don't understand, then," Ruth replies. "You always say that I . . ."

"Dammit, Ruth. It's too little too late. I don't care whether you cleaned the kitchen or not. It's over."

"But what will Joey and I do."

"Don't hang Joey on me, Ruth. He's Pete's kid. I think the world of Joey, but talk to Pete about what to do about him. He's always been more help to Joey than you have, anyway. As for you, Ruth, I quit caring a long time ago."

Ralph disconnects. Ruth reaches for two more Valium. She calls him back.

"You will some day, Ralph."

"I will what?"

"You'll care what happens to me."

"Dammit, Ruth, are you threatening me again? Are you talking about suicide again?"

"Ralph, I just want you to care." She disconnects, turns over, and drifts off to sleep.

She sleeps until noon, and awakens groggy and numb. Turning to the telephone, she calls Dr. Baker. The answering service replies. "No. No message," she tells them. She begins to cry, again.

Why aren't therapists available when you need them? She goes downstairs to get some vodka. "I just want to feel numb," she says out loud. She washes two Valium down with the vodka.

She dials Carolyn's number at work. "Hi, Ruth," Carolyn says. "Love to talk, but I'm supposed to be in a meeting right now."

"Oh. I just thought since you're such a good friend. . ."

"Do you want something in particular? You sound pretty down, Ruth, but I can't talk now, I'm supposed to be in a meeting. . ."

"Ralph's talking like he might leave me. . ."

"Ruth! I have to go to the meeting. Let me call you back tonight."

"For some reason, he says that I'm not a good mother. . ."

"Ruth! I'm sorry, but I must go. Goodbye."

Carolyn disconnects. Ruth pours another vodka.

"I just want to feel numb," she says. "Just numb."

Maybe it would have been different if they had made love last night. It's been so long. But if Ralph knew how much she loved him, that wouldn't be so important. She pours herself another vodka. "Numb. I just want to feel numb." At last, she goes to sleep.

Groggily, she awakens. It's three-thirty. Joey. Where's Joey? Staggering down the stairs, she finds his note on the refrigerator door. A little ladybug magnet holds the note to the door. The bug looks alive. Holding herself back from the bug, she tries to read the note. She sees only the "six o'clock" part. "Ralph will be home by then, too," she decides.

The sleeping pills. She finds them in the linen cabinet where Ralph has hidden them. In the bathroom, she stares at the face in the mirror. "Whose face is that?" she wonders.

"I don't want to feel anything," she tells the face in the glass. The bottle of pills is half empty. She swallows all those remaining. In bed once again, she cries herself to sleep. It doesn't take long.

Chapter 26

APATHIC ASCENT TO NIRVANA

Carl Goldman, our Apathic Type Suicide, unconsciously believes he is Transcendent. His sole unconscious goal in life is to rise above it. In his futile attempt to manifest his Transcendent Fantastic Self, Carl strives for ultimate detachment, independence, and self-sufficiency. Carl intellectually, spiritually, or aesthetically moves away from mundane life. Yet rather than realize his impossible transcendence, Carl ironically becomes but a prisoner to the ambivalence, inertia, and detachment resulting from his futile efforts to attain it.

Because Carl believes he transcends real limitations, he must be convinced there are no actual restrictions on his beliefs, behavior, or relations with others. He must believe he is free to think, behave, or relate to other people in ways beyond the confines of his own real existence. Therefore, Carl attempts to detach himself from his expressions of Self-Hatred, Vindictiveness, and Hopelessness.

Although Carl can usually ignore the origins and character of his Self-Hatred and Vindictiveness, he unconsciously designs their expressions to reinforce his illusions. The consequences to Carl's life on account of his expressions of Self-Hatred and Vindictiveness are grave. But they nevertheless support his illusions of transcendence.

255

However, Carl's expressions of Hopelessness and their consequences pose him an entirely different dilemma. He devotes a great
deal of time and effort to devising his abstract values. But they become so hopelessly abstract that they contradict his very existence. He
expresses his chronic discontent only as spiritual, intellectual, or wan-
derlusting detachment. But it contradicts his ability to rise above life
as a process. His hopeless resignation would seem to sustain his transcendence. But it merely proves the impossibility of his attaining it
precisely by virtue of his need to resign.

Rather than reinforce his illusion of transcendence, Carl's expressions of Hopelessness actually contradict it. How can Carl express
Hopelessness in a life he believes he transcends? To avoid the contradiction, Carl devises defenses designed to insulate him from it.

By employing Stoic Detachment, Carl can participate in life but
still believe he transcends it. Nothing happening to Carl can seriously
affect him. By Generalizing his Hopelessness, he disowns it. All life is
hopeless, not just his. By employing Nihilism, he strikes out at life as a
process. How better could he prove he transcends it?

To be sure, Carl's defenses have their debilitating effects. Each
level of defense becomes increasingly self-destructive. But Carl can
usually devise rationalizations, for from the paramount advantage of
a metaphysical perspective, all things below can be explained.

This appears to work very well for Carl. He may rave about intellectual honesty, artistic merit, the follies of mankind, but he bears a
certain inner serenity. Often others envy him his detachment. If only
things were not so crucial for them. However, regardless of Carl's serene perspective, the fundamental paradox of his dilemma remains.
Carl cannot transcend mundane existence and still exist.

Never sensing the hopeless irrationality of his unconscious basic
premise, Carl wrestles with its syllogistic logic. "I am my Transcendent Fantastic Self," he unconsciously vows, "free of all contingencies
of life. But life inherently involves contingencies. Therefore, in order
to be my Fantastic Self, I must be free of life."

This logical progression underlies Carl's unconscious impetus to
suicide. Unable to transcend mundane existence and still exist, Carl
starts off in a state of absolute Hopelessness. He represses his Hopelessness but still must express it in mundane life. He must then devise
defenses insulating him from the consequences of its expressions, regardless of how self-destructive his defenses become. Finally, just because Carl cannot resolve his existential Hopelessness, he suicides on
its account.

PRECIPITATING FACTORS

The Apathic Type suicides primarily on account of Hopelessness. Self-Hatred and Vindictiveness each play a part, as we will see, but their roles are secondary to the main. Because of Carl's detachment, he can survive them. However, because Carl cannot resolve his impossible riddle, he is infinitely vulnerable to its consequences. The haunting pervasiveness of Carl's existential despair undermines his every effort to transcend it.

Consequently any event, situation, or condition focusing on the inevitable contingencies of mundane life and thereby contradicting Carl's illusions of his transcending it can precipitate a suicidal crisis for him. Often, just the prospect of his encountering such contingencies will suffice.

To be sure, Carl encounters contradictions to his transcendence every day, but, through his defenses, he manages to rationalize them away. Yet despite his defenses and rationalizations, a situation can arise not so easily dismissed. It may contradict his transcendence in a way in which he is unconsciously accustomed to believing he manifests it. It may come as a culmination of years of concentrated but futile efforts to attain what he unconsciously perceives as a truly transcendental position, only to come up against its mundane reality.

The situation may contradict his imagined transcendence in a new or unique way for which he has not developed sufficient defenses. A sudden challenge to his illusions can catch him unaware, doubling the despair it causes him by proving his lack of transcendental foresight.

Finally, and most ironically, the situation may result from his escalation of defenses to the degree they contradict the illusions of transcendence he employs them to defend. His stoic detachment may grow so pronounced he has no earthly contacts left to transcend. His generalized hopelessness may become so profound that even he cannot rise above it. His nihilism may grow so self-destructive it puts him in a situation where he must depend upon others.

Most often, the contradictions are cumulative. He can spend years searching for that one transcendental moment, only to discover its mundane reality when finally it arrives. He then escalates his defenses to protect him from the resulting despair, only to encounter new contradictions resulting from his escalated defenses. Then the accumulated contradictions could be just enough to cause him to terminate his existence.

REACTION TO CRISIS

Carl unconsciously designs his life to demonstrate his belief he transcends it, designing his defenses to help maintain this impossible illusion. Without being aware of his true mission, Carl drifts on his own inertia, ambivalently vacillating between detaching himself from the course of life and moving into contact with it. He exaggerates all these characteristics when faced with a suicidal crisis.

Because Carl's expressions of Self-Hatred and Vindictiveness reinforce his illusions of transcendence, he escalates them when confronted by a suicidal crisis. His unconscious but automatic escalation of these expressions adds a confusing note to his suicidal crises. But Carl does not suicide because of Self-Hatred or Vindictiveness. Events such as worldly failure or rejection in love cause Carl little shame or humiliation. Instead, they elicit his despair, thus triggering his Hopelessness, by virtue of their proving he is subject to the ordinary contingencies of life after all.

But Carl's escalated expressions of Self-Hatred and Vindictiveness add to his Hopelessness by the despair they cause him. Consequently, Carl must further escalate his defenses. His Stoic Detachment usually keeps him merely uninvolved. Now he carries it to the extreme of depersonalization. His Generalizing usually just makes life as a mundane process seem futile. Now it surfaces as existential terror. His Nihilism usually only renders his life sparse and vacuous. Now he must destory its reality or be destroyed by it.

All these consequences combine to motivate Carl towards suicide. Caught in the grip of existential terror, feeling ripped apart by powerful but unseen impulses, losing touch with what reality he was previously able to maintain, Carl fluctuates between trying to solve his dilemma and trying to rid himself of it. Like a chained and frustrated god, Carl struggles with the fetters of reality binding him to it.

His overwhelming impulse is to flee. But where? To some exotic land? To a dark and eremitic cave? To the other side of sanity? But in none of these can Carl manifest his threatened transcendence. There is only one place Carl can metaphysically actualize his illusions. Carl must ascend to Nirvana.

SUICIDAL METHODOLOGY

All these complexities render Carl's motivation to suicide the most difficult to recognize and understand. Even from his detached

APATHIC ASCENT TO NIRVANA 259

perspective, Carl cannot usually see it for what it really is. And because of its esoteric nature, the ways he finds to enact it may not look like suicide at all. Since he believes he transcends existence, Carl suicides best by simply ceasing to exist.

However, ceasing to exist through suicide is Carl's only logical culmination. Since life has no intrinsic meaning to him, it is but a hopeless distraction. To Carl, suicide is the only reality.

Furthermore, suicide is the only way Carl can avoid having to face the absurdity of his secret mission. By suiciding, Carl can demonstrate his belief that life itself is absurd, not just his mission in it.

Finally, suicide is the only way Carl can metaphysically actualize his Transcendent Fantastic Self. In a life devoted to transcending it, suicide constitutes Carl's ultimate transcendental act.

Because of its transcendental nature, Carl can simply drift off into his suicide. It may come in a senseless accident or a set of circumstances one would be inclined to say couldn't happen again in a million years. It may result from a common situation or event which, by some unique and inexplicable twist, proves to be fatal for him. His suicide nearly always expresses his solitary alienation. He may die a derelict's death, refusing help that is just around the corner. He may come to his end in an impersonal public hospital from alcoholism or another severe addiction. He may get himself killed in connection with some esoteric cause, or like Melville's nihilistic Ahab, he may be dragged down to his demise, entangled in the noose that ties him to the very forces of life he aims at destroying.

But whatever strange and unique way Carl finds to end his existence, he rarely leaves a suicide note. In the absence of an actual note, he may leave some kind of legacy behind such as a manifesto condemning the futility of mundane life or a tome exalting the virtues of higher pursuits. He might make an offhand parting deposit of his few prized products or possessions with a stable friend.

Outside of a few fading memories of a handful of people, these may constitute the only substantial evidence that Carl Goldman ever existed. But only Carl's hopelessly earthbound Empirical Self ceases to exist. His immortal Transcendent Fantastic Self ascends to the universal All.

CARL'S SUICIDE

Carl is getting drunk. "Do you know," he says to Phil sitting next to him in the bar, "that our whole universe: our solar system, our galaxy, no, all the galaxies, quasars, black holes, the whole damned thing, could just be a bunch of molecules in the thumbnail of some gigantic creature that. . ."

"Come on, Carl," Phil turns on his stool, "let's go. You've had enough."

"Look, Phil. I'm serious. I mean we wouldn't even know, would we?"

"Carl," Phil sounds impatient behind his smile, "when you start talking like this, I know from the old days that it's time to go home."

"That's what I like about you, Phil," says Carl, as he steps down from his stool, "you're so damned solid. What happened to the times when we would sit for hours in a bar and talk about things that really matter? You weren't so solid, then."

"That was thirty years ago, Carl. Those things may have mattered to me then, but not now."

"I understand. You're right. Thirty years. It really has been that long. You've got your business, your family, your home, all those solid things to be concerned with. Me? I still worry about being molecules in a giant's thumbnail."

They are out on the street. The winter air is cold and sobering. "I don't know about that," Phil says. "You're solid, too, but in your own way."

"Sure I am," Carl replies sarcastically. "I blew-off school, and you got an MBA. I blew-off marriage, and you have a family. I blew-off the ad agency, and you have your own company. I've knocked all around, and you have a nice home. I seldom have a dime, and you have a safe deposit box full of stocks and bonds. Sure, I'm really solid."

"Who is to say," Phil says rather ponderously, "which one of us is better off? I'm going up to my hotel room, alone," counters Phil, "and you're going back to Taos and to Lisa. Tomorrow morning, I have to catch a plane for Atlanta. You'll get up late and at your leisure paint another picture that will be published in TIME. I'm not complaining about Joan. She's been a good wife and mother for twenty-five years, but you've had other women, and now Lisa. . ."

"Yeah, Lisa. What's the difference. . ."

". . . who seems just right for you. Same interests, artistic, young, what more do you want?"

Carl feels subdued. Phil has never talked to him like this before. He suspected it, but he hadn't realized how much Phil envied him. Now, knowing it, it embarrasses him. "Sure. By the way, Phil," he says, trying to break through his embarrassment, "did you ever realize that our universe, I mean the whole damned thing, could just be a few molecules in the thumbnail. . .''

For a moment, they laugh together. Then Phil looks around the lobby, straightening his coat and tie, recovering his decorum. "Well, Carl," he says, "I hope it won't be three more years before I see you again. If Joan hadn't heard where you were, I wouldn't have known to call you to meet me in Santa Fe. From now on, keep us posted where you'll be."

"Sure," Carl replies, putting his hand on Phil's shoulder. He feels Phil stiffen under his touch. "Sure. I'll keep you posted." Turning to leave as Phil enters the elevator, he thinks to himself, "no I won't. Thirty years is long enough for us to envy each other."

The old Jag is cold on the drive back to Taos. Carl fidgets with the heater controls, but he knows it is useless. The heater hasn't worked for the last three winters. Lisa wanted him to take her Rover into Santa Fe, but he wouldn't feel right driving her car.

Cupping his hands, he warms them with his breath, almost missing a turn. "That's right, baby," he says, as the Jag responds to the wheel. "Fifteen years old, and you can still handle the curves with finesse."

Typical of Phil to stay in the Hilton with the beautiful old La Fonda just a few blocks away. How can he be so stuffy? "All these years I've wished I was more like him. Now, I discover he wishes he was more like me. What a joke life is."

Leaving the expressway, he turns onto 68 towards Taos. The Jag starts making a new noise. "Haven't heard this one before, baby. What's going wrong with you now?"

He hopes Lisa will be sleeping when he gets there. "I wish she could just let me be, sometimes. Why does she always want me to talk to her or make love to her?" Passing through Pilar, he notices only two other cars on the road. "Where is everybody? Do they know something I don't?" At Taos he gets his answer. Heavy snow begins to fall.

"Please be asleep, Lisa. I don't want to feel like a human vibrator again. I just plug in my batteries and you get your jollies. But not tonight." The snow falls heavier as he turns off the highway to Lisa's. The noise in the Jag is louder. "Come on, baby. Just a little bit further." The old car coughs on the hill. It almost stalls. Then, over the ridge, the noise subsides. "That-a-way, baby. I knew you could make it!" Pulling into the drive, it makes one more loud cough before he turns the ignition off.

Hurrying into the house, he realizes Lisa is asleep, but most of the lights are on. There is hot coffee in the kitchen, wood burning in the fireplace. "What does she expect for this?" Mug of coffee in hand, he strolls around the house turning off lights.

Six months before, when Lisa first showed him the house, he felt as warm as the glowing cinders. The natural richness of it, its quietness, its shadows, everything about it reminded him of a place he had always known but had never seen. The old books, the leather chairs, the rugs. He felt as though he had lived quietly among them in some long ago forgotten life.

"We have so much in common," Lisa said then. "Your painting. My sculpture. We might even do some things together. College kids come here every summer. Perhaps we can have some workshops with them. You could make some money, that way." Lisa was concerned about his not having any money. She had her inheritance to go with the house.

He had stayed, yet they hadn't worked together. The workshops never got organized. Now, as he looked around, he realized he had stayed only because of the house.

Peering out the window, he sees the Jag collecting a blanket of snow. Suddenly, he is overcome by grief. She looks as though she is being buried. "Don't die, now, baby. You're the last thing I have left." He is sobbing. He hasn't cried in years. Now he can't stop.

On the opposite wall hangs *Oedipus at Colonus,* its abstractly mottled colors subdued in the light. "Why that name?" a few people asked when he finished painting it fifteen years ago. "Because I can't think of anything else to call it," he replied, laughing. They thought he was joking. He wasn't. Some others would gaze at the wildly abstract eight by ten foot canvas and say, like the stylish young Junior Leaguer put it, "I can see blind old Oedipus sitting there in his eternal grief with Antigone at his side, and . . . what was the other girl's name?"

That year, TIME published an article about the Taxco artist's colony. *Oedipus* was among the paintings reproduced, one column wide, black and white. Carl's one great moment.

Then, the commercial art studio in San Francisco. Ad accounts, mag illustrations, deadlines. And Caryl. "Life in the fast lane," he called it afterwards. Lunch on the Hill. The refurbished townhouse. For the first and last time, money in the bank. But he knew it wouldn't last. At the peak, he walked away.

"What do you mean, 'you're quitting'?" Caryl asked. "How can you quit when you are doing so well?"

"I don't want it. I never really did," he answered. "I don't want you, either."

The next day, he was gone. A month later, bought out by three employees. Three months later, divorced. Not much money left, but enough to get along on for a while.

Now softly sobbing, Carl hears Lisa say, "Hi!" She is standing at the doorway smiling, in a negligee.

"Lisa. It's three A.M. Why are you up?"

That concerned look on her face. Why does she have to look so concerned? "What's wrong, dear? Are you crying?"

"No. No, it's the fire. I stirred it and smoke got in my eyes." He was glad she asked. Now he can wipe his face without embarrassment.

"How's your friend? Have you really known him for thirty years?"

"He is fine. And, yes I have. In that order."

"Are you angry?" Still showing concern.

"Lisa, why don't you go back to bed? Don't let me disturb you. Go back to sleep."

She smiles on her way to the kitchen. "You're not disturbing me, dear. I think I'll get some coffee. You look like you need some company."

With Lisa out of the room, Carl raises his arms, looks at the ceiling, and shakes his head in exasperation.

Coming back with coffee, she is still smiling. "Here. Look at the rough I did for the brochure about our show." Lisa is standing over him dangling the pasted-together draft in front of him. "I thought that the article from TIME would make a good introduction for your work."

"Oh, Lisa. It's too late to think about all that. And anyway, I don't know if I really want us to do that show. Your sculpture and my paintings are just too different to be shown together. And besides, the stuff in TIME is really just a lot of shit." Carl turns from Lisa and stares into the fire.

He seems so withdrawn, Lisa thinks to herself. He's been more and more withdrawn since they first started talking about their upcoming show together. "I don't know what's been wrong with you tonight, Carl. When you left for Santa Fe you were in a foul mood, and you still are," Lisa says, trying to sound at once scolding and kidding. "We planned to do this show together. You made a commitment to making it work. And besides, the art in TIME is *good*. You're great. It's not just commercial success that matters. Anyhow, what's wrong with that? Picasso was a sharp businessman. . ."

"Never mind, Lisa," Carl shoots back. "I just don't want to be

bothered by those stupid little details right now. Just get off my back."
He grabs the brochure and crumpling it, tosses it into the fire.

Lisa feels like she has been slapped. Looking at Carl, she wonders how he can be so uncaring about her feelings and their work together; so willing to live in his own little emotional world, never allowing her to get close to him.

"Carl, just tell me what you want. I will do anything to help you. I
know how unhappy you are," Lisa pleads.

"I don't want your help. I just want to be left alone," Carl responds quietly and slowly.

Lisa sinks to her knees, feeling the weight of the futility in trying
to talk with Carl.

"Did you know it was snowing?" Lisa asks, trying to placate Carl's
moodiness and change the subject.

"Yes. It started on my way back."

"Last year, I was snowed in for two weeks. They don't clear all the
roads back this way, and. . ."

Alarmed, Carl wheels from the fireplace. "Here? You get snowed
in here? For two weeks?"

"Not every year, but last year the snow was unusually heavy. It
was so beautiful, looking out. And it's so warm and cozy inside."

His alarm turns to panic. He turns and runs to the bedroom,
pulling his clothes from the dresser. Then, suitcase off the shelf, he
furiously begins to pack.

Lisa comes in, her smile quickly fading into bewilderment. "What
in the world are you doing?"

"What does it look like? I'm getting out of here!"

"I don't mean tonight, dear. We probably won't get snowed in tonight. It's too early. I mean later in the winter. . ."

"I'm not waiting! I don't want to get snowed in. Now or later."
He's crying again, not knowing why.

"But, Carl, you said you loved this house; that you've always
dreamed of having a place like this and a life like this."

"Your house is great, Lisa, but I'm leaving."

Crossing to him, Lisa takes his hand. "I've told you before, Carl.
It's not just my house. It's our house."

He stiffens. "Let go!" Looking straight into her eyes, he says, "get
your clinging clammy paws off of me. Now!"

Stunned, she backs away as though he had hit her with his fist.
Softly, she almost whispers, "you can't leave tonight Carl. What about
the snow and the roads? It's below freezing outside. You don't have

snow tires. You don't even have a heater. Wait until morning. You'll see how beautiful it is."

He keeps packing. "They may not clear the road tomorrow. I'm leaving now while I can still get out."

"But your car. . ."

The Jag. He remembers the new noise. He knows the Jag won't make it but he says, "She'll make it, somehow. If not, I'll walk. I'll crawl if I have to."

"Carl, you will freeze to death. Don't you realize that?"

"Around here?"

"Yes, around here! Just last winter, three people over on Red River pass. . ."

"I don't care. I'm leaving."

"Where are you going?"

"I don't know."

"What about your paintings?"

"I'll send for them."

"What about me?"

"I'll write."

She's crying. "No you won't. You won't do any of that. You'll die out there." She sinks to the floor. Suitcase packed. Clothes in the bag. Looking down at her sprawled on the floor, he feels like vomiting. He barely resists a compulsion to kick her. She disgusts him.

When Lisa looks up, he is gone. Forever.

Chapter 27

SOCIAL SUICIDE

Suicidal societies commit suicide for the same reasons and in similar ways as do individual Suicides. But like most individual Suicides, most suicidal societies eventually compromise with the logic of the syndrome, never consciously aiming at absolute self-destruction. However, the smaller, younger, or more cohesive societies among them are highly susceptible to immediate and premeditated social suicide.

These societies often speak of their fixed attribute with blatant naiveté. Their conscious belief in their Social Fantastic Self is as out in the open as a suicidal child's. Yet as the suicidal society grows larger or more mature, its expressions and defenses begin to set in. Resignation always contains a meliorating effect. Defensive evasion, displacement, and compromise dull and disguise its unconscious intent.

As the suicidal society grows aged, its primary attribute pales in the light of its imagined immortality. In the face of its degeneration, belief in its immortality comes to the fore. Yet regardless of relative age or size, the unconscious suicidal goal remains intact. The potential for actual suicide resides within every suicidal society.

Social Suicidal Crises

Precipitating factors, reactions to crisis, and suicidal methodologies of a society are also similar to those of the individual Suicide. First, a situation, event, or condition contradicts the fixed attribute of its Social Fantastic Self when the society expects confirmation. Second, the results of the situation or event break through the society's usual defenses. Third, the society escalates its expressions of secondary motivations and customary defenses to such a level as ironically contradicts its imagined fixed attribute. Finally, as with the individual, most truly lethal social crises are accumulative.

The Antipathic society reacts to its crisis with arrogant and indiscriminate hostility, desperately trying to regain its omnipotence. It escalates its defenses to Self-Hatred by evading recognition of the true situation, growing more paranoid on account of its externalizations, and by making token concessions.

The Synpathic society reacts to its crisis with massive demonstrations of its being abused, inadequate, and deprived, desperately trying to validate its innocence. It escalates its defenses to Vindictiveness by withdrawing from the contingencies of the real situation, by internalizing its vindictive rage against others, and by making surrogate sacrifices.

The Apathic society reacts to its crisis with amplified expressions of ambivalence. It vacillates between impersonal hostile acts against outsiders and overtures of an esoteric brand of love for humankind, desperately trying to demonstrate its transcendent disregard for its own and others' existence. It escalates its defenses to Hopelessness, growing even more paranoid in its detachment, further promoting its generalized hopelessness, and striking out at all signs of life with vehement nihilism.

Methodologically, the Antipathic society often makes careful and meticulous plans and preparations for its own demise. Usually surrounded by similar Antipathic societies, it rarely wants for acceptable rationalizations to explain its behavior. But regardless of how sane its course may appear from an all-against-all perspective, its ultimate goal invariably shows through. It may even frankly advertise its suicidal goal, convincing its constituents and outsiders of the logic of its course. After all, what greater mark in history can a society make than intentionally to plan for and execute its own worldly destruction as a tribute to its immortal omnipotence?

The Synpathic society often rehearses its suicide. It practices it through low lethal attempts or symbolic suicide rituals. As with the individual Synpathic, its rehearsals have the added value of intimidating outsiders through threats of harm to itself. Its rehearsals can grow so ritualized that their inherent suicidal intent is virtually lost on its adherents behind a screen of accumulated pretense. However, despite any ritualized accretions, the Synpathic society must let all outsiders know beyond doubt that its eventual suicide is strictly on their account.

Like the Apathic individual, the Apathic society can find strange ways to do itself in. It may dissipate into nonexistence on account of its taboos against material production, reproductive sex, and other self-sustaining endeavors. It may get itself destroyed in the crossfire between other battling systems, or come to its violent end after igniting a rebellion it cannot sustain. But whatever means it finds to end its existence, it nearly always leaves behind an enigma. Usually, no one can even recall what it stood for, let alone why it had to die.

Thus, the suicide of each type occurs in accordance with the complexities of its role. But all have one basic factor in common. Only through suicide can the society attempt metaphysically to actualize its Social Fantastic Self. And only when seen as this mass manifestation of its Social Fantastic Self can the social suicide phenomenon make sense. For the suicidal society's headlong plunge towards its own destruction can be traced every step of the way.

First, the normally unconscious belief in the Social Fantastic Self surfaces into common awareness. The members come to an open agreement, or at least an implicit one, that the society they collectively comprise is omnipotent, innocent, or transcendent, and consequently immortal. This common belief is usually focused on a central figure or leader, real or mythological or both, who personifies it, articulates it, and symbolizes it to the society and to the rest of the world. It often appears as though this leader is responsible for convincing the society in its belief. We have already seen how each suicidal society chooses leaders or symbolic figures who personify its existing beliefs about itself. The Antipathic society chooses leaders who promise to make it more powerful, more self-reliant, more industrious. The Synpathic society focuses on figures or leaders who promise eternal innocence. The Apathic chooses those who lay claim to knowledge of the abstract and eternal All. Each suicidal society picks its own leaders on the basis of its own beliefs. And each eventually grants its leaders ultimate power over the system strictly on this account.

Second, the society grows more cohesive and homogenous

around this chosen symbolic figure or leader. The dissenting elements are suppressed, ostracized, or destroyed. The lifestyle of the remaining constituents grows insidiously uniform. Conformity to the ideal and dedication to its realization become the manic and exclusive themes.

Third, the society becomes more isolated and inclusive. Outsiders are eyed with the same degree of suspicion, regardless of their apparent amity or enmity. Constituents not fully epitomizing the ideal are suppressed or eliminated. A wall of paranoid suspicion is drawn around the system, isolating it physically or psychologically from the outside world.

Finally, its real suicidal intent surfaces. Just becoming more powerful, more benign, or more detached is never enough. Only the absolute will do. As insane as the idea objectively appears, the society irrevocably commits its own mundane destruction in the name of its impossible ideal.

THE THIRD REICH

No better example of a suicidal society's headlong plunge to its own destruction can be found than in the birth and death of the German Third Reich.[1] Being one of the most powerful, feared, and victorious societies of all time would not suffice. Nothing short of its absolute self-destruction in the name of its metaphysical omnipotence would do.

The Third Reich chose its leader in the popular elections of July 31, 1932. The National Socialist (Nazi) Party won a substantial plurality in the German Reichstag. Its leader, Adolf Hitler, was made Chancellor a few months later. Hitler had pursued the popular vote with promises to end the existing runaway inflation and economic slump. But he actually garnered victory through appeals to the society's existing unconscious but commonly held beliefs in collective omnipotence, racial superiority, and historic glory through retaliatory victory over old enemies.

The virtually unchallenged authority granted to Hitler by his society while he led it to a certain social suicide stands as a blazing example of a salient principle of the Suicide Syndrome. For history tragically demonstrates that the popularity of many propositions can be measured by their appeal to the belief in the attributes of the Fantastic Self.

Certainly there could be no doubt as to Hitler's popular appeal. His popularity and power rose in direct proportion to his blatant allusions to the omnipotence of his followers. The sales of his book, exhorting them to their manifest destiny, made him a millionaire. His speeches, praising them as supermen, raised them to the heights of mob ecstasy. His demeanor, comically fatuous to outsiders, personified the impossible dreams of unlimited power and glory upon which the Third Reich was founded. His arrogance, hostility, and goose-stepping rigidity might have appeared preposterous to others. But his society rallied behind him in their mutual march to suicidal oblivion.

The Third Reich spent the next few years growing into a cohesive and homogenous social system under his leadership. Dissenting elements were suppressed or eliminated. Constituents not fitting the Aryan ideal were disenfranchised and imprisoned, later to be destroyed. The lifestyle of the remaining majority grew stultifyingly uniform.

By 1936, Hitler had delivered on his promises and his society was grateful. The Third Reich was in economic recovery while the rest of the world still struggled with the remnants of depression. It was powerful while they were weak. It was celebrating its unity while they were agitated by dissension at home. It was on the road to immortal glory while they remained preoccupied with divisive elections, labor unrest, and social diversity.

But the Third Reich was already preoccupied with the next step towards its suicide. All outsiders became suspect. Preposterous claims, hostile warnings, ominous threats isolated the Third Reich. Finally, its publicly advertised intent became a stark reality in the following years of bloody destruction.

For by 1941, the Third Reich had destroyed almost everything in reach and had attained the acme of power. It had conquered virtually all of Europe and was allied with the only real power in the Far East. Great Britain was on its knees with only its meager air power and a sympathetic American president to count on. The Third Reich had conquered more people, more industrial capacity, more agricultural land, more national territory than a modern Charlemagne could have dreamed.

If worldly conquest and undisputed power had been the Third Reich's goal, now would have been the time to consolidate its gains and unify its conquests. It was the most powerful society on the face of the earth. But worldly conquest, material wealth, territorial expansion, and undisputed power were obviously not the real goals of the

German Third Reich. For on more than one occasion, its Leader had identified the three-phased course of action that he and his generals all agreed would most certainly constitute *selbmorden.*

This agreed course to suicide would be, one, to attempt to conquer Russia, two, intimidate the United States into conflict, and, three, to be thereby forced into a two-front war. At the peak of its power, the Third Reich took this exact course of action.

By the dawn of April, 1945, the Third Reich and its Leader had gone to their mutual suicides. Certainly, not all of the Third Reich's constituents died in its social suicide. But 9 million of them did, including the over 3 million German Jews it destroyed as a token concession to its omnipotence while in its death throes. Its major cities were in ruin; its economy laid waste; its countryside scorched; its culture dismantled. Its leadership was eliminated by suicide, execution, or imprisonment. Only the paradoxical sympathy of some of its enemies prevented the absolute destruction of all its people and its homeland.

For even when defeat was obvious, the Third Reich persisted in following the exhortations of its Leader, "Surrender is forbidden. The fight is to the death."

For a fight to its death was exactly the goal of the Third Reich in the first place. It superficially seemed to succeed the First Reich of Charlemagne and Barbarossa and the Second of Bismark and the Kaiser. But the Third Reich actually aimed at the berserkers of Odin —the ecstasy of battle to the death—and ultimately, Valhalla, the Hall of the Immortal Slain in Battle.

THE PEOPLES TEMPLE

November 18, 1978.[2] The bloated corpses of over 900 members of the Peoples Temple lay in a grotesquely colorful array in a clearing of the Guyana jungle. The stench of decaying human flesh rose in macabre incense to the Suicide Syndrome in its socialized form.

Outwardly, these people had sought comfort, meaning, and direction to their lives through the otherwise humane goals of mutual love, racial tolerance, and universal understanding. But unconsciously, they had rallied around their common experience of being abused, inadequate, and deprived, to seek eternal salvation through collective self-destruction. Together, they joined in a mass demonstration of the metaphysical actualization of the Innocent Fantastic Self.

Just as the Third Reich chose a leader who personified its beliefs about itself, so the Peoples Temple coalesced around its chosen spokesman. And just as the Third Reich gladly abdicated the course of its fate to the will of Adolf Hitler, so the Peoples Temple joyously placed its fate in the hands of Reverend James Warren Jones.

Certainly no one could question Reverend Jones' original altruistic fervor, nor doubt his sincerity in carrying it out. For Jim Jones was not content with simply mouthing idealistic euphemisms. He put his ideals to work in church, community, even in his own home.

There is little wonder, then, that his faithful flock congregated around him; that they called him back from a happy, nuclear bomb-proof escape in Brazil to lead them; that they followed him from a repressive experience in the Midwest to greener pastures in California; that they accompanied him on the fateful voyage to the promised land in Guyana; that they attributed to him suprahuman messianic powers.

For Jim Jones personified the symbiotic love, universal understanding, and altruistic benignity of the Innocent Fantastic Self. And the effects upon him of his flock's adulation demonstrated another fundamental principle of the Suicide Syndrome. The corrupting effects of absolute power lie in its apparent confirmation of the leader's Fantastic Self.

For while the congregants of the Peoples Temple sought confirmation of their collective innocence through Jim Jones' leadership, he found apparent confirmation of all his Fantastic Self's attributes in their compliant adulation. Confronted by their unquestioned belief in him, by their absolute obedience to him, by their irrevocable faith in him, Jim Jones' previously unconscious belief in his personal omnipotence, innocence, and transcendence elevated into his awareness. Jim Jones began consciously to see himself as his true Fantastic Self. And he began to behave accordingly.

Paradoxically, his consequent behavior only reinforced his followers' faith in him. Now isolated from the rest of the world in the Guyana jungle, the Peoples Temple formed into a cohesive and compact system under his messianic leadership. It cleared the jungle foliage away for its crops, it organized a flourishing functional system, built neat and substantial housing, installed health facilities. But it also began to suppress or ostracize its few remaining dissenters. It grew increasingly paranoid toward outsiders. It hinged all its functions on faith in its leader. And, finally, its real suicidal intent came to the surface.

In its final weeks, all the characteristics of Synpathic crises came to the fore. It automatically escalated expressions of Self-Hatred and Hopelessness and defenses to Vindictiveness. Public confessions of imaginary guilt, self-inflicted punishments, penance for fleshly desires, condemnation of sexuality mixed with perverse expressions of it, and ritualized surrogate sacrifices began to characterize the daily life of the Peoples Temple.

Then came the *White Night* pseudosuicide ritual. Night after night, upon the beckoning of its leader, members of the Peoples Temple lined up to drink the mystic potion. Was it poison? Was it not? Who knows? Who cares? Leave it to eternal fate in the personage of Father—Dad—Reverend Jim Jones.

Finally, the humiliating visit by Congressman Ryan and his party of news reporters triggered the inevitable. Hysterical Vindictiveness flashed to the surface with the murders at the airstrip. Back in the jungle clearing, the rehearsed ritual finally became a reality. Few resisted the cyanide-laced Koolaid at the last moment and those who did were shouted down by the masses.

"We are only passing on to a higher life," exhorted the Peoples Temple's messiah before he cried out to his dead mother and fired his own fatal shot. Only a couple of scroungy dogs and an uncommitted few were left to attest to the carnage.

THE SLA

Most Apathic societies do not raise their nihilism to the obvious degree of the SLA.[3] For despite the unconscious destructiveness characterizing Apathic transcendentalism, the vast majority of Apathic societies restrain their opposition to the surrounding social establishment merely to rising above it intellectually, aesthetically, or spiritually.

However, even in this context, Apathic destructiveness shows through. Instruments of mass destruction have an eerie unconscious attraction to the transcendent. Following their characteristic premium on the abstract, they can devote their esoteric energies to the development of the most awesome tools of destruction with serene stoic detachment.

Yet the obliteration of mundane existence is the unconscious goal of every Apathic system. And nowhere could this goal be more apparent than in the acts of a small band of insurgents who called themselves the SLA. Each word of its name—Symbionese Liberation Army —symbolizes one of the primary attributes of the Fantastic Self. And after all these years, no one can point to anything else the SLA could have stood for or any other reason that it believed it had to die.

It would be easy to dismiss the SLA as simply a small band of ruffians unrealistically out to win political power, but they made no efforts towards power. Despite their overtures, they really were not out to aid and abet the downtrodden, as was the early Peoples Temple. Nor were they obviously out for personal gain or to effect comprehensive social change. Nor, finally, were they just after notoriety. They had attained that long before they chose to die. Entirely to the contrary, their ultimate goal of social suicide became more obvious at every step of their course towards attaining it.

Very few people took notice of the Symbionese Liberation Army until the publicity following its kidnapping of Patricia Hearst, of the well-known publishing fortune. Several months before, it had claimed the murder of a San Francisco public school official, for "crimes against the children." But the SLA remained a mysterious unknown.

However, in the months following the February, 1974, kidnapping of the "daughter of a corporate enemy of the people," the SLA made itself notorious. It was, said its leader, one Donald De Freeze who called himself Cinque, against "all forms of racism, sexism, ageism, capitalism, fascism, individualism, possessiveness, and competitiveness." But, despite its typically sweeping Apathic indictment, it offered no suggestions as to how to alleviate these evils.

An insight into the premeditated fate of the SLA could easily have been surmised from its leader's assumed name. For Cinque was originally the name of a fictional Negro slave who led an abortive rebellion against hopelessly superior odds, leading to his and his followers' violent deaths.

But now having chosen its obvious course, the SLA was busily working towards a similar fate. The few dissenting persons were ostracized. The remainder shaped their group into a hard core of conformity. Even their kidnap victim was pressed into membership and given a new name, Tania, to demonstrate her conformity.

In the following months, the SLA went through the ambivalent tactics typical of Apathic crises. In March, it coerced the Hearst family into distributing millions of dollars worth of food to the needy, thus illustrating its esoteric concern for humankind. In April, it demonstrated its hostility through an armed robbery of a Hybernia, California bank. Then, the SLA seemed to disappear into Apathic obscurity.

But not for long. Most certainly to its surprise, the SLA went undetected by state and federal law enforcement forces while housed in San Francisco. So, naturally, it moved to East Los Angeles where it could more easily be found. To assure detection, a couple of members robbed a small store of a few items, shooting up the place in the process. Then the SLA moved into a house where it intimidated the residents but allowed them periodically to leave the premises.

At last, the word got around. The previously baffled police were informed that the hard-core five of the SLA were sequestered in the house at 1466 East 54th Street.

Surrounded by 350 heavily armed police, the SLA made its ultimate decision. As to the true nature of that decision there could be no doubt. They had several hours to surrender before the shooting started. None of them had committed a capital crime and they faced only trial and incarceration at worst. Even if their probable suspicions of being shot at upon emergence from the house were well-founded, at least they might have had a chance. Finally, to signify the decision, they allowed two persons who were not members of the group to leave the house before the shooting started. That evening, over a thousand rounds of spent ammunition later, the house on 54th Street burned to the ground with the SLA inside.

Part VIII

PREVENTING SUICIDE

Chapter 28

CRISIS MEDIATION

That impossible metaphysical moment passes, and those human beings who once existed exist no more. Survivors mourn for a while, researchers add numbers to their data, life in the real world goes on.

What happened to the Antipathic Suicide? Murdered by a figment of his own imagination. The Synpathic? Victimized by her own vindictive rage against others. And the Apathic? Destroyed by the inexplicable consequences of his own imagined dilemma. Terminating a life unconsciously devoted to the impossible actualization of an illusionary Fantastic Self, suicide constitutes its final impossibility.

Yet the terrible tragedy of the Suicide Syndrome shows through the stupid irony of it all. For the more convinced the Suicide is in his Fantastic Self, the more compelled he becomes towards attempting its metaphysical actualization in the face of its contradiction in real life.[1]

However, by definition, every suicidal crisis must end with a decision. Each time the Suicide is confronted with a crisis, he must decide either to attempt the metaphysical actualization of his Fantastic Self or to stay alive. In the overwhelming majority of cases, he decides to stay alive. Indeed, given the widespread prevalence of the Suicide Syndrome and the almost infinite number of suicidal crises it generates, the relative incidence of overt suicide is extremely small. Nevertheless, as we have seen, a potentially lethal crisis can occur at any time in the life of any Suicide.

ASSESSING LETHAL POTENTIALITY OF SUICIDAL CRISES

The lethal potentiality of a suicidal crisis is directly related to three interdependent sets of variables: precipitating factors, reaction to crisis, and suicidal methodology.

The intensity of the precipitating factors is the obvious first set of criteria by which the lethal potentiality of a crisis must be gauged. But this intensity can only be measured from the subjective experience of the Suicide. What it boils down to with the adult Suicide is how greatly the event, situation, or condition contradicts his belief in his Fantastic Self, and the adequacy of his defenses against the contradiction.

As we know, most potentially lethal crises are accumulative. An event contradicts expected confirmation, customary defenses prove inadequate, and the Suicide then escalates his defenses to the degree that they paradoxically add to the contradiction. All this must be taken into account when assessing lethal potentiality.

How determined or accustomed is the Suicide in gaining illusionary confirmation of his Fantastic Self in the specific area it has been contradicted? How deeply entrenched are his expectations in this area? How strongly are they reinforced? How profound or unexpected is the contradiction? How inadequate are his customary defenses? And, finally, to what extent do his escalated defenses add to the contradiction?

With the younger or elderly Suicide, stages of syndrome development enter the picture. How necessarily committed to his belief in his Fantastic Self is the suicidal child and how greatly have environmental conditions or events contradicted it? What prevailing conditions prevent the preadolescent from repressing his conviction in his Fantastic Self and what event elicits its manifestation? What pervasive factors intervene in the adolescent's resolution and what situation brings this difficulty to a head? What defenses does the postadolescent lack and how has his resolution been contradicted? Finally, what special challenge to his immortality, beyond the obvious, has occurred with the older Suicide and how does it hook into his old motivations?

In all cases, only the subjective evaluation of the precipitating factors in the light of the Suicide's own experience can be considered. That which is crucial to one Suicide can be virtually insignificant to another. To be sure, contradictory defenses as manifested in the Suicidal Lifestyle are particularly important. But only to the extent that they contradict his belief in his Fantastic Self. Chronic consequences such as highly fatuous rationalizations, depression, alcoholism, sexual disturbances, and suicidogenic factors can add considerable weight to these contradictions, as we have seen. However, the immediate lethal potentiality must still be measured with regard to the immediate precipitating factors.

The second set of variables, reaction to crisis, is equally important in determining lethal potentiality. But just consideration of the Suicide's own reaction to crisis is never enough. The reaction of his environment to his reaction to crisis must also be taken into account.

We know that the adult Suicide reacts to his crisis by escalating his defenses and expressions of secondary motivations in order to regain confirmation of his Fantastic Self. But how have the people in his environment reacted to these escalations?

For example, the Antipathic strikes out at others in a crisis as a result of these escalations. Have those around him crumbled before his powers, reconfirming his imagined omnipotence? Or have they effectively resisted or escaped his attacks, thus further denying him his illusions? The Synpathic cries out for help. Have those in her environment responded in ways that would reconfirm her innocence? Or have they reacted in ways which would further deny it? The Apathic strikes out at mundane life. Have those in his environment reconfirmed his customary mode of ascending it or have they denied his transcendence of mundane life by further entangling him in its noose?

In addition, how has the Suicide reacted to the reactions of those in his environment? Has he continued to escalate his defenses and secondary expressions in return? Have they, in turn, escalated their denials? Has this potentially fatal interplay been building up to the point where, strictly because of everyone's defenses, no one can seem to break the cycle? How long and how fervently has it been building?

With the younger and elderly Suicide, again, stages of development must be considered. The environment's reaction to the critical issue of each developmental stage must be taken into account when assessing lethal potentiality.

In all cases, this comprehensive picture of the Suicide in relation to his environment is paramount. Quite often, just one person apparently plays a more prominent role. But it would be a serious error, and one often made, to measure the lethal potentiality of a suicidal crisis strictly from a dyadic point of view. Reactions of the seemingly most unimportant people or institutions in the Suicide's environment can have a profound effect on the lethal potentiality of his crisis.

Suicidal methodology is the third set of variables determining the lethal potentiality of a crisis. For, obviously, the Suicide must utilize a lethal method in order for him to commit suicide.

To be sure, the Suicide is surrounded by potentially lethal instruments in his everyday life. But the mere presence of a lethal method in no way satisfies our criteria. Several other factors must also be taken into account.

First among these is compatibility with type, age, and experience. For example, men in our society are predominately Antipathic Types. They usually use more violent means than our predominately Synpathic women. By the same token, young boys, who are usually taught the use of guns if only through toys, would be more inclined to use such violent means than would young girls. This certainly does not preclude the possibility of male Antipathics using more passive means or female Synpathics using more violent means. But compatibility with type, age, and experience is a factor which must be considered.

Second is the immediate availability of a compatible method. The Suicide who talks of killing himself with a gun he does not have is obviously not as potentially lethal as one who has a gun in hand. One who speaks of overdosing, with nothing more than a few aspirin on hand, is obviously not as potentially lethal as one who has 50 Seconal on the bedside table. And so on.

Third is the Suicide's familiarity and confidence regarding the method available. It is extremely important to the potentially lethal Suicide that he is familiar with and has confidence in his proposed method. He wants to be certain his method will be fatal and relatively immune to accidental abortion or forceful interference by intruders. This is one reason why the use of kitchen knives, common household chemicals, or elaborate contrivances can often be ruled out.

Fourth is the potential pain or physiological trauma of available methods. This is especially true of the Synpathic Type who does not want her suicide to "hurt," even for a moment. Neither the Antipathic nor the Apathic are quite so concerned about trauma. However, all potentially lethal Suicides are concerned with finding a methodology which promises as quick or as painless a death as possible.

Fifth is the definitiveness of the Suicide's planned method.

Vague and nebulous allusions to committing suicide are obviously not as potentially lethal as definitive plans. While any Suicide can kill himself in any way on impulse, arrival at a definitive plan always increases the lethal potentiality.

Finally, the degree of reinforcement of the Suicide's planned method is a very important factor. Very few Suicides actually commit suicide without having at least mulled over the method, thus reinforcing it, for a considerable period of time. A definitive method, incorporating a familiar means which is immediately available and which the Suicide has heavily autoreinforced through real or imagined rehearsals, poses very high lethal potentiality. Environmental reinforcement by family, friends, and society at large adds to it. And actual rehearsals through nonfatal attempts constitute the most potentially lethal reinforcement of all.

The vast quantity of variables contained in these three sets of criteria can be overwhelming. They render it infinitely difficult, if not virtually impossible, to predict any actual suicide with any proven degree of reliability.[2]

It is crucial, therefore, whether or not life-sustaining aid is rendered to any Suicide who even just vaguely appears potentially lethal. For every suicidal crisis, regardless of its lethal potentiality, is amenable to crisis mediation.

INAPPROPRIATE INTERVENTIONS

Forceful intervention, however, is almost always inappropriate. The exception would occur in such instances as that of a very young child who has not yet learned of the fatal consequences of his actions, the Suicide whose rationalizations have inaccessibly escalated beyond the realm of consensual reality, the Suicide who has already embarked upon a sure lethal course and is relatively helpless to reverse the process alone, or the Suicide who is so narcotized that further decision making is impossible for him.

The Suicide's reaction to forceful intervention usually conforms with type. The Antipathic is vehement over intrusion on his control. The Synpathic is resentful and feels abused, inadequate, and deprived in relation to the intervenors. The Apathic resorts to philosophic claims in regard to his suicidal rights. Not surprisingly, even the imagined prospect of forceful intervention can elicit all these reactions in any Suicide who just contemplates an attempt.

Of course, what the Suicide is really adamant about is interference with the anticipated actualization of his Fantastic Self. When confronted by the obvious fact that he can always commit suicide in the future, he will most likely deny it. He argues that he may "never get up the nerve" again or that he may "never be able to make the decision" again. But behind these rationalizations lies the contradiction of his Fantastic Self inherent in forceful intervention which can intensify the lethal potentiality of immediate or future crises. This is why forceful intervention should be avoided in all cases short of immediate impending death.

Incarceration in custodial institutions, alone, is equally inappropriate. Custodial care may appear to have the advantage of removing the Suicide from environmental elements precipitating his crisis or the escalation of his reaction to it. But, by the same token, it places the crisis beyond resolution by the Suicide.

Furthermore, custodial care cannot be completely suicide-proof. This holds true even for the best-run hospitals or jails and despite special precautions conjunctive with "suicidal status" designations. The multitude of opportunities for suicide under such conditions has been amply demonstrated.[3] Indeed, the data show that hospitalized psychiatric patients commit suicide six to ten times more often than people on the outside.[4]

Finally, custodial care not only reinforces the Suicide's rationalizations regarding the extrinsic origins of his suicidal impulses from which he apparently must be protected. It also adds an obvious contradiction to the Suicide's Fantastic Self, increasing his shame, humiliation, and despair, and the suicidal motivations they generate. Thus, many Suicides kill themselves while on furlough from the hospital or shortly after discharge.[5]

Medical interventions, alone, also prove equally inappropriate. To be sure, physical trauma resulting from nonlethal attempts warrant immediate medical treatment. But the suicidal crisis that brought the physical trauma about is not a legitimate medical issue. The only conceivable advantage to the use of pharmaceuticals lies in their possibly rendering the Suicide more "accessible" to crisis mediation, but even this possibility is open to question. And, of course, getting his hands on a lethal prescription is the crowning achievement of many a Suicide.

Medical claims establishing electric convulsive therapy as the treatment of choice for suicidal crises have generally been discounted. However, even lobotomies have been tried to relieve suicidal impulses. But the British advocate of this radical measure admits that his last two patients "died by suicide" sometime after surgery.[6]

The only redeeming factors regarding all forms of such inappropriate interventions lie in the crisis mediation which often takes place conjunctive with them. But this mediation process sometimes occurs unnoticed. If so, the inappropriate intervention is usually erroneously credited for the crisis eventually subsiding.

But crisis mediation is the only way a suicidal crisis can be fully resolved. For every suicidal crisis necessarily requires a decision in order to be resolved. Consequently, mediation between opposing options automatically takes place, whether recognized or not. And it most likely can best occur without these inappropriate interventions. The Suicide can, and usually does, mediate his own crisis. But when confronted with a crisis beyond his own powers of mediation, he will need help through Crisis Mediation. Crisis Mediation consists of four distinct but overlapping stages: communication, confrontation, catharsis, and commitment.

COMMUNICATION

Frank and open communication with an objective and understanding other person is the obvious first step. But this is not easy. Once in a crisis, the Suicide is not usually prone to initiate frank and open communication with anyone. This is not to say that he will not or cannot communicate his suicidal intent. Much to the contrary, he can, and he usually does, at the very least hint at his suicidal intentions, to almost everyone with whom he comes into contact. But he rarely finds, nor does he expect to find, objective understanding for his plight.

Furthermore, it is virtually impossible, especially in the absence of knowledge of the syndrome, for people in the Suicide's immediate environment to be objective and understanding. Indeed, the people in the Suicide's immediate environment—family, friends, or co-workers—are usually so involved in the interpersonal consequences of his suicidal motivations and reaction to crisis that there is little possibility for objectivity and understanding. They usually react to his suicidal intimations with disbelief, anxiety, hostility, or fear.

Thus, the best person for the Suicide to turn to is a professional or paraprofessional trained in crisis mediation. Ideally, this mediator's capacities would include excellent counseling skills plus empathy, objectivity, experience with suicidal crises, and a thorough knowledge of their origins and complexities.

However, effective communication can only be established after the Suicide has been convinced that this mediator will not resort to other, inappropriate, interventions. For the mediation processes to follow can only occur in an ambience of mutual understanding and trust.

The obvious first goal of this communication phase is to establish just such a reasonable degree of mutual understanding and trust. Here, also, the mediator tries to obtain a picture of the Suicide's general situation, an estimated assessment of lethal potentiality, identification of stage or type, and other factors bearing on the usual counseling situation.

Confrontation

After this trusting and empathic communication is established, the Suicide is confronted with his suicidal impulses contingent with his crisis and then with the precipitating factors which brought his crisis about. This need for the Suicide actually to confront his immediate suicidal impulses might seem redundant, but this is never the case.

For instance, the reality of his suicidal behavior may be considerably obscured to him. This would be particularly true for the naive child or that Suicide whose rationalizations have extended well beyond consensual reality. But it is also true of the normally well-oriented adult Suicide involved in a severe crisis. For the complexities of the syndrome inherently obscure or confuse the real life and death issues of suicide.

Even when the Suicide does acknowledge his immediate suicidal impulses, he often tends to not confront them as his own. He will talk about his impulses as though they come from out of the blue, originating from some inexplicable extrinsic force that he can only fight against or succumb to, but over which he has no control. He will speak of his suicidal impulses as though he is afflicted with them. It is as if they originate in some mysterious flaw or disease with which he was born or has inexplicably contracted. He will say that it is only reasonable for him to feel suicidal, given the conditions of his life. Or he will say that it is only natural, in view of the human condition.

Knowing the real origins of his suicidal impulses, it is easy for us to understand his tendency to evade responsibility for them. Nevertheless, it is absolutely essential to effective crisis mediation for the Suicide not only to be confronted with his suicidal impulses, but for him to experience them as his own.

Frank, open, friendly, and matter-of-fact confrontation works best. "Are you thinking about killing yourself?" the Suicide is asked. "How do you plan to kill yourself?" "When?" This kind of direct confrontation contains a number of inherent advantages.

One, it provides real information to the mediator as to the lethal potentiality of the crisis. This is especially true if the Suicide feels confident that the mediator will not over-react to mention of specific plans with anxiety, fear, or especially, inappropriate intervention.

Two, such confrontation brings the entire crisis down into the realm of matter-of-fact reality. This is why the phrase, "kill yourself" is far more effective than "commit suicide," which, as we know, contains an inherent metaphysical quality. And it is obviously preferable to such evasive euphemisms as "do something to yourself," or "do something you can't undo," or especially, "do something foolish."

Three, such frank, matter-of-fact, and anxiety-free confrontation invites the Suicide to discuss his impulses with the mediator in a like manner. He can abandon his own evasions and euphemisms and confront his actual behavior in a concrete way.

Finally, such confrontation opens the door to investigation of the precipitating factor of his suicidal crisis. For even though Self-Hatred, Vindictiveness, and Hopelessness are the unconscious motivations for suicide, they cannot precipitate suicidal crises. A suicidal crisis can only be precipitated by an event, situation, or condition which elicits these motivations by virtue of the shame, humiliation, or despair it generates.

This distinction is very important to crisis mediation for two reasons. First, there is no possibility of raising, and therefore no reason to attempt to alleviate the Suicide's real unconscious Self-Hatred, Vindictiveness, and Hopelessness in crisis mediation. This is not to say that the Suicide in a crisis may not be aware that he harbors exaggerated expectations of himself, others, or life. But this awareness, again, stems from such expressions as inner dictates, external claims, and abstract values, not from his unconscious motivations per se. His unconscious motivations are simply not accessible in times of severe suicidal crisis.

Second, this distinction is important because it is essential for the Suicide to focus on the actual event, situation, or condition that precipitated his suicidal crisis in order to mediate it. But the Suicide often resists focusing on this specific precipitating situation. He will either deny knowledge of any specific reason he feels suicidal or he will dwell on generalizations. Since he cannot understand the real nature and origins of his suicidal motivations, his resistance usually stems from his not wanting to admit that he feels suicidal over some event that he or others might consider insufficient cause for suicide— possibly even trivial.

However, as we have seen, there is no such thing as a trivial event in the life of a Suicide. What the Suicide cannot see is that any event, regardless of its importance or consequence for the course of his life in real terms, has the potential for eliciting his unconscious suicidal motivations.

So rather than focusing on the specific event, the Suicide tends to generalize. Most of his generalizations can be traced directly to the Suicidal Lifestyle. He will talk in general terms about his loneliness, isolation, and lack of friends. He will discuss his unhappy marriage, a succession of unhappy love affairs, or the absence of love in his life. He will complain of generalities in regard to his sex life. He will generally blame his drinking, his consummate lack of success, his always getting into trouble, his comprehensive illness or disability. Or he will paint a total picture of his life as one of misfortune and of loss. He may say that his life is not worth living because of its shallow boredom or because he "can't get motivated" to change it. He may lay claim to overwhelming guilt or complain in general terms of the stress and strain of his entire existence. He may even point to depression, emotional suffering, or anxiety as cause for his suicidal feelings, but still in the most general terms.

But regardless of these generalizations, every suicidal crisis is always precipitated by a specific event, situation, or condition of recent origin. Even when the Suicide designates his depression or anxiety as grounds for his suicidal impulses, a precipitating factor is present. What happened that elicited his depression? Why has he become so anxious? No suicidal crisis can be fully resolved without focusing on this specific precipitating factor.

It is, therefore, imperative that these camouflaging generalizations be put aside in favor of focusing on the specific event. Often, just encouraging the Suicide to relate the details of the course of his everyday life the last few weeks, days, or hours will uncover this event. If not, persistence is in order.

Usually, there is considerable trial and error involved in uncovering the precipitating factor. More often, there is a chain of events following the original which also must be brought to light. But in all cases there is a specific situation that causes the Suicide shame, humiliation, or despair by virtue of its contradicting his Fantastic Self and thereby precipitates his crisis. And this precipitating factor must be confronted by the Suicide in order for him successfully to mediate his crisis.

CATHARSIS

After the Suicide has confronted his suicidal impulses and focused on their precipitating circumstances, catharsis of his real suicidal motivations is called for. His mere recognition is never enough. Even though the Suicide might feel extremely relieved as a result of being able frankly to discuss his suicidal impulses and the situation precipitating them, he still must nondestructively discharge the motivations underlying them in order to eventually resolve his crisis.

However, eliciting this catharsis has its difficulties. In the first place, he may experience such relief from the communication and confrontation phases that he might not want to continue the mediation process. Also, as we know, one reason he experiences suicidal impulses is to avoid facing the very motivations he needs to bring into conscious awareness and discharge. And, finally, since he believes he cannot truly hate himself if he is Antipathic, cannot truly be vindictive towards others if Synpathic, and cannot be absolutely hopeless if Apathic, he experiences no conscious reason to express these motivations, even verbally. But to free himself of his immediate suicidal impulses, he must discharge the motivations underlying them in a nondestructive way.

This holds equally true for childhood crises. However, their verbal expression may be beyond the child's level of development. Therefore, the suicidal child is induced to act out his impulses in the least destructive way through play therapy or other vicarious methods.

The preadolescent is induced to express his motivations verbally, if feasible, or act them out nondestructively. Verbal expressions of his imagined powers are blandly accepted, indeed even elicited, in order for him to discharge the pain resulting from his repressing them.

The adolescent can be quite verbal with just a little inducement, provided he feels safely accepted. Therefore, his verbal attacks on those who are interfering with his resolution are elicited and accepted

290 THE SUICIDE SYNDROME

without judgment. Although he may seem to grow more destructive the more he expresses it, the opposite is the case. His destructiveness subsides the more he verbally discharges it.

The postadolescent or adult Suicide is induced to experience the catharsis of the primary suicidal motivation corresponding to his type. But with the postadolescent and many adults, identification of type may be difficult. However, a good rule of thumb is that his primary motivation is usually the one he least expresses on his own. If he freely verbalizes expressions of Vindictiveness and Hopelessness without inducement, then verbal expressions of Self-Hatred must be induced, and so on.

Such self-castigation may seem to be an unlikely antidote to suicidal impulses. And for the Synpathic Type, especially, this would certainly hold true. It would also be somewhat true for the Apathic Type. But he may need to discharge a measure of Self-Hatred before he can get around to his real motivations, which we know to be Hopelessness.

However, it is just this unlikely gambit that holds the most promise for the Antipathic Type. Since his suicidal impulses derive from Self-Hatred, he must verbally discharge his self-murderous rage in order to relieve them. This is not an easy tactic to induce him to try. And, because of the Antipathic Type's propensity to quick action rather than just talk, it does have its risks. It is therefore extremely important that the Antipathic Type not have a gun or other immediately lethal method conveniently at hand while experiencing his catharsis.

For while the Antipathic Type may start off directing his verbal attacks at other people, his work, society, or life in general, he is no fool. Sooner or later, especially with subtle inducement, he will get around to himself. An empathetic focus on his role in the precipitating events will often help him turn the tide: but usually not without a preliminary verbal assault on the mediator. Indeed, it may be the obvious irrationality of his assault on the mediator that induces him to see that it is at himself that his rage is really aimed.

In contrast to the Antipathic Type, the Synpathic dwells on Self-Hatred. Inducing her to turn away from expressions of Self-Hatred and Hopelessness to verbal expression of her real suicidal motivations poses a challenge. But since the Synpathic Type's Vindictiveness holds the greatest danger to herself, its catharsis is essential. However, even though such catharsis would automatically neutralize her crisis, she really believes she cannot be vindictive. Inducing her to discharge her Vindictiveness is a difficult task indeed.

Certainly, she may complain of other people's cruel and harsh treatment of her, but she lodges her complaints as victim, adding to her unconscious rage. The strategy here is to put her literally on the offensive. She is encouraged verbally to victimize in absentia the people whom she believes victimize her.

This is not to say that sympathy for her role as victim does not seem to have a neutralizing effect. The Synpathic Type basks in sympathy for her plight. And she gains considerable comfort from it. But sympathy for her plight, however comforting, cannot help her discharge her rage, which must be discharged, in order for her crisis to be resolved.

Rather than sympathy for her plight, or at least in addition to it, empathy with her rage is far more effective. As irrational as her rage may appear from an objective point of view, some of its overwhelming self-destructiveness can be experienced from an empathic sharing.

Eliciting the Antipathic's catharsis of Self-Hatred or the Synpathic's catharsis of Vindictiveness is certainly difficult. But either may seem like downhill coasting when compared with the difficulty of inducing the Apathic Type's catharsis of Hopelessness. To be sure, he may dwell on the existential futility of the human condition, even the folly of his own individual course of life. But this brand of pessimistic ridicule stems from his philosophic detachment. Life in general is hopeless—not just his mission in it.

Philosophical discussions in crisis mediation are inherently ineffectual. But no one could be more inclined to indulge in them than the Apathic Type. Their only possible advantage lies in the direction of Schopenhauer's dilemma: if every possibility is futile, then the act of suicide must be futile, too.

Once confronted by the impossibility of even his suicide transcending reality, the Apathic Type may be willing to focus on the precipitating factors of his crisis and the profound subjective despair they entail. What brand of transcendence has he been striving for? How did it fail him?

As he begins to discharge the despair contingent with his dilemma, his suicidal impulses automatically diminish. Although he pictures himself the pessimistic cynic, in truth the Apathic Type is a closet optimist. Real transcendence, he believes, is just around the corner.

In all cases, verbal or otherwise nondestructive discharge of the content of suicidal motivations is the keystone to effective crisis mediation. Often, just the Suicide vicariously experiencing the mediator's empathetic expression of this content helps. Better yet, this tactic tends to relieve the Suicide's inhibitions in his own verbal expressions.

The Suicide need not and cannot discharge all his primary motivation to suicide. However, each Suicide needs to express only enough of that motivation to keep himself alive. It is as if his "cup runneth over," and by allowing himself to express a modicum of his Self-Hatred, Vindictiveness, or Hopelessness he is able to discharge his suicidal impulses. To be sure, once the dam is broken, the catharsis will flow. And it is this very catharsis that makes it possible for the Suicide to decide to stay alive.

COMMITMENT

Finally, the Suicide makes his decision. If the communication, confrontation, and catharsis phases have been effective, he decides to stay alive rather than to kill himself. The more effective these processes, the easier his decision to live.

In fact, the Suicide can gain such profound relief from these previous processes, he tends to avoid making a conscious and deliberate decision to live. He just takes the decision for granted or he believes that actually to verbalize it would be superfluous or even absurd. But it would be a grave error not to elicit and consequently reinforce a specific and verbalized decision. A conscious and deliberate decision to live is an essential conclusion to effective crisis mediation.

However, the Suicide's decision to live must be a strictly unilateral one. Promises made to the mediator not to commit suicide, or so-called therapeutic contracts, contain inherently dangerous contradictions. The more interpersonal factors are involved in his crisis, the truer this is.

Childhood and adolescent suicidal crises cannot be fully resolved by promises to family members or their adult surrogates not to commit suicide. Indeed, such promises can, and usually do backfire, simply by virtue of the oppressive element they inherently contain. Resentment returns in the form of additional suicidal impulses, whether the young Suicide acts on them or not.

The same holds true for Synpathic crises. Relations with other people are the essential ingredients of her suicidal motivations in the first place. Promises to others not to harm herself, even when made to one who has demonstrated empathy and understanding, only add fuel to her unconscious vindictive fire. "I'm sorry to let you down, but

I just can't help myself," she would say to the mediator in absentia as she later executes her unconscious suicidal revenge.

Even the Antipathic and Apathic Types eventually react negatively to such agreements. Such promises or contracts obviously contradict Antipathic omnipotence and Apathic independence, counteracting their effectiveness. In order to be effective, therefore, each Suicide's decision to live must be a unilateral one.

Furthermore, the Suicide's decision to live upon the resolution of his crisis must be a reasonable one. Natural lifetime commitments never to attempt suicide, or indefinite, open-ended commitments are impractical, if not impossible, at this stage, even if the Suicide seems willing to make them. A unilateral commitment not to harm himself, regardless of what the situation may be or how he feels about it, but only for a specified period of time, is the only truly effective commitment the Suicide can reasonably make.

The period of time involved can vary tremendously. Of course, the longer the better, still provided it is reasonable. With the child or adolescent, some future milestone may be selected. The commitment may be made, say, until the end of the school year, until he turns eighteen, until one year after he leaves home, or any other such event. With the adult Suicide, similar milestones can be chosen, but usually, simple chronological periods—years, months, weeks, or even just days or hours if necessary—work best. The important factors are that the decision to stay alive is his and his alone, and that it is made for a reasonable period of time.

The Suicide resolving a crisis is often reluctant to make such a commitment. His reluctance usually indicates that the crisis mediation phases leading up to the present one were not thorough enough. These must be repeated to the extent necessary to elicit a sincere and positive commitment. Assurances that he can always decide to kill himself upon termination of the selected time period can be helpful. After all, compared with normal life expectancy, what percentage does the time of his commitment represent? Negotiations to elicit the longest reasonable period of time are in order, provided further emphasis is placed on the decision being his and his alone.

Once the Suicide makes his decision, he states it clearly and sincerely. Vague or apparently insincere statements or those which imply coercion such as, "OK, I won't do it until then," are ineffective. A sincere and concise statement would be such as, "I will not kill myself or do any harm to myself or to anyone else until such and such a date, regardless of how bad the situation gets or how suicidal I feel, and I won't decide to kill myself then without consulting with the mediator or another qualified counselor first."

Reinforcement of this decision is imperative. Continued, friendly conversation about the Suicide's future based on the assumption of the irrevocability of his commitment is one method. Eliciting his abbreviated repetition of it is another. A suggestion that he might want to re-establish contact sometime in the future, just to report on how he is getting along, is still another. Repetition by the mediator, in bland, matter-of-fact words in the course of conversation, is still one more way to reinforce his commitment.

As the crisis mediation process comes to a close, the Suicide learns that he has discovered a real ally of his real living self. Communication with another who displays empathic and knowledgeable understanding of his crisis, who helps him confront it, who experiences his catharsis objectively, and who shows a genuine interest in his unilateral commitment to stay alive automatically reinforces the same kind of treatment for himself on his own behalf in the future.

Should he incur future suicidal crises, and he most likely will, he will be more inclined to seek similar help in resolving them. Or, better still, he will be more inclined to repeat the mediation process on his own with similar positive results.

Chapter 29

ALLEVIATING THE SYNDROME

The Suicide will most likely survive his crisis. Indeed, he may survive many crises of varying severity, either succumbing to the more covert modes of self-destructiveness or sustaining his life to its natural end. But even though he may survive the crises stemming from it, the Suicide Syndrome takes a terrible toll on the quality of his life. After probably gaining some insight into this toll, following repeated crises he may decide he wants to get out of the Suicide Syndrome.

But in this the Suicide usually needs help. It is feasible for him somewhat to alleviate the syndrome on his own. But only if he has a thorough working knowledge of it, familiarity with the process of its alleviation, and a good understanding of the intrapsychic processes involved. However, even then, his getting help in the process is far more practical for several reasons.

One, the Suicide had a great deal of help in getting into the syndrome in the first place. He accordingly can use help getting out of it. Two, even though he may have a working knowledge of the syndrome, many of its unconscious intricacies will escape his awareness. Three, alleviating the syndrome can be a very painful and disruptive process. Understanding companionship and immediate reinforcement of constructive moves is virtually essential. And last, the processes involved are often deviously deceptive. When the Suicide believes he is making genuine constructive moves can be the very time he may merely be shifting self-destructive modes of expression.

Having a competent professional counselor, psychologist, or suicidologist thoroughly familiar with the syndrome and its alleviation to help avoid these pitfalls and to provide reinforcement is crucial and decisive. For the only way for the Suicide to alleviate his syndrome is for him meticulously to reverse each of its processes, eventually relinquishing his belief that he is his Fantastic Self.

INADEQUATE AMELIORATION

Paradoxically, the Suicide usually seeks counseling or psychotherapy for the exact opposite goal. Unable to actualize his unconscious Fantastic Self in everyday life and having suffered for it, the Suicide enters counseling or psychotherapy with the secret hope of finding the "key" to its actualization.

At the very most, he looks to counseling or psychotherapy to help relieve him of the unhappy consequences of his secret conviction; certainly never to relieve him of the unconscious conviction itself. He may seek relief from anxiety, guilt, or depression, for example. He may want assistance with overcoming his alcoholism, chronic trouble with authority, his overwhelming reaction to loss. He may look for help with his sexual difficulties or in resolving his disturbed love relations. He may even identify his mental anguish as an area in which he seeks relief. He may seek counseling or psychotherapy in order to become more aggressive and less passive, more independent and less driven, more involved and less alienated.

Whatever the nature of his complaints, however, he rarely comes into counseling or psychotherapy openly complaining of his suicidal impulses. This is true even though he may have suffered intense suicidal crises in the past. He either assumes the counselor or psychotherapist already knows he is suicidal or he conceals his suicidal impulses for defensive reasons of his own.[7]

By the same token, the counselor or psychotherapist may tend to ignore the suicidal impulses of his client. This is especially true in the absence of the client's specific mention of them. He may take for granted that his client is suicidal on account of other problems, rather than the reverse, and that the impulses will subside as counseling or therapy progresses. He may discount the seriousness of his client's impulses or focus only on their manipulative aspects. Or he may fail to realize that his client is suicidal at all.

For this reason, the counselor or psychotherapist is often drawn into the interpersonal contingencies of his client's suicidal motivations. This can not only impair progress. It can result in great risk to his client's life.

It is imperative, therefore, that the counselor or psychotherapist openly confront his client's suicidal impulses very early in the therapeutic process, whether his client mentions them on his own or not. And it is imperative that the counselor or psychotherapist elicit his client's unconditional unilateral commitment to stay alive, at least for the projected counseling or therapy period, whether his client admits to suicidal impulses or not.

Fortunately, most currently popular behavioral and psychotherapeutic theories and methodologies have a temporary ameliorating effect on the processes of the Suicide Syndrome. Behavioral changes, for instance, diminish the autoreinforcing effects on the syndrome of the particular behavior extinguished. Improvement of communication with others and reduction of banal scripts and games contain similar ameliorating effects. An understanding of historical material and catharsis of current self-destructive motivations associated with it meliorates immediate self-destructiveness. Enhanced cognizance of feelings, behaviors, and relations in the here and now helps decrease the Suicide's dangerous inner dichotomy. A more realistic subjective assessment of the Suicide's condition in relation to the real ways of the world tends to diminish reinforcement of his unconscious convictions. Just his experiencing sympathy and understanding from a concerned other person or group can help relieve his estrangement.[8]

Similarly, the use of certain prescribed drugs appears to ameliorate some consequences of the syndrome. Antidepressants, tranquilizers, and mood stabilizers all possess temporary meliorating effects. Extended hospitalization can also appear meliorative. This is especially true should the Suicide weather the immediate contradiction to his Fantastic Self inherent in custodial care. But as he grows more "hospital-wise" his chronic suicidal patterns inevitably return.[9]

Finally, incidental change in life course or environment often results in superficial ameliorating effects. Favorable changes in social conditions, economic status, or education can often add the appearance of positive consequences, but only in the short run.

But in all these respects, amelioration of consequences cannot constitute alleviation of the syndrome bringing them about. Psychotherapeutic methods not specifically aimed at alleviation of the comprehensive syndrome cannot eradicate it merely through relief from some of its consequences. Medications cannot actually alter the course of the syndrome without seriously impairing those salient human qualities from which it paradoxically stems. Custodial care cannot modify the unconscious motivations eliciting its imposition. Incidental change in life course or environment cannot eliminate the secret motivations which usually bring them about. The only way the Suicide Syndrome can truly be alleviated is through a comprehensive process specifically designed expressly for that purpose.

DEVELOPMENTAL STAGES

It would seem that the Suicide Syndrome would be readily amenable to alleviation in its earliest developmental stages. And this would certainly hold true for childhood and preadolescent stages were it not for the obvious problem of the young Suicide's environment. Indeed, the younger the Suicide, the more influential his immediate environment on the development and reinforcement of his syndrome. And, unfortunately, the younger he is, the more difficult it is for his environment to be changed.

There is no such thing as a suicidal child who does not derive from a suicidogenic environment. Therefore, some kind of environmental change is a prerequisite for alleviation of the syndrome in the very young Suicide. The suicidal child or preadolescent must either be moved from his current environment to a less pernicious one or his current environment must undergo radical change if his syndrome is to be alleviated.

All the complex ramifications of the Suicide Syndrome in the parent or parent surrogate must be taken into account when attempting to alleviate the syndrome in a child or preadolescent. As a general rule, the younger the suicidal child, the more the process must shift from focusing on him to focusing on the adults who shape his environment.

Fortunately, by the time it reaches the adolescent phase, the syndrome is more amenable to alleviation on its own account. In fact, once mutual trust and understanding is established, the adolescent syndrome can best be tackled without parental involvement. Certainly, the contaminating elements may still be present in the adolescent's home environment. But by encouraging him to look forward to the day he will be free from this lends him the impetus to work on his syndrome for himself.

Much the same process employed for the adult Suicide is applicable to the adolescent, postadolescent, and elderly Suicide. Of course, developmental factors must still be taken into account. For example, the postadolescent's defenses are not as fully developed as the adult's. He therefore does not cling to them with the same degree of tenacity. But by the same token, he is more immediately vulnerable to his raw suicidal motivations.

On the other hand, the elderly Suicide's defenses are strongly developed and tenacious. They have obviously served him well: that is, except in the face of his mortality. Social conditions again play a major role with the elderly Suicide. But the central task in alleviating his syndrome is his coming to terms with the immutable finality of his impending death.

In all cases, it is of paramount importance that the Suicide comes to understand that the counselor, psychologist, or suicidologist helping him alleviate his syndrome is dedicated to his real best interests and to those alone, and that he is an advocate for the Suicide's real living self against all other influences. For only on the basis of an exclusive and confidential alliance between the mediator and the Suicide's real living self can the difficult task of alleviating the Suicide Syndrome take place. This is because the alleviation of the syndrome must culminate in the Suicide relinquishing his conviction in his Fantastic Self in its favor. But the process cannot start there. As desirable as this may seem and as expedient as it may appear, the Suicide obviously cannot forego this conviction early in the process, even though he may be intellectually aware that this conviction lies at the heart of his syndrome.

The alleviation of the Suicide Syndrome essentially consists of a slow, meticulous reversal of the total process and all its illusions. This need for disillusionment is rarely apparent on the surface, especially in the beginning. For instance, because of his arrogance, the Antipathic Type is not prone to seek counseling or psychotherapy on his own in any case. But the rare instances when he might seek help usually follow periods of discouragement when he appears already thoroughly disillusioned.

Disillusionment would seem to be the last thing the Synpathic Type would need. She usually seeks help when overcome by her feelings of being abused, inadequate, and deprived, a far cry from the apparent need for disillusionment. The Apathic Type believes he has no illusions, especially about himself. The rare instances when he might seek help would be to improve his adjustment to his already disillusioned picture of the follies of life.

But in every case, alleviation of the syndrome constitutes a systematic dispensing with the Suicide's illusions, culminating with the principle illusion—his Fantastic Self—upon which all his other illusions are founded. The Suicide who is unaware of the syndrome and of his belief in his Fantastic Self and who seeks help only with the consequences of his belief shows a certain serendipitous wisdom. For the analysis of these consequences is exactly where the alleviation process must start.

LIFESTYLE ANALYSIS

In keeping with the reversal of the process, the systematic alleviation of the Suicide Syndrome begins with an objective analysis of the Suicide's personal style of life. In the course of this analysis, the Suicide comes to understand that those facets of his everyday life which seem to be cause for his complaints are, in fact, consequences of a far more comprehensive and fundamental process of which he is the author.

In the course of his lifestyle analysis, no possible consequence of the Suicide Syndrome can be overlooked. It is not enough for him simply to examine those aspects constituting cause for initial complaints or presenting problems. Every aspect of the Suicidal Lifestyle must bear examination, whether the Suicide consciously experiences it as reason for complaint or not. All facets of the Suicide's conceptual, affectual, behavioral, sexual, interpersonal, and social life must be brought to light as subject for thorough and objective examination.

It is enough, however, for the Suicide simply to accept these merely as consequences of a more fundamental process. He need not attempt to uncover the details of this process at this stage. Indeed, his preoccupation with causation can severely hamper investigation. And the Suicide often uses just such a preoccupation as a defensive gambit against a more thorough investigation. He tries to discover why he does what he does rather than face and fully analyze exactly what it is he is doing.

Other defenses to a thorough investigation usually consist of rather transparent rationalizations. It is only "normal" to harbor insatiable ambitions. It is only "natural" continually to sacrifice for love. It is only "reasonable" to value abstract concepts, aesthetics, or ideals as superior to personal, interpersonal, or social goals.

Social conditions are often used as grounds for further rationalizations. To be sure, it must be conceded to the Suicide that society does prescribe certain roles, statuses, and mores. But the Suicide must also come to recognize what rewards he believes he personally obtains by virtue of his adherence to the prescriptions. Just how real or how spurious are they? And how strongly does he choose to contribute to the perpetuation of such a system?

Only after a thorough analysis of his lifestyle is the Suicide ready to proceed to a more advanced phase of work. However, regardless of how thorough or objective this analysis is, he will soon discover the need to return to this phase for further investigation. For as the Suicide delves into his defenses and expressions, their consequences in shaping his lifestyle will grow increasingly more apparent, thus providing further material for lifestyle analysis.

DEFENSES

As a result of the Suicide's lifestyle analysis, he begins to confront his defenses. He first examines his evasions. He looks at what he evades, how he evades it, and most important, what his evasions cost him in real life terms.

The Antipathic examines his checks and avoidances. He tries to ferret out what exactly causes him additional shame. He looks at how he holds himself back to evade the shame contingent with what he perceives as a failure or defeat. He comes to understand that as long as he keeps checks on active strivings, he cannot attain even a modicum of his real life goals.

The Synpathic faces her passive withdrawal. She sees how it protects her from what she experiences as humiliation. When she laments that there is no one whom she can trust, she must confront the real issue: trust them to do what? Finally, she recognizes how her withdrawal precludes even an opportunity for fulfillment of her desires.

The Apathic looks at his stoic detachment. He sees that this game can only satisfy his illusions about himself. He looks at why he automatically interprets real involvement in real life as cause for further despair. He recognizes that he cannot possibly gain genuine gratification through anything from which he holds himself apart.

The Suicide then confronts his more destructive displacement defenses. The Antipathic begins to recognize how he externalizes self-condemnation onto other people. He sees that this tactic can only bring him their hostility and lack of cooperation in return. The Synpathic begins to recognize how she internalizes her rage against others. It slowly but surely dawns on her how much she suffers strictly on this account. The Apathic begins to recognize the roots of his hopeless interpretation of life. He sees that life as a process can only remain an exercise in futility as long as he generalizes his own futile mission upon it.

Gradually, as the Suicide confronts his displacement defenses, he begins to comprehend just exactly what beliefs about himself he has been so valiantly trying to protect. And he begins to wonder if protecting nothing more than an illusion is worth the debilitation his defenses automatically entail.

However, this comprehension must come from the Suicide strictly on his own. A direct assault on his rather paranoid displacement defenses can only result in their automatic escalation. But once the Suicide does begin fully to recognize their spurious content on his own, reinforcement is most certainly in order.

Armed with this insight of his merely having been defending an illusion, the Suicide confronts his most destructive compromising defenses. At this point, review of recent historical material can be valuable. What loss has the Antipathic Type recently incurred? What happened to cause him shame immediately prior to the loss? What illness, rejection, or misfortune has encumbered the Synpathic Type? What condition causing her humiliation preceded it? What real interpersonal or vocational gain has the Apathic Type discarded or procrastinated away? What was there about it beforehand that elicited his despair?

Throughout confrontation with his defenses, the Suicide's overwhelming impulse is to fall back on old rationalizations justifying them or to invent new ones. Often, he puts the cart before the horse, focusing on the consequential shame, humiliation, or despair his defensive moves elicit rather than recognizing what elicited his defensive moves to begin with. However, each rationalization or secondary defensive evasion must be examined for what it really is.

Finally, as his defenses begin to fall by the wayside, he may become temporarily but imminently more suicidal. It is, therefore, of paramount importance that his commitment to stay alive for the term of his alleviation process be heavily reinforced at this time. And it is of equal importance that he have access to or the opportunity for such reinforcement at virtually any reasonable time. As he begins to examine his expressions, these intense suicidal impulses will rapidly subside.

SECONDARY EXPRESSIONS

At almost the same time that the Suicide examines his defenses, he also looks at his expressions of secondary motivations. These also tend to reinforce his illusion of his fixed attribute. He consequently finds that he clings to them as tenaciously as he clings to his defenses.

It is particularly difficult for the Antipathic to recognize the nature of his expressions of Vindictiveness, let alone relinquish them. After all, the more potently he expresses them, the more powerful he must be. But he tends to see it the other way around. Since he is so powerful, it is only natural for him to assert himself, condemn others, retaliate against them when they cross him.

It is therefore essential for him to see how he uses these expressions mainly to further his illusions of omnipotence. If he did not impose his claims on others, would this really prove he is weak? If he did not hold them in contempt, would this really demonstrate his inadequacies? If he did not retaliate against them, would this really mean he is impotent?

The same holds true for his expressions of Hopelessness. If he did not impose his values on life, would he really succumb to a perverse and chaotic world? Without his chronic discontent, would he actually become a shiftless nobody without goals? Without his resignation, would facing his humanity be too much for him to bear?

In contrast, you would think that the Synpathic would welcome recognition and riddance of her expressions of Self-Hatred. But because of their reinforcing effects on her illusions of innocence, she resists relinquishing them every step of the way. Even when she does recognize her inner dictates, her self-accusations and self-condemnation, her self-defeat and self-punishment, she feels helpless. After all, she can't help being the way she is.

It is therefore imperative that the Synpathic accept the obvious fact that her own feelings are subject to her own control. This is extremely difficult for her to do. In principle, she believes her feelings are foisted on her by outside forces, other people, her innate condition. Persevering work on this illusion is essential.

What external forces make her think other people value her the more she gives to them? Who decides that she must hold herself down and cater to other people's wishes? What innate condition makes it necessary that she punish herself and render herself dependent and ineffective? Only after the Synpathic takes responsibility for her own rules of behavior and recognizes that her feelings are her own handiwork can she begin to relinquish her expressions of Self-Hatred.

The same holds true for her expressions of Hopelessness. She alone determines her values and she alone expects them from life as reward for her innocence. Only when she owns her own discontent can she stop feeling abused on account of it. And only when she understands that she designs her own resignation can she see that she devises it just to protect her illusions.

The Apathic discovers the same degree of difficulty in relinquishing his expressions of Self-Hatred. Since he shapes his inner dictates to accentuate his transcendence, to forego them would contradict it. His self-accusations and self-contempt are aimed at his own mundane qualities. To forego them means accepting mundaneness. His self-defeat and self-punishment exempt him from mundane affairs. To forego them would mean to participate in the ordinary.

Likewise with his expressions of Vindictiveness. How ordinary must he become to relinquish his claim to immunity? Must he also possess mundane qualities to cease accusing and condemning others for theirs? And would he not drown in the amalgamated mass of "them" if he did not retaliate by rising above others?

Indeed, the Suicide clings to his secondary expressions with such tenacity that the only way he can even begin to relinquish them is persistently to evaluate how much they actually cost him in real life terms. Only after persistent and thorough accounting at this ledger can he come to realize that he employs them at great personal loss purely for the sake of illusion.

PRIMARY EXPRESSIONS

As the Suicide begins to loosen his defenses and question his secondary expressions, the illusory grounds of his primary expressions come to the fore. At this point, once again, he may experience the full force of his suicidal motivations. And, once again, his commitment to stay alive may require considerable reinforcement.

This is especially true of the Antipathic Type. He might weather the undermining of his defenses and secondary expressions and still secretly maintain a modicum of his omnipotence. But once he faces his expressions of Self-Hatred, he faces his illusions at their core.

All that he has believed himself to be is wrapped up in his inner dictates. And these must be dissected, one by one. It is not enough that he examine those the violation of which cause him shame from vivid experience. He must examine all possible injunctions and taboos in detail, whether he has experienced them as dictates or not.

This is most certainly a difficult thing for him to do. For with every inner dictate discovered, a little of his omnipotence automatically slips away. In sharp contrast to his normal experience, the harder he works, the less powerful he will feel. Uncharacteristically, he can experience himself as the dregs of humanity, utterly worthless, and contemptible.

It would never be worth it to him if he could not see real autonomy at the end of his struggle. For without his inner dictates, for the first time in his life he can be his own man. To be sure, he may have believed he was his own man before. But just a glimpse at the nature of his inner dictates proves the fallacy of that former belief.

But as he examines and loosens his inner dictates, his other expressions of Self-Hatred automatically diminish. As his illusion of omnipotence slips away, so do his self-accusations and self-contempt. And as his inner sovereignty grows, his need for self-defeat and self-punishment rapidly disappears.

Nevertheless, examination of his customary modes of these expressions promotes his repudiation of them. While this discovery paradoxically revives his shame, the effect is temporary. The more he dispenses with these expressions, the greater his genuine autonomy grows.

Correspondingly, the examination of the Synpathic Type's expressions of Vindictiveness automatically humiliates her. But with her defenses weakened, she suddenly sees all her vindictive claims for what they really are. With every conceivable claim examined, her benign innocence begins to dissipate into the blue from whence she believed it came. But only when she sees how she has had the worst of the bargain will she be willing to loosen her claims. Her discovery that other people have known about them all along helps. But the discovery of her own self-punishing reaction to their frustration provides her the greatest impetus to relinquish them.

The material, emotional, and imaginary support the Synpathic can garner from her claims can be considerable. And for this reason, if for no other, they can be difficult for her to renounce. That any real advantages need not be lost upon renunciation could be brought to her attention. She need not deviously expect and demand satisfaction from others in order to make real gains in real life.

However, the strongest motive for renouncing her claims comes from her recognition of the price they inevitably cost her. She comes to realize that she cannot shuck her feeling abused, inadequate, and deprived—indeed, cannot avoid actually being abused, inadequate, and deprived—and still maintain her claims.

Review of her defenses also helps here. Remembering the pain of her withdrawal, internalized vindictiveness, and surrogate sacrifices and their inevitability in face of her frustrated claims serves as a powerful extinguisher. This is true, especially in view of the useless pretense of it all. She sees that her exaggerations of altruistic love in lieu of genuine empathy have fooled no one but herself. Those close to her have seen right through it. Those more distant don't care.

As her claims loosen, so do her contempt and accusations towards others. These stem both from her unconscious Vindictiveness and from frustrated claims. As her empathy grows while her claims decrease, her contempt and accusations subside.

Finally, the emergence of true empathy automatically decreases her need for vindictive retaliation. However, seeing how she has suffered from it the most—in fact, may be the only one who really has suffered—serves as her most powerful impetus to relinquish it.

It is in this exact vein that the Apathic Type can best examine his expressions of Hopelessness. Who, and who alone, suffers on account of them? Who suffers emptiness on account of his abstract view of life? Who cannot find real gratification because of his chronic discontent? Whose life ends fruitless because of his hopeless resignation?

Only from this personal perspective can the Apathic truly confront his expressions. To take a more philosophical approach can only end where it begins. Of course, more general questions can make a little more sense to him now. Of what use are art, science, or religion without people to profit from them? What is freedom if not to garner real gains in real life for those who make real use of it? Of what import is the abstract meaninglessness of life to those who actually live it? But the real cogency must lie just with him. What of his abstractions? What of his wanderlust? What of his void?

Just exactly when in the process that the Apathic recognizes he cannot transcend himself is hard to pin down. But he clings to his expressions of Hopelessness as his last vestige of the All. Yet even he

ALLEVIATING THE SYNDROME   307

must confront the real futility of his private mission. Stripped of his defensive rationalizations, his real rationality finally wins out. Having basked in his idealizations of truth for so long, he can only come to terms with the real truth of himself.

And when he does, he finds a brand of freedom the like of which he never dreamed he could find. He finds a freedom *to*, not just a freedom *from*. All his expressions drift away to his imaginary never-land. And in their place grows a spontaneous will to live.

COMMON CHARACTERISTICS

Just as the Suicide's common characteristics automatically develop as consequences of the Suicide Syndrome, they also automatically begin to subside as the alleviation process progresses. An occasional glance at them in detail during the process, however, speeds their subsidence along.

As his pride subsides, the Suicide discovers that he begins to shed the extreme vulnerability he had heretofore just taken for granted. Situations or events causing him so much conscious or disguised shame, humiliation, or despair beforehand, can now be experienced in a far more pellucid light. Indeed, his recognition of his diminished vulnerability operates as a powerful impetus for him to continue to relinquish his remaining pride.

A similar process operates with respect to his compulsiveness and perfectionism. Almost automatically, he begins gradually to devote more of his energies to his real best interest, and in a more reasonable mode. He discovers an enhanced discrimination regarding his personal capacities, the directions of his efforts, the character of his hopes and his desires. His growing awareness of this brand of inner sovereignty and confidence adds impetus to his foregoing both his compulsiveness and perfectionism.

Likewise with his narcissism and obsessiveness. The more he begins to comprehend what maintaining his image has cost him in real life terms, the more his fascination with it declines. He grows concerned with his real situation in real life in real terms. He starts to appreciate his real assets, real limitations, and real potential.

These processes, in turn, help diminish his arrogance and egocentricity. Now seeing his true condition as simply that of another bona fide human being struggling with his own illusions, automatically has a neutralizing effect on both these characteristics. His attitudes grow steadily more egalitarian. He begins to move closer and closer to social mutuality.

Finally, he more accurately perceives the irrationality of it all. Whereas before it all seemed so normal, so logical, so predetermined, it now begins to look a touch absurd. Glimpses of his former irrationality often elicit renewed shame, humiliation, or despair, but only temporarily. Some humor and a review of the irrational conditions of his childhood situation that launched him on his course will usually bring relief.

The more the Suicide evaluates how much these common characteristics have cost him in real life terms, merely for the sake of his illusions, the sooner he will be willing to forego them. And the more rapidly he foregoes the common characteristics founded on it, the more responsive he will become to finally giving up the fundamental illusion of his Fantastic Self.

GIVING UP THE GHOST

Slowly but surely the Suicide comes to realize that he has spent his major time and effort in the pursuit of an impossible illusion. His over-riding impulse is to seize upon the entire structure of the syndrome in a last-ditch attempt to reinstate it. At the very least, he will cling to an old inner dictate, the remnant of a diminished claim, traces of a questionable but well-entrenched abstract value.

But if his work thus far has been thorough, there is no way for him even to begin to put the pieces back together. Having come this far, he now faces the ultimate step. While his struggles may delay the inevitable, he eventually must confront the necessity of relinquishing his belief in his Fantastic Self.

Other avenues may temporarily appear open to him. And at this point, he can be extremely prone to embarking on at least one of them. Even though he cannot rebuild exactly as it was the structure of the syndrome he has so painfully dismantled, it does appear that he could rebuild another similar to it. He attempts this by simply shifting to another of his Fantastic Self's attributes. He gives up his former omnipotence but fixates a new transcendence. Or he abandons his transcendence and fixes on innocence. Or he foregoes his innocence but embraces omnipotence.

His subsequent exhilaration is intense but short-lived. For fixating a new primary attribute automatically entails reconstituting a whole new set of characteristics, motivations, expressions, and defenses. The inherent artificiality of this move eventually comes to light. Having experienced the impossibility of his Fantastic Self, none of its attributes can satisfy him now.

The last remnants of Self-Hatred, Vindictiveness, and Hopelessness quickly follow suit. How could he have been so stupid to have believed himself omnipotent? How could she have been so naive as to suffer for the illusion of innocence? How could he have been so irrational as to reach for an impossible transcendence? After these last traces of self-condemnation subside, he turns on others. They—parents, teachers, ministers, society at large—are despicable for having launched him on such a course. And after condemning them, he turns on life. What an absurdity life must be that humans must encounter its meaninglessness.

These last hurrahs of old motivations often usher in a profound sense of grief over the loss of his Fantastic Self. His grief over the loss can take a number of circuitous forms. It may appear as though his old depression or other self-destructive defenses are coming back. But these detours only postpone the inevitable. Sadly, he buries the ghost of his illusion.

In the wake of his grief follows an even more profound sense of relief. No longer must he adhere to expressions that seem to originate from out of the blue. No longer must he employ defenses that impair the quality of his life. No longer must he look forward to an impossible promise of the future. He can indulge in life here and now.

When he looks around at others still struggling with their illusions, he may grow rather smug with his new-found autonomy. But his complacency is not long-lasting. A touching moment here, an intimate glimpse there, a broader understanding of human struggles everywhere, soon elicit a new sensitivity. As his empathy with others develops, so does his spontaneous experience of life. No longer devoting his energies to the maintenance of a fantasy, he turns them towards the betterment of a real existence. Work is aimed at real personal and social improvement. Relations with others are aimed at real mutual well-being. His imaginative powers are unleashed for the generation of real usefulness, the creation of real beauty, the enhancement of real human life.

At last, armed with his real intrinsic qualities—and with the resolve of Camus' Dr. Rieux—the former Suicide confronts that which plagues the everyday human condition.[10] He looks toward a life beyond the Suicide Syndrome.

Chapter 30

BEYOND THE SUICIDE SYNDROME

Suicidal crises can be mediated, but the cultural pervasiveness of the syndrome still prevails. To be sure, we can employ these expeditious measures to preserve individual human life or to enhance it, even in the face of such arduous odds. But can we not create a comprehensive human environment that functions beyond the Suicide Syndrome?

The cultural pervasiveness of the syndrome is certainly obvious enough for anyone to see. If humanity's historical and contemporary milieu demonstrates anything, it is our enculturated belief in an omnipotent, innocent, transcendent, and consequently, immortal Fantastic Self.

This grand illusion would constitute nothing more than an ironic joke on its adherents were it not for the consummate destructiveness at which it automatically aims. Of course, the syndrome takes its toll in tragic human deaths. And it takes an even broader toll in tragic human lives. Yet humanity as a whole has survived.

But now, after long struggling with its unconscious motivations to humanity's self-annihilation, we have at last devised a method by which we can attain it. Thus, our invention, proliferation, and esca-

lated production of nuclear weapons constitutes the one truly significant development in the long history of our enculturation of the Suicide Syndrome. It provides us a suicidal methodology of global
proportions. And the more this suicidal methodology is reinforced
through a growing confidence and familiarity with it, threats or plans
to use it in a crisis, and rehearsals of its use, the more liable we become
to committing global suicide.

Most urgent, of course, is for us to find a way mutually to lay
aside our means to global self-destruction and to mediate recurring
crises. No issue in human affairs could rationally claim a higher priority than this. Indeed, that this issue has been persistently neglected in
favor of pursuing the illusion of attaining an impossible omnipotence
stands as a glaring tribute to the cultural pervasiveness of the Suicide
Syndrome.

Its eradication would have seemed desirable in the past; but now,
for us to strive toward creating a human environment that functions
beyond the Suicide Syndrome is imperative for the survival of humanity.

What kind of human environment could we strive for that would
function beyond the Suicide Syndrome? It would be an environment
that would reinforce the development of genuine autonomy, empathy, and spontaneity in our youth. This would entail the removal of
arbitrary familial and social criteria for individual performance in favor of innocuous trial-and-error learning. It would entail recognition
and unconditional satisfaction of bona fide needs in lieu of teaching
spurious strategies for gaining their satisfaction. And it would require
the reinforcement of organismic growth instead of imposing artificial
inhibitions on it.

We would strive for creating an environment that would not prescribe social roles based on the principles of the syndrome. This
would mean cultural recognition and reinforcement of each individual's intrinsic human value and integration into the whole, regardless
of gender, physical characteristics, or genetic constitution. Men would
not be taught to pursue power in order to conquer life rather than
live it. Women would not be taught passively to submit to life rather
than actively experience it. Neither would be taught to idealize and
glorify the abstract in lieu of valuing the real.

We would strive for a human environment that would reject expressions of Self-Hatred, Vindictiveness, and Hopelessness rather
than reinforce them. This would necessitate dispensing with environmental reinforcement of inner dictates operating under the guise of

self-discipline, moral edict, or artificial mores. It would mean abolishing cultural support of vindictive claims manifested as racial prejudices, class rights, or posing as the natural socioeconomic order. It would require our rejection of culturally propagated values prizing the impossible.

Such an environment would call for cultural support of genuine inner confidence in lieu of self-accusations and self-contempt, mutual appreciation of others in lieu of overtly or covertly accusing and condemning them, the celebration of organismic life in lieu of organized discontent with its mundane reality. And it would mean placing emphasis on authentic self-interest ahead of spurious self-punishment, empathic tolerance ahead of vindictive retaliation, attainable potential ahead of resignation from the impossible.

We would strive for a human environment that does not put a premium on the common characteristics stemming from the belief in the Fantastic Self. We would recognize individual and collective pride for the hollow and self-destructive pretense it is. We would see human life as an integral part of the comprehensive natural process rather than measure all existence from an anthropocentric point of view. We would celebrate our animal nature rather than narcissistically worship an artificial and glorified self-image.

We would realistically accept our humanity rather than reach for an impossible and thereby self-depreciating perfection. We would endeavor to recapture our intrinsic responses rather than compulsively attempt to actualize an impossible dream. We would revel in our real qualities rather than arrogate characteristics to our individual and collective selves that we cannot possibly possess. And we would strive towards the rational life as the only genuine mode of human experience.

We would aspire to a human environment that would consciously recognize and inherently discourage the incipient destructiveness of the Suicidal Lifestyle. This would entail piercing through our rather transparent rationalizations for the ways in which we treat ourselves and others. It would mean disposing of our endemic but pitiable rationalizations for suicide, euthanasia, and publicly condoned individual murder known as capital punishment, and mass murder known as war.

It would mean dispensing with our perverted view of our own nature, our prejudices of others, and of our cultural denials of the natural processes of life that result in philosophies ranging from Existentialist *angst*, through dogmatic asceticism, to Machiavellian cynicism.

It would require our admission that anxiety is not an intrinsic human condition; that suffering, despair, and guilt are not conditions foisted on us by the gods; that shallowness and the lack of motivation to render life more fruitful for us all stems not from natural design; but that all of these derive, instead, from our impossible beliefs about ourselves.

It would mean dispensing with artificial inhibitions on our organismic sexuality and the frustrations and perversions they entail. It would require a new perspective of our usual modes of pairing as consequences of cultural attitudes, socioeconomic systems, and our individual spurious needs rather than requisites to genuine fulfillment. And, it would require cognizance that we are not born alienated from each other but that our loneliness and isolation results from our culturally conditioned prejudices, competitiveness, and artificiality.

Finally, we would strive for a human environment that would found its social systems on mutual well-being rather than on the imagined attributes of the Social Fantastic Self. This, of course, would redirect social energies to the cause of the general human welfare rather than waste them in the attempt to manifest an impossible illusion.

Such a social system would function in the mutual best interests of all its constituents, not just in the apparent best interests of some. It would relate to other social systems with equanimity, amity, and mutual regard. And it would look to its own existence solely as a consequence of the human propensity for association for mutual betterment.

The creation of such a human environment might seem to be unrealistic, idealistic, and contrary to human nature. But just the opposite is the case. It is only as a consequence of the enculturated endorsement of the impossible ideal at the expense of the achievable reality that we have come to regard human nature as cynically as we often do. For this picture of human nature derives solely from the encultured belief in the Fantastic Self and the consummately destructive process stemming from it.

However, the belief in the Fantastic Self has a powerful, albeit artificial appeal. But this attraction comes only as a consequence of our self-made environmental conditions necessitating it. There is no possibility that human beings, by nature, must believe themselves to be omnipotent, innocent, and transcendent, and consequently, immortal. And there is no possibility that human beings, by nature, must destroy themselves on this or any other account.

Certainly, the creation of such a human environment would require a degree of social control. But no one could rightly deny that stringent controls already operate in every existing society. Indeed, we have already seen how each social system controls its constituents in both subtle and blatant ways. And we can readily see how each system lends its constituents the illusion that each of them is free of its control in contrast to other constituents or, more especially, in contrast to constituents of rival social systems. Thus, the issue in our creating an environment beyond the Suicide Syndrome is obviously not one of control. The issue is who controls, how, and to what end.

Shall control rest with the Antipathic who will most assuredly march us to our self-annihilation under the banner of an imagined omnipotence? Shall it belong to the Synpathic who leads us to the mass extermination of our real selves in favor of an impossible innocence? Shall it rest with the Apathic who must obliterate our collective existence in order to attain an illusionary transcendence? Or shall we grasp control of our own lives, wresting it from these advocates of death, and found a human environment that functions beyond the Suicide Syndrome?

GLOSSARY

This Glossary contains only those terms peculiar to the Suicide Syndrome. Other terms whose meanings may be misinterpreted as to their use in this book are usually defined in the Notes.

ABSTRACT VALUES—The primary expression of unconscious Hopelessness consisting of arbitrary values imposed on life in the abstract.

ACCUSATIONS AND CONTEMPT TOWARD OTHERS—The secondary expression of unconscious Vindictiveness consisting of blaming others for not relating to the Suicide as his Fantastic Self.

ADOLESCENT RESOLUTION—The selective fixation of one of the Fantastic Self's Attributes and repression of the other two, resulting in Type.

ANTIPATHIC TYPE—That Suicidal Type who fixates Omnipotence and represses Innocence and Transcendence: who moves against his feelings; who is empirically characterized by hostility, arrogance, and rigidity; and whose primary Suicidal Motivation is Self-Hatred.

APATHIC TYPE—That Suicidal Type who fixates Transcendence and represses Omnipotence and Innocence: who moves away from his feelings; who is empirically characterized by ambivalence, detachment, and inertia; and whose primary Suicidal Motivation is Hopelessness.

APPARENT IRRATIONALITY—One of the Common Characteristics of all Suicidal Types: specifically, the Suicide's concepts, affects, and behaviors which appear irrational except when viewed in the light of his unconscious conviction that he is his Fantastic Self.

ARROGANT SUPERIORITY—One of the Common Characteristics of all Suicidal Types: specifically, the Suicide's concepts, affects, and behaviors resulting from his arrogating the Attributes of his Fantastic Self to his Empirical Self, thereby rendering him superior to other people.

ATTRIBUTE, FIXED—That Attribute of the Fantastic Self respectively fixated by each Suicidal Type, specifically as follows:

Suicidal Type	*Fixed Attribute*
Antipathic	Omnipotence

Synpathic

Apathic

Innocence

Transcendence

ATTRIBUTES—Absolute metaphysical characteristics of the Fantastic Self; namely, Omnipotence, Innocence, and Transcendence.

ATTRIBUTES, REPRESSED—Those Attributes of the Fantastic Self respectively repressed by each Suicidal Type, specifically as follows:

Suicidal Type	*Repressed Attributes*
Antipathic	Innocence and Transcendence
Synpathic	Omnipotence and Transcendence
Apathic	Omnipotence and Innocence

CHECKS AND AVOIDANCES—The Antipathic Type's evasion defense against Self-Hatred consisting of avoiding situations eliciting shame and employing checks on active strivings in order to evade a shameful defeat.

CHRONIC DISCONTENT—The secondary expression of unconscious Hopelessness consisting of the Suicide's chronic dissatisfaction with the reality of himself, other people, and the course of his life.

COMMON CHARACTERISTICS—Those personality characteristics common to all Suicidal Types, namely: unconscious Pride, Egocentricity, Narcissism, Compulsiveness, Obsessiveness, Perfectionism, Arrogant Superiority, and Apparent Irrationality.

COMPULSIVENESS—One of the Common Characteristics of all Suicidal Types: specificially, compulsive ideation, affects, and behaviors resulting from the absoluteness of the Attributes of the Fantastic Self.

DEFENSES—Defensive measures employed by the Suicide to protect his Fixed Attribute from expressions of his primary Suicidal Motivation and consisting of evasion, displacement, and compromise, respectively.

DEFENSES TO HOPELESSNESS—Defensive measures employed by the Apathic Type Suicide designed to protect his illusion of Transcendence from his expressions of Hopelessness; namely, Stoic Detachment, Generalizing, and Nihilism.

DEFENSES TO SELF-HATRED—Defensive measures employed by the Antipathic Type Suicide designed to protect his illusion of Omnipotence from his expressions of Self-Hatred; namely, Checks and Avoidances, Externalizing, and Token Concessions.

DEFENSES TO VINDICTIVENESS—Defensive measures employed by the Synpathic Type Suicide designed to protect her illusion of Innocence from her expressions of Vindictiveness; namely, Passive Withdrawal, Internalizing, and Surrogate Sacrifices.

EGOCENTRICITY—One of the Common Characteristics of all Suicidal Types: specifically, ideations, affects, and behaviors resulting from the exclusivity of the Fantastic Self.

EMPIRICAL CHARACTERISTICS—The predominant characteristics of each Suicidal Type's Empirical Self, specifically as follows:

Suicidal Type	Empirical Characteristics
Antipathic	Hostility, Arrogance, and Rigidity
Synpathic	Abused, Inadequate, and Deprived
Apathic	Ambivalence, Detachment, and Inertia

EMPIRICAL SELF—The Suicide's true phenomenological personality as empirically experienced by him and other people in everyday life.

EXPRESSIONS OF HOPELESSNESS— Behaviors, affects, and concepts in the Suicide's everyday life expressing repressed Hopelessness; namely, Abstract Values, Chronic Discontent, and Hopeless Resignation.

EXPRESSIONS OF SELF-HATRED—Behaviors, affects, and concepts in the Suicide's everyday life expressing repressed Self-Hatred; namely, Inner Dictates, Self-Accusations and Self-Contempt, and Self-Defeat and Self-Punishment.

EXPRESSIONS OF VINDICTIVENESS—Behaviors, affects, and concepts in the Suicide's everyday life expressing repressed Vindictiveness; namely, External Claims, Accusations and Contempt toward Others, and Vindictive Retaliation.

EXTERNAL CLAIMS—The primary expression of unconscious Vindictiveness consisting of demands and restrictions lodged against other people aimed at their control and exploitation in the service of the Suicide's Fantastic Self.

EXTERNALIZING—The Antipathic Type's displacement defense against Self-Hatred consisting of projecting the hatred of his Empirical Self onto other people.

FANTASTIC SELF—Unconscious self-concept endowed with the metaphysical Attributes of Omnipotence, Innocence, and Transcendence, and which is therefore conceived as immortal.

GENERALIZING—The Apathic Type's displacement defense against Hopelessness consisting of generalizing personal hopelessness onto life as a process.

HOPELESSNESS—One of the three Suicidal Motivations; results from the despair contingent with the existential impossibility of the Fantastic Self.

HOPELESS RESIGNATION—The tertiary expression of unconscious Hopelessness consisting of the Suicide resigning from the active pursuit of actualizing his Fantastic Self in real life.

INNER DICTATES—The primary expression of Self-Hatred consisting of injunctions and taboos aimed at total control of the Suicide's Empirical Self by his tyrannical Fantastic Self.

INNOCENCE—One of the three metaphysical Attributes of the Fantastic Self; manifested in everyday life as altruism, benignity, and lovableness.

INTERNALIZING—The Synpathic Type's displacement defense against Vindictiveness consisting of introjecting Vindictiveness against others onto the Suicide's Empirical Self.

LETHAL POTENTIALITY—The probability of a lethal outcome of a Suicidal Crisis measured by three interdependent sets of variables; namely, Precipitating Factors, Reaction to Crisis, and Suicidal Methodology.

NARCISSISM—One of the Common Characteristics of all Suicidal Types: specifically, love of the Fantastic Self.

NIHILISM—The Apathic Type's compromise defense against Hopelessness consisting of overt and covert hostile acts against life as a process.

OBSESSIVENESS—One of the Common Characteristics of all Suicidal Types: specifically, the Suicide's unconscious preoccupation with manifesting his Fantastic Self.

OMNIPOTENCE—One of the three metaphysical Attributes of the Fantastic Self; manifested in everyday life as power, mastery, and control.

PASSIVE WITHDRAWAL—The Synpathic Type's evasion defense against Vindictiveness consisting of physical, affectual, and intellectual withdrawal from people and situations that elicit humiliation.

PERFECTIONISM—One of the Common Characteristics of all Suicidal Types: specifically, ideations, affects, and behaviors resulting from the absoluteness of the Attributes of the Fantastic Self.

PRECIPITATING FACTORS—Situations, events, or conditions which precipitate a Suicidal Crisis.

PRIDE, UNCONSCIOUS—One of the Common Characteristics of all Suicidal Types: specifically, contingencies of autoreinforcement of the Fantastic Self.

PRIMARY (SUICIDAL) MOTIVATION—That Suicidal Motivation which is primary to each Type, as follows:

Suicidal Type	*Primary Motivation*
Antipathic	Self-Hatred

Synpathic   Vindictiveness

Apathic   Hopelessness

REACTION TO CRISIS—The Suicide's automatic reaction to a Suicidal Crisis consisting of the escalation of Defenses and expressions of Secondary Motivations.

SECONDARY (SUICIDAL) MOTIVATIONS—Those Suicidal Motivations which are secondary to each Type, as follows:

Suicidal Type	*Secondary Motivations*
Antipathic	Vindictiveness and Hopelessness
Synpathic	Self-Hatred and Hopelessness
Apathic	Self-Hatred and Vindictiveness

SELF-ACCUSATIONS AND SELF-CONTEMPT—The secondary expression of unconscious Self-Hatred consisting of blame placed on the Suicide's Empirical Self by his Fantastic Self.

SELF-DEFEAT AND SELF-PUNISHMENT—The tertiary expression of unconscious Self-Hatred consisting of defeats and punishments inflicted upon the Suicide's Empirical Self by his Fantastic Self.

SELF-HATRED—One of the three Suicidal Motivations; results from the shame contingent with the impossibility of the Suicide manifesting his Fantastic Self.

SOCIAL FANTASTIC SELF—Social self-concept endowed with the metaphysical Attributes of Omnipotence, Innocence, and Transcendence.

STOIC DETACHMENT—The Apathic Type's evasion defense against Hopelessness consisting of psychic detachment from mundane conditions eliciting despair.

SUICIDAL CRISIS—Impending decision to attempt the metaphysical actualization of the Fantastic Self.

SUICIDAL LIFESTYLE—That style of life founded on or dominated by the Suicide Syndrome.

SUICIDAL METHODOLOGY—The specific means of attempting or committing suicide, usually associated with Type.

SUICIDAL MOTIVATIONS—The three exclusive motivations to suicide; namely, Self-Hatred, Vindictiveness, and Hopelessness.

SUICIDAL SOCIETY—Any social system founded on or dominated by the principles of the Suicide Syndrome.

SUICIDAL TYPE—That personality type as determined by the selective fixation and repression of the Attributes of the Fantastic Self; namely, the Antipathic Type, the Synpathic Type, and the Apathic Type.

SUICIDE—The termination of one's own existence.

SUICIDE, A—Any person who lives in accordance with the Suicide Syndrome whether he ever consciously considers committing suicide or not.

SUICIDE SYNDROME—The human self-destructive process.

SUICIDOGENIC FACTOR—The social reinforcement of Suicidal Motivations and their expressions taken in proportion to the absence of social reinforcement of the specific defenses against them.

SURROGATE SACRIFICES—The Synpathic Type's compromise defense against Vindictiveness consisting of vindictive acts against the Empirical Self as a surrogate for other people.

SYNPATHIC TYPE—That Suicidal Type who fixates Innocence and represses Omnipotence and Transcendence: who moves towards her feelings; who is empirically characterized by feeling abused, inadequate, and deprived; and whose primary Suicidal Motivation is Vindictiveness.

TOKEN CONCESSIONS—The Antipathic Type's compromise defense against Self-Hatred consisting of concessionary losses sustained by the Empirical Self designed to placate the hateful Fantastic Self.

TRANSCENDENCE—One of the three metaphysical Attributes of the Fantastic Self; manifested in everyday life as freedom, objective independence, and self-sufficiency.

VINDICTIVENESS—One of the three Suicidal Motivations; results from the humiliation contingent with the impossibility of other people ratifying the Suicide's Fantastic Self.

VINDICTIVE RETALIATION—The tertiary expression of unconscious Vindictiveness consisting of overt or covert retaliatory acts against other people.

NOTES

INTRODUCTION

1. Gernsbacher, L. M. (1978). Intrapsychic and Situational Variables in Suicidal Ideations in a General Population. Unpublished study. When asked, "Have you ever felt like committing suicide?" 93 of 146 subjects (63.7 percent) replied "Yes." Participants in this study included 34 clerical and administrative employees of a utility company, 28 high school seniors, 26 undergraduate students, 37 graduate students, and 21 members of a business and professional men's service club. There was no significant variation in the proportion of "Yes" answers among these groups or on account of age, marital status, employment status, household income, education completed, or gender. When asked, "Do you believe most people, at least one time in their lives, have felt like committing suicide?" 113 (77.4 percent) replied "Yes." Interestingly, this total included all but one of the 93 subjects answering "Yes" to the question about themselves. More interestingly, of all the groups, the graduate (psychology) students had a much higher ratio of "Yes" answers for "Most people" than for themselves. In other words, the graduate psychology students, as a group, believed other people were more suicidal than they were, even though about the same proportion of those students replied "Yes" regarding themselves. I call this the "arrogance factor."

2. Linden, L.L., & Breed, W. (1976). The demographic epidemiology of suicide. In E.S. Shneidman (Ed.). *Suicidology: Contemporary developments.* New York: Grune & Stratton.

3. Shneidman, E.S., Farberow, N.L., & Leonard, C.V. (1961). *Some facts about suicide.* Public Health Service Publication No. 852. Washington, DC: Government Printing Office.

4. *Newsweek,* December 4, 1978; *Time* Magazine, December 4, 1978.

5. Public Health Papers (1968). *Prevention of Suicide.* Geneva: World Health Organization.

6. Freud, S. (1959). *Collected papers.* New York: Basic Books.

7. Becker, E. (1973). *The denial of death.* New York: Macmillan.

8. Shneidman, E. S. (1975). Suicide. In A.M. Freedman, H.I. Kaplan, & B.J. Sadock (Eds.). *Comprehensive textbook of psychiatry.* Baltimore: Williams & Wilkins. This psychiatric textbook contains 247 articles, but only psychologist Shneidman's article touches on suicide. In fact, the word "Suicide" is absent from the Glossary.

9. Jones, E. (1961). *The life and work of Sigmund Freud.* New York: Basic Books.

10. Robert, M. (1966). *The psychoanalytic revolution* (K. Morgan, Trans.). New York: Harcourt, Brace, & World.

11. American Psychiatric Association (1968). *Diagnostic and statistical manual of mental disorders* (2nd ed.). Washington, DC: Author.

12. American Psychiatric Association (1980). *Diagnostic and statistical manual of mental disorders* (3rd ed.). Washington, DC: Author.

13. Shneidman, E.S. in A.M. Freedman, H.I. Kaplan, & B.J. Sadock (1975). A massive psychiatric handbook containing only one article about suicide, authored by Shneidman.

14. Menninger, K.A. (1938). *Man against himself.* New York: Harcourt, Brace.

15. Horney, K. (1950). *Neurosis and human growth.* New York: Norton.

16. Adler, A. (1967). *Symposium on suicide: Discussions of the Vienna Psychoanalytic Society.* New York: International Universities Press.

17. Durkheim, E. (1951). *Suicide, a study in sociology.* Glencoe, IL: Free Press. (Original work published 1897)

18. Shneidman, E.S. (1980). The reliability of suicide statistics. *Suicide and Life-Threatening Behavior, 10* (2), 67-69.

19. Gibbs, J.P., & Martin, W.T. (1964). *Status integration and suicide: A sociological study.* Eugene, OR: University of Oregon Press.

20. Maris, R.W. (1981). *Pathways to suicide: A survey of self-destructive behavior.* Baltimore: Johns Hopkins University Press.

21. Baechler, J. (1979). *Suicides* (B. Cooper, Trans.). New York: Basic Books.

22. Douglas, J. (1967). *The social meanings of suicide.* Princeton, NJ: Princeton University Press.

23. Shneidman, E.S. (1973). Suicide. *Encyclopaedia Britannica* (14th ed.). Chicago..

PART I GENESIS OF THE SUICIDE SYNDROME

1. The word "unconsciously" is used in this book in a phenomenological sense rather than in an existential sense. Herein, "unconscious" simply means "immediately unaware," and "his unconscious" simply means that collection of experiences of which "he" is at present unaware.

2. The word "learn" is used herein as the adaption of behavior to experience, although the experience may be "unconscious."

3. The word "mind" I also use phenomenologically rather than existentially. In this book, the "mind" is not substantial, but operational.

4. Berne, E. (1961). *Transactional analysis in psychotherapy.* New York: Grove Press. Berne attributed these qualities to his child ego state, rather than seeing them as essential characteristics of the fully integrated mature adult.

5. Karen Horney's (1950) analogy of a Frankenstein's monster depicts the process well.

6. I use the word "repress" in this book as roughly analogous to "forget."

7. The Superman concept serves as an obvious symbolization of the Fantastic Self in literature and mythology.

8. This term, "Empirical Self," is borrowed from Horney (1950) who in turn borrowed it from William James. Readers more familiar with Horney's later work will recognize my debt to her for a great deal more than just this term.

9. Erikson, E. (1968). *Identity, youth and crisis.* New York: Norton. Although Erikson correctly assigned this search for identity to adolescence, it may reappear later at any time of stress.

PART II SUICIDAL TYPES

1. The behavioral equivalent for the way I use the word "pride" would be "contingencies of autoreinforcement" and the equivalent for the term "unconscious pride" would be "unobserved contingencies of autoreinforcement." While I have not found this obvious conclusion in the literature, everything leading up to it can be found in Skinner (1953, 1969, 1974).

2. My use of the word "egocentricity" can best be equated with "self-image-centered."

3. Narcissism is not herein defined as "love of self" which implies an impossible dichotomy, but rather as "love of self-image," or, more accurately, "love of unconscious self-concept."

4. See Fasteau, M.F. (1975). *The male machine.* New York: Dell.

5. The incidence of mistaking or misinterpreting suicides for accidents is endemic. Nowhere is this more true than with the Antipathic male.

6. See Trip, C.A. (1975). *The homosexual matrix.* New York: McGraw-Hill.

PART III THE MURDEROUS TYRANT WITHIN

1. It would be superfluous, if not virtually impossible, to catalogue here all the religious, philosophical, psychological, and common wisdom interpretations of this impossible dichotomy from earliest classical literature to our contemporary scene.

2. The Fantastic Self, inner dictates, and other expressions of Self-Hatred can best be differentiated from the psychoanalytic oppressive Superego as operational as opposed to existential. It is exactly this existential impossibility of the Fantastic Self that makes the Suicide Syndrome a *suicide syndrome.*

3. See Berne, E. (1964). *Games people play.* New York: Grove Press; and Freud, 1959.

4. Franz Kafka's *The Trial* (1956) captures the process with beautiful artistic insight.

5. For a poignant and vivid description of this kind of comprehensive self-destructiveness, see Menninger, 1938.

PART IV THE ULTIMATE WEAPON

1. While Freud certainly recognized the connection of exaggerated claims with hysteria, his preoccupation with mechanistic and instinctual origins precluded his recognition of their origins.

PART V THE DESPAIR OF BEING ALIVE

1. See Beck, A.T., & Kovacs, M. (1975). Hopelessness and suicidal behavior. *Journal of the American Medical Association, 7,* 1146-1149. Beck's group has repeatedly demonstrated hopelessness as more consistently associated with suicide in contrast with depression, and has devised some rather ingenious ways of measuring hopelessness. Nevertheless, in the best empiricist tradition, the origins of hopelessness seem to have been ignored.

PART VI THE SUICIDAL LIFESTYLE

1. In the behavioral view, thinking is simply another form of human behavior. For more on suicidal rigid thinking, see Neuringer, C. (1964). Rigid thinking in suicidal individuals. *Journal of Consulting Psychology, 28* (1), 54-58.

2. Shapiro, D. (1965). *Neurotic styles.* New York: Basic Books. Shapiro insightfully finds different styles of perceiving as grounds for the conventional personality disorders. However, he does not investigate the origins of these styles.

3. Shneidman has long contended a syllogistic fallacy in suicidal thinking, but without looking for its roots. See "The Logic of Suicide," in Shneidman, E.S., & Farberow, N.L. (1957). *Clues to suicide.* New York: McGraw-Hill.

4. This fundamental "gamble" underlies all the gambling aspects of suicide, such as a solitary game of Russian roulette. For more on the gambling aspects of suicide, see Lester, G., & Lester, D. (1971). *Suicide: The gamble with death.* Englewood Cliffs, NJ: Prentice-Hall.

5. See Berne, 1964.

6. Simonton, O.C., & Simonton, S.S. (1975). Belief systems and the management of the emotional aspects of malignancy. *Journal of Transpersonal Psychology, 7* (1), 29-47.

7. LeShan, L. (1962). Cancer mortality rate: Some statistical evidence of psychological factors. *Archives of General Psychiatry, 6,* 333-335.

8. See Frank, M.G. 1965, Porterfield, A. L. 1960, & Selzer, M. L. & Payne, C.E. 1962.

9. Criteria following Abel, T. (1970). *The foundation of social theory.* New York: Random House.

10. Mead, G.H. (1934). *Mind, self and society.* Chicago: University of Chicago Press. Similar to what Mead would call "significant symbol."

11. With a bow to Stengel, 1964a, for this analogy.

PART VII SUICIDAL CRISES

1. Data for this section are generally derived from Shirer, 1960, and Speer, 1970. Shirer, W.L. (1960). *The rise and fall of the Third Reich.* New York: Simon & Shuster. Speer, A. (1970). *Inside the Third Reich.* New York: Macmillan.

2. Cult of death. (1978, December 4). *Newsweek,* p. 23.

3. *Newsweek,* July 27, 1977; *Time* Magazine, July 27, 1977.

PART VIII PREVENTING SUICIDE

1. Witness Roman (1980). Indeed, Jo Roman's 200-page suicide note is a page-by-page testimony to the veracity of the Suicide Syndrome. Contrast it with the truly splendid literary contribution made by Alvarez, 1972.

2. Much frustrating work has been devoted to devising a reliable "lethality scale" by researchers and clinicians. Most have been to no avail.

3. See Reynolds & Farberow, 1976.

4. Shneidman in Freedman, Kaplan, & Sadock, 1975.

5. James, I.P., & Levin, S., 1964; Bolin et al., 1968.

6. Kelley, D. (1975). What's new in psychosurgery. In S. Arieti & G. Chrzanowsky (Eds.). *New dimensions in psychiatry.* New York: Wiley.

7. I conducted an informal survey in two therapy groups conducted by a psychotherapist friend. Eleven of the twelve members said they had experienced "serious" suicidal impulses or ideations immediately prior to entering therapy. The twelfth, who denied suicidal impulses, said that one reason he entered therapy was to learn to take better care of himself after incurring three serious auto accidents. When asked why the group members had not told the therapist about their suicidal impulses, most replied, "He didn't ask."

8. See Wolpe, 1973, Berne, 1964, 1966, Fromm-Reichman, 1950, Menninger, 1958, Perls et al., 1951, Rogers, 1951, and other psychotherapeutic methodology references.

9. Farberow, N.L., Shneidman, E.S., & Leonard, C.V. (1961). Suicide among mental hospital patients. In N.L. Farberow & E.S. Shneidman (Eds.). *The cry for help*. New York: McGraw-Hill.

10. Camus, A. (1972). *The plague* (S. Gilbert, Trans.). New York: Vintage Press.

BIBLIOGRAPHY

Alvarez, A. (1972). *The savage God*. New York: Random House.

Baechler, J. (1979). *Suicides* (B. Cooper, Trans.). New York: Basic Books.

Beck, A.T., & Kovacs, M. (1975). Hopelessness and suicidal behavior. *Journal of the American Medical Association, 7*, 1146-1149.

Bolin, R.K., Wright, R.E., Wilkinson, M.N., & Linder, C.K. (1968). Survey of suicide among patients on home leave from a mental hospital. *Psychiatric Quarterly, 42* (1), 81-89.

Bosselman, B.C. (1958). *Self destruction: A study of the suicidal impulse*. Springfield, IL: Charles C. Thomas.

Choron, J. (1972). *Suicide*. New York: Scribner.

Donne, J. (1930). *Bianthanatos Reproduced from the First Edition*. New York: The Facsimile Test Society.

Douglas, J. (1967). *The social meanings of suicide*. Princeton, NJ: Princeton University Press.

Durkheim, E. (1951). *Suicide, a study in sociology*. Glencoe, IL: Free Press. (Original work published 1897)

Erikson, E. (1968). *Identity, youth and crisis*. New York: Norton.

Farber, M. (1968). *Theory of suicide*. New York: Funk & Wagnalls.

Farberow, N.L. (Ed.). (1968). *Proceedings: Fourth International Conference for Suicide Prevention*. Los Angeles: Suicide Prevention Center.

Farberow, N.L., & Shneidman, E.S. (Eds.). (1961). *The cry for help*. New York: McGraw-Hill.

Frank, M.G. (1965, July). Suicide in automobile accidents. *Medical College Bulletin, 147*, 1-4.

Freedman, A.M., Kaplan, H.I., & Sadock, B.J. (1975). *Comprehensive textbook of psychiatry*. Baltimore: Williams & Wilkins.

Fromm, E. (1973). *The anatomy of human destructiveness*. New York: Holt, Rinehart, & Winston.

Fromm-Reichman, F. (1950). *Principles of intensive psychotherapy*. Chicago: University Press.

Gibbs, J.P., & Martin, W.T. (1964). *Status integration and suicide: A sociological study*. Eugene, OR: University of Oregon Press.

Grollman, E.A. (1971). *Suicide prevention, intervention, postvention*. Boston: Beacon Press.

Hankoff, L.D., & Einsidler, B. (Eds.). (1979). *Suicide: Theory and clinical aspects*. Littleton, MA: PSG Publishers.

Horney, K. (1937). *The neurotic personality of our time.* New York: Norton.
Horney, K. (1939). *New ways in psychoanalysis.* New York: Norton.
Horney, K. (1945). *Our inner conflicts.* New York: Norton.
Horney, K. (1950). *Neurosis and human growth.* New York: Norton.
James, I.P., & Levin, S. (1964). Suicide following discharge from psychiatric hospitals. *Archives of General Psychiatry, 10* (1), 43-46.
Klagsbrun, F. (1976). *Too young to die: Youth and suicide.* Boston: Houghton Mifflin.
Kubler-Ross, E. (1969). *On death and dying.* New York: Macmillan.
Lassh, C. (1979). *The culture of narcissism.* New York: Norton.
Lester, G., & Lester, D. (1971). *Suicide: The gamble with death.* Englewood Cliffs, NJ: Prentice-Hall.
Lum, D. (1974). *Responding to suicidal crisis.* Grand Rapids, MI: William B. Eerdmans.
Maguire, D.C. (1973). *Death by choice.* New York: Shocken Books.
Maris, R.W. (1981). *Pathways to suicide: A survey of self-destructive behavior.* Baltimore: Johns Hopkins University Press.
McGee, R.K. (1974). *Crisis intervention in the community.* Baltimore: University Park Press.
Menninger, K.A. (1958). *Theory of psychoanalytic technique.* New York: Basic Books.
Montagu, A., & Barnet, S.A. (1974). *Man and aggression.* New York: Oxford University Press.
Nelson, M.C. (Ed.). (1977). *The narcissistic condition.* New York: Human Sciences Press.
Perls, F., Hefferline, R.F., & Goodman, P. (1951). *Gestalt therapy.* New York: Julian Press.
Porterfield, A.L. (1960). Traffic fatalities, suicide and homicide. *American Sociological Review, 25,* 897-901.
Resnik, H.L.P. (Ed.). (1968). *Suicidal behaviors: Diagnosis and management.* Boston: Little, Brown.
Reynolds, D.K., & Farberow, N.L. (1976). *Suicide: Inside and out.* Berkeley: University of California Press.
Rogers, C.R. (1951). *Client-centered therapy.* Boston: Houghton Mifflin.
Roman, J. (1980). *Exit house.* New York: Seaview Books.
Rubin, T.I. (1975). *Compassion and self-hate.* New York: David McKay.
Savage, M. (1975). *Addicted to suicide.* Santa Barbara, CA: Capra Press.
Selzer, M.L., & Payne, C.E. (1962). Automobile accidents, suicide, and unconscious motivation. *American Journal of Psychiatry, 119,* 237-240.
Shneidman, E.S. (Ed.). (1969). *On the nature of suicide.* San Francisco: Jossey-Bass.
Shneidman, E.S. (1973). *Deaths of man.* New York: Quadrangle/New York Times.
Shneidman, E.S. (Ed.). (1976). *Suicidology: Contemporary developments.* New York: Grune & Stratton.

Shneidman, E.S. (1980). The reliability of suicide statistics. *Suicide and Life-Threatening Behavior, 10* (2), 67-69.

Shneidman, E.S., & Farberow, N.L. (Eds.). (1957). *Clues to suicide.* New York: McGraw-Hill.

Shneidman, E.S., Farberow, N.L., & Litman, R.E. (1970). *The psychology of suicide.* New York: Science House.

Skinner, B.F. (1953). *Science and human behavior.* New York: Macmillan.

Skinner, B.F. (1969). *Contingencies of reinforcement.* New York: Appleton-Century-Crofts.

Skinner, B.F. (1974). *About behaviorism.* New York: Knopf.

SLA holocaust. (1977, June 27). *Newsweek,* p. 9.

Sprott, S.E. (1961). *The English debate on suicide: From Donne to Hume.* La Salle, IL: Open Court.

Stengel, E. (1964a). Suicide and social isolation. *Twentieth Century, 173,* 24-36.

Stengel, E. (1964b). *Suicide and attempted suicide.* Baltimore: Penguin Books.

Stone, H.W. (1972). *Suicide and grief.* Philadelphia: Fortress Press.

Temoche, A. (1971). *Suicide and known mental disease.* Cambridge, MA: Harvard University Press.

Wechsler, J.A. (1972). *In a darkness.* New York: Norton.

Wekstein, L. (1979). *Handbook of suicidology.* New York: Brunner/Mazel.

Wolpe, J. (1973). *The practice of behavior therapy* (2nd ed.). New York: Pergamon Press.

INDEX

334 THE SUICIDE SYNDROME